WHO BENEFITS FROM PRIVATISATION?

Privatisation has captivated governments, policy makers and bureaucrats of both developed and developing countries over the past few decades. It has led to the shifting of billions of dollars' worth of assets from public to private ownership, the restructuring of industries, and the loss of thousands of jobs. Has it all been worth it and who has benefited?

This edited collection examines the impact of privatisation and the lessons to be learnt from it for the purpose of regulatory reform. The contributors analyse the benefits and losses of privatisation in a variety of countries from economic, legal and consumer perspectives and address fundamental questions such as whether private ownership necessarily leads to better incentives for management and productivity.

The book contains illustrative case studies of the Australian telecommunications industry, the deregulation of the Swedish taxi and postal industries and Californian telecommunications industries and discusses consumer responses to the privatisation of key utilities in the UK. The impact of privatisation in developing nations is also addressed, with particular reference to India and Malaysia.

Dr Moazzem Hossain is former Senior Research Officer of the Australian Bureau of Agricultural and Resource Economics and currently senior lecturer in Economics at Griffith University, Australia.

Mr Justin Malbon is a barrister, consumer advocate and senior lecturer at Griffith University, teaching commercial law and international trade law.

The contributors are: Michael Whincop, Stuart Rowland, Allan Brown, Colin Meek, Michael Shames, Maria Bengtsson, Agneta Marell, Andrew Baldwin, Winnie Goh, Jomo Sundram, Hiranya Mukhopadhyay, Eileen Webb and Charles Sampford.

ROUTLEDGE STUDIES IN THE MODERN WORLD ECONOMY

1 INTEREST RATES AND BUDGET DEFICITS
A study of the advanced economies
Kanhaya L. Gupta and Bakhtiar Moazzami

2 WORLD TRADE AFTER THE URUGUAY ROUND
Prospects and policy options for the twenty-first century
Edited by Harald Sander and András Inotai

3 THE FLOW ANALYSIS OF LABOUR MARKETS
Edited by Ronald Schettkat

4 INFLATION AND UNEMPLOYMENT
Contributions to a new macroeconomic approach
Edited by Alvaro Cencini and Mauro Baranzini

5 MACROECONOMIC DIMENSIONS OF PUBLIC FINANCE
Essays in honour of Vito Tanzi
Edited by Mario I. Blejer and Teresa M. Ter-Minassian

6 FISCAL POLICY AND ECONOMIC REFORMS
Essays in honour of Vito Tanzi
Edited by Mario I. Blejer and Teresa M. Ter-Minassian

7 COMPETITION POLICY IN THE GLOBAL ECONOMY
Modalities for co-operation
Edited by Leonard Waverman, William S. Comanor and Akira Goto

8 WORKING IN THE MACROECONOMY
A study of the US labor market
Martin F. J. Prachowny

9 HOW DOES PRIVATISATION WORK?
Edited by Anthony Bennett

10 THE ECONOMICS AND POLITICS OF INTERNATIONAL TRADE
Freedom and trade: Volume II
Edited by Gary Cook

11 THE LEGAL AND MORAL ASPECTS OF INTERNATIONAL TRADE
Freedom and trade: Volume III
Edited by Asif Qureshi, Hillel Steiner and Geraint Parry

12 CAPITAL MARKETS AND CORPORATE GOVERNANCE IN JAPAN, GERMANY AND THE UNITED STATES
Organizational response to market inefficiencies
Helmut M. Dietl

13 COMPETITION AND TRADE POLICIES
Coherence or conflict
Edited by Einar Hope

14 RICE
The primary commodity
A. J. H. Latham

15 TRADE, THEORY AND ECONOMETRICS
Essays in honour of John S. Chipman
Edited by James C. Moore, Raymond Riezman and James R. Melvin

16 WHO BENEFITS FROM PRIVATISATION?
Edited by Moazzem Hossain and Justin Malbon

17 TOWARDS A FAIR GLOBAL LABOUR MARKET
Avoiding the new slavery
Edited by Ozay Mehmet, Errol Mendes and Robert Sinding

18 MODELS OF FUTURES MARKETS
Edited by Barry Goss

WHO BENEFITS FROM PRIVATISATION?

Edited by
Moazzem Hossain
and Justin Malbon

ROUTLEDGE

London and New York

First published 1998
by Routledge
11 New Fetter Lane, London EC4P 4EE

Simultaneously published in the USA and Canada
by Routledge
29 West 35th Street, New York, NY 10001

Typeset in Garamond by RefineCatch Limited, Bungay, Suffolk
Printed and bound in Great Britain by
Biddles Ltd, Guildford and King's Lynn

British Library Cataloguing in Publication Data
A catalogue record for this book is available from the British Library

Library of Congress Cataloging in Publication Data
Who benefits from privatisation? / [editors] Moazzem Hossain and Justin Malbon.
p. cm. – (Routledge studies in the modern world economy; 16)
Includes bibliographical references and index.
1. Privatization. 2. Privatization – Case studies. I. Hossain, Moazzem, 1950– . II. Malbon, Justin. III. Series.
HD3850.W47 1998
338.9 – dc21 98–15337
CIP

ISBN 0–415–17189–X

CONTENTS

TABLES

FIGURES

CONTRIBUTORS

Mr Justin Malbon: Senior Lecturer, School of Law, Griffith University, Nathan, Australia.

Mr Michael Whincop: Lecturer, School of Law, Griffith University, Nathan, Australia.

Mr Stuart Rowland: Barrister at Law, Brisbane, Australia.

Dr Allan Brown: Senior Lecturer, School of Economics, Griffith University, Nathan, Australia.

Mr Colin Meek: Senior Researcher, UK Consumers' Association, London, UK.

Dr Michael Shames: Executive Director, Utility Consumers' Action Network, California, USA.

Dr Maria Bengtsson: Faculty, Umea Business School, University of Umea, Umea, Sweden.

Ms Agneta Marell: Faculty, Umea Business School, University of Umea, Umea, Sweden.

Dr Andrew Baldwin: Faculty, Umea Business School, University of Umea, Umea, Sweden.

Ms Winnie Goh: Senior Lecturer, Metropolitan College, Subang Jay, Kuala Lumpur, Malaysia.

Professor Jomo Sundram: Professor of Economics, Faculty of Economics and Administration, University of Malaya, Kuala Lumpur, Malaysia.

Dr Hiranya Mukhopadhyay: Senior Economist, National Institute of Public Finance and Policy (NIPFP), New Delhi, India.

Dr Moazzem Hossain: Senior Lecturer, School of International Business, Griffith University, Nathan, Australia.

Ms Eileen Webb: Lecturer, Law School, Griffith University, Nathan, Australia.

Professor Charles Sampford: Professor of Law, National Institute for Law Ethics and Public Affairs, Griffith University, Nathan, Australia.

PREFACE

Privatisation was the policy fashion of the 1980s and 1990s. It captivated governments in both developed and developing economies. The USA was also affected despite a relatively low pre-existing level of government ownership of industries and utilities. There the monopoly and virtual monopoly utilities were 'deregulated' and subjected to competition. The attraction of privatisation to governments that owned vast profit-making utilities was obvious. Asset sales led to huge injections of cash into their treasuries allowing them to fund election promises without having to increase taxes (and sometimes allowed tax reductions). This undoubtedly improved the re-election prospects of the privatising governments.

Privatisation also brought pain. Governments invariably introduced efficiencies into their utilities to make them more attractive for sale. This usually involved laying off hundreds, and sometimes thousands, of workers. In many instances the public was sceptical about the benefits that privatisation would bring. They were assured by their governments that privatisation would bring competition and improved efficiency, which itself would lead to competitive prices and improved service delivery. The question is, has it? The answer, which is examined in this book, reveals varied outcomes. In some cases consumers have benefited, in others the benefits have not materialised.

This book considers the alleged and real benefits of privatisation in a number of countries, including the UK, Australia, India, Malaysia, New Zealand and Sweden. It also considers the US deregulatory experience. In addition, the public obligations of privatised corporations and the economics of privatisation are considered and regulatory measures are proposed for the protection of consumers from some of the consequences of privatisation.

The genesis of this book was a conference the editors organised in Brisbane, Australia, in March 1996. The conference considered the lessons Australia could learn from countries that had preceded her with privatisation, and what could be learnt from the Australian experience itself. Speakers attended from around Australia and from Malaysia, New Zealand and the UK. This book includes a number of papers from the conference as well as chapters solicited from commentators in the USA, Sweden and India.

We thank our editorial assistant Robyn White for her high quality word-processing skills and patience. Finally, we also thank our families for their understanding and support.

Moazzem Hossain and Justin Malbon
Brisbane, December 1997

1

INTRODUCTION

Moazzem Hossain and Justin Malbon

The industrial policy issues of developed and developing countries have been affected by both trade liberalisation strategies prompted by the GATT Uruguay Round, the privatisation movement initiated in the UK and by the World Bank and the IMF. Like trade liberalisation, the privatisation agenda was endorsed by both the more developed and developing countries. Developing countries have adopted one of three basic approaches to privatisation: the 'big-bang' approach of Latin American and Caribbean countries, the 'go-slow and institutional' approach of the Asian and East Asian countries and the 'marketisation' political approach of the East European countries. The more developed nations, on the other hand, directed their strategies towards industries such as airlines, banking, post and telecommunications and utilities (electricity, water and gas). Most of the OECD nations are currently undertaking privatisation to achieve further economic development and are involved in various stages of full privatisation of the industries mentioned above.

Why, then, has privatisation been so widely and comprehensively adopted throughout the world? The rationale more commonly put is that privatisation will:

- raise funds and reduce borrowing to improve a nation's effective economic management;
- increase efficiency at the enterprise level;
- reduce government and bureaucratic interference in the day-to-day business of an enterprise;
- increase the share in enterprise ownership;
- create competition in the market; and,
- promote discipline in the market place (Gould 1990).

Privatisation involves selling state-owned enterprises (SOEs) or government business enterprises (GBEs) and other government activities to the private sector (Edadan 1997). The purported aim of the process is to ensure a GBE operates on a commercial basis or is subject to fair competition

(Treedson 1996). The most common privatisation mechanisms include direct sale of a GBE, public offer of a GBE, concession sale, joint venture, management buyouts, liquidation and lease (Thein 1990). In many nations, regulators have been established for the privatisation process to protect the interests and activities of three major players, namely consumers, privately owned new companies and governments.

In Australia three major GBEs were privatised, namely the national flag carrier (Qantas), a major bank (Commonwealth Bank) and most recently one-third of Australia's telecommunications company (Telstra). At the state level the major utilities are either privatised or are being privatised. In April 1995 the Council of Australian Governments (COAG) adopted a package of proposals known as the National Competition Policy which were based on the recommendations of the Independent Committee of Inquiry into National Competition chaired by Professor Fred Hilmer (Hilmer 1993). The Hilmer recommendations, however, went beyond proposals for corporatisation and privatisation of GBEs, and recommended a range of microeconomic reforms which potentially reach into some core government activities.

The scope and rapidity of the privatisation process and its profound implications for the people prompted the editors to organise a conference entitled 'Corporatisation and Privatisation: In Whose Interest?', held in March 1996 in which the experiences of a number of countries were reviewed. We decided to take a multidisciplinary approach to the topic, since privatisation involves not only economic rationalism but also raises legal and political issues. The conference considered the implementation of Australia's competition policy and the experiences of New Zealand, the United Kingdom and Malaysia.

This book includes a number of papers from the conference as well as chapters solicited from commentators in Europe, the USA, South Asia and Southeast Asia. The title of the present book asks: who benefits from privatisation? Most chapters either directly or indirectly attempt to answer this question in light of the privatisation experiences of a number of nations.

Specifically, Chapter 2 argues that privatisation should not be confused with deregulation, as it has been in some countries, most notably New Zealand. Rather, privatisation offered a challenge for regulatory reform. Privatisation highlighted the failure of the pre-existing regulatory system to pay sufficient regard to issues of efficiency and accountability. Privatisation has not, however, been the panacea it promised. It delivered substantial amounts of public assets to private owners without sufficient regard being paid to the impact on consumers in remote areas and poorer consumers. There is very little empirical evidence to show that consumers overall have benefited from the process. The privatisation process does, however, offer the opportunity to learn from experiences around the world to introduce or refine regulation of utilities.

Chapter 3 questions the theoretical claim that privately owned corporations will perform more efficiently than publicly owned corporations because of the way incentives for productive efficiency operate in each case. Whincop and Rowland argue that the relationship between efficiency claims and the governance of privatised enterprises, is poorly understood. They offer theoretical considerations for clarifying the relationship. In particular they deal with the relationship between the effects of capital and factor markets, the governance of corporations, and corporate law. Corporate law, they believe, is an essential influence on the governance and, therefore, the efficiency of a privatised corporation. Their analysis focuses on the changes that have taken place in Australia's corporate law. These changes are significant because they suggest that the structure of corporate law is moving away from the norms by which it historically has been dominated. They argue that it is moving towards norms that are more typical of public law.

Chapter 4 investigates privatisation issues arising from Australia's telecommunications industry. Before presenting a case study, Brown discusses privatisation's theoretical contribution to the debate about economic efficiency and the fiscal imbalances of modern economies. In this part of the paper he finds that judging the benefits of privatisation is complex and is affected by a number of factors, including the profitability of the enterprise in the post-privatisation period, the amount of underpricing of a privatised enterprise and the transaction costs during privatisation. Profitability in the post-privatisation period can either be due to improved productive efficiency or to charging high prices. If the increase in profits results from the privatised firm charging higher prices, then allocative efficiency in the economy generally will decline. Underpricing and transaction costs will reduce the proceeds to the government from privatisation. Underpricing is likely to increase proportionally with the size of a public float and may occur because of restrictions on eligibility for shares and the perceived sovereign risk facing the privatised firm, but will be minimised by the use of tender process and the sale of shares in tranches. There will be a direct loss of national wealth to the extent of the premium on shares sold to foreign interests. In the second part of the paper, Brown examines the privatisation process and outcomes of privatisation of Australia's telecommunications industry. The privatisation process began with the introduction of competition, initially in the value-added services, in 1991, creating a duopoly in mobile services. Subsequently, a licence was granted to a second general telecommunications carrier called Optus Communications, which competed with the government-owned carrier, Telstra. In the mobile services, however, a triopoly was created by granting a licence to Vodafone. Other competitors were granted general telephony licences in July 1997. Telecommunications policy since 1991 has largely been directed to bringing about 'sustainable competition' in the industry, which has involved the imposition of restraints on Telstra to prevent the abuse of its market power. By 1995, Optus had captured 14 per cent of both domestic (STD) and international (IDD) markets and 30 and 37 per cent of the mobile analogue and mobile digital markets, respectively. However, in the face of increasing competition, Telstra has been a leading performer among Australian GBEs. Telstra's total revenues grew steadily over 1992 and 1996 from A$12.2 to A$15.2 billion (in nominal A$ terms), while after tax profit increased substantially from A$0.3 to A$2.3 billion. With Telstra's economic performance in mind, Brown, in the third and final part of his paper, explores the outcomes of Australia's privatisation of Telstra. He considers the asset value of Telstra, the savings in public debt interest, underpricing and transaction costs, foreign investment and allocative efficiency. He concludes that, from an economic perspective, there is little sense in supporting or opposing Telstra's privatisation *per se*. The economic issues are complex and privatisation involves potential benefits as well as costs. The balance of benefits and costs depends crucially on the timing of the sale and the terms and conditions on which the sale proceeds, and, crucially, the regulatory environment created, the level of foreign interest and the achievable net sale proceeds. After Brown's chapter was completed, one-third of Telstra was sold by public float in November 1997.

The UK experience of privatisation of utilities is considered from the consumers' point of view in Chapter 5. Meek argues that when the Thatcher administration embraced the privatisation strategy it promised that privatisation would introduce greater competition in the utility industries making the industries efficient which in turn would bring prices down. In brief, privatisation would deliver consumer benefits. In practice, however, the goal of consumer benefits was either suspended or abandoned entirely due to priority given to other objectives. In fact, competition in the domestic market was actually prohibited in the gas, water and electricity industries when they were privatised. Consumers experienced limited competition in the telephony sector in the outset. In the absence of competition the government turned to regulators. The regulators were given statutory powers to impose price controls on the privatised monopolies and were expected to wither away when competition developed. In this context Meek examines the performance of several utilities, post-privatisation. British Gas (BG) was privatised in 1986, but competition was initially limited to very large users and then gradually extended. British Telecom (BT) was privatised in 1984 and is currently in competition with various national and local companies. Despite the growth in competition, all companies depend on interconnection agreements with BT. Water was privatised in England and Wales in 1989. No attempt has been made to introduce competition at the domestic user level; however, competition is encouraged for very large industrial users. Electricity was privatised in 1990 and 1991. While competition has so far been limited to large commercial users, it will be extended in 1998 to domestic users. In the second part of his chapter, Meek explains the major barriers to competition in the various utility industries. These are: dominance of incumbent firms, the restriction upon consumers gaining appropriate market information on services and prices, and the excessive regulatory powers in the hands of regulators. He finishes this part by highlighting the impact of regulatory mechanisms on vulnerable and disadvantaged consumers. In the final part, Meek makes some observations about the future direction of the privatisation movement in the UK. He observes that, with all their limitations, the regulators have won a number of important battles over the years. The gas regulator has managed to ensure that the gas price formula is targeted to benefit domestic users, the telecommunications regulator has established a range of comparable performance indicators for the consumers to compare costs of calls under various companies, and has ensured that various options and ranges of services are available to consumers so that more households now have access to phones at affordable rates.

Chapter 6 examines the Californian experience of exposing the telecommunications industry to competition and regulatory reform and proposes regulatory reforms which should be made in the light of that experience when California exposes the electricity industry to competition. His primary concern is to ensure that the market mechanism, which is claimed will deliver greater consumer benefits than a regulated monopoly, function effectively, particularly for residential consumers. The problem for residential consumers is the lack of meaningful information available for them to make rational choices about which 'competitive' services they should use. The costs involved in gathering and making sense of the information will outweigh the benefit of obtaining the information unless the regulatory parameters are set correctly. Shames outlines a wide range of regulatory and other options to ensure that market information is available to consumers in a meaningful and cost-effective way.

Bengtsson, Marell and Baldwin present two Swedish case studies on deregulation in Chapter 7. The case studies address two industries: taxi cabs and postal communications. Before providing the empirical analysis, the authors offer a theoretical basis to explain how business-induced barriers can become a major hindrance to achieving privatisation goals. They discuss ways of identifying business-induced barriers and resource advantages and describe theoretically how barriers to entry affect the intensity of competition in both pre- and post-deregulation stages.

In their empirical analysis Bengtsson, Marell and Baldwin first consider deregulation of the taxi-cab industry in Sweden which took place in 1990. Deregulation was extensive in comparison to the deregulation of the industry in a number of American cities, and of local and regional bus traffic in the UK. The primary purpose of the taxi-cab deregulation in Sweden was to guarantee free entry into the market and to generate healthy competition. Deregulation also introduced free price-setting and the abolition of the maximum fare rate. Their case study results suggest that immediately after deregulation prices rose sharply, but began to fall within a year of deregulation. They note that customer loyalty to an established company is greater than to a new entrant. The case study on the postal industry begins with the observation that the Swedish Post Office has been a monopoly business for more than 300 years. The industry was subject to competition in 1991 when a duopoly was introduced. The introduction of the duopoly was instrumental to a deregulation of the postal service in 1993. The outcome of the deregulation has been positive. Prices have dropped markedly where competition exists. The third and final part of the chapter attempts to analyse the relationship between entry barriers and deregulation outcomes. In the pre-deregulation period the postal industry enjoyed the following entry barriers: monopoly operation, advantages of scope, economies of scale and customer loyalty. The taxi-cab industry enjoyed the entry barriers of company familiarity and monopoly operation in designated areas. The study found that in the post-deregulation era the postal industry is still enjoying the same entry barriers it had during the pre-deregulation period except that deregulation has brought competition regarding some products and some locations, and as a result led to price reductions. This was at the expense of price rises in low population areas outside Stockholm and other metropolitan cities. In the taxi-cab industry, post-deregulation prices dropped for subsidised trips negotiated by the public sector; however, for the privately paid trips, prices either have increased or remained the same. The authors conclude that in their view some features of predatory pricing can be observed in both industries in the post-deregulation period. Therefore, the deregulation measures are not consistent with the goal of attaining operative efficiency and gaining intense competition within the industry. This is due mainly to the existence of business-induced barriers that existed even after deregulation.

In Chapter 8, Goh and Sundram provide an assessment of Malaysia's privatisation experience. Malaysia announced its commitment to a privatisation strategy in its Privatisation Master Plan (PMP) in 1991. By 1994, the government was able to earn a one-off revenue of about RM2,063 million from divesting shares of enterprises to the public. One of the most important features of the Malaysian privatisation agenda is to further inter-ethnic wealth distribution by way of ensuring Bumiputera participation in share acquisition of at least 30 per cent. The postal services were corporatised in 1992. Since corporatisation, the postage rates for small parcels with weights exceeding 100 grams have increased tremendously. The objective of faster delivery remained unattainable. In some cases the delivery time has even increased during the post-corporatisation period. The authors note several adverse outcomes of privatisation, including the pricing structures of privatised industries such as Highways, Passenger Railways, Medical Stores and Telecommunications. The authors argue that there is considerable scepticism about the benefits of privatisation in Malaysia. In most cases the transfer of ownership brought high user costs and reduced quality of services. The privatisation process adopted by the government lacks accountability, which has contributed to its poor outcomes. The objective of inter-ethnic redistribution of wealth has, however, been achieved as a substantial amount of wealth has been shifted to the Bumiputeras.

Chapter 9 does not address the issue of privatisation directly but quantitatively analyses the outcome of economic reforms (privatisation being one of the reform measures) in the Indian manufacturing sector. Mukhopadhyay argues from a macroeconomic point of view that the major goals of economic reform measures were not achieved, even after five years of their introduction. In terms of GDP growth, the objective of 7 per cent sustainable rate of growth was not achieved. The economy has failed to achieve positive revenue results, when judged by the tax-to-GDP ratio. Exports and industrial growth have had mixed fortunes. After an initial surge, export growth has declined in recent years (a 6.2 per cent decline occurring during the first ten months of 1996–7). The most alarming development is the shadow of recession which hovers over the industrial sector. Mukhopadhyay quantitatively examines this by employing an econometric model of private consumption behaviour. His investigation shows that private consumers have postponed their consumption for the future owing to higher real interest rates. To avoid such an environment the author makes the following recommendations to the Indian authorities: first, the real interest rate (lending rates) should be reduced by lowering the inflation expectation permanently during the transition of liberalisation and privatisation; second, various uncertainties that are associated with the non-transparent nature of economic policies should be minimised as early as possible; finally, maximum priority should be given for removing infrastructural bottlenecks.

In Chapter 10, Hossain examines telecommunications privatisation in India. The Indian telecommunications market is the world's second largest, after China. India's expansion programme of its existing network will need around US$22.5 billion of investment over the next five years. To attract such a huge investment capital the Indian authorities have brought substantial reform measures within the industry. These are: complete freedom of telecom equipment manufactures, privatisation of services, and liberalisation of the rules relating to foreign investment and technology imports. The production line of telecom equipment is now being freed for private production. The telecom services were privatised particularly for value-added services such as Cellular, Pager and e-mail services. Foreign carriers including AT&T, BT, Sprint, Telstra and Deutsche Telekom have invested jointly with Indian counterparts in various telecom services. The chapter concludes that, while price elasticity is critical for assessing future demand, wide discrepancy is believed to exist in elasticities across the country. The present telecom network is highly skewed and almost 25 per cent of telephone lines in India are confined to two cities – Delhi and Bombay. These two cities also have the highest telephone density – over nine times the national average. Future demand for telephones is expected to be driven primarily by the metropolitan and large cities and by the states which are currently growing rapidly, including Maharastra, Gujarat, Karnataka, Tamil Nadu, Andhra Pradesh and Uttar Pradesh.

In Chapter 11, Webb examines the implementation of competition policy in Australia, particularly with regard to the community services sector. The competition reforms in Australia have gone beyond those in any other country in terms of reach. Indeed, the reforms have extended beyond that proposed by the Hilmer report, which prompted a great deal of microeconomic reform in Australia. Government-funded voluntary and non-voluntary community services groups have been subjected to reviews and have been required to become competitive in circumstances where competition is unlikely to deliver community benefits. She cites the example of meals on wheels which delivers food to the homes of the frail and elderly. The organisation has been forced to contract out its services leading to the more 'efficient' delivery of food at the expense of providing vital human contact to people who are usually socially isolated.

Chapter 12 reflects upon the earlier contributions to the book and suggests reasons for caution in too readily adopting privatisation for achieving public sector reform. Sampford cautions that the ideological assumptions of the privatisation debate can themselves undermine achieving the proclaimed benefits of privatisation along with the transaction costs of privatisation and the effects of transferring wealth from the public sector.

References

Edadan, N. (1997) 'Privatisation Strategies in Developing Countries: External Debt and Domestic Economic Prospects', *Economic and Political Weekly*, XXXII, 27: 1608–19.

Gould, J. (1990) 'Challenges of Privatization and Corporatization: The UK Experience', Conference paper presented in Singapore, Singapore.

Hilmer, F. (1993) *The Report of the Independent Committee of Inquiry into National Competition* (the 'Hilmer Report'), Canberra: Australian Government Publishing Service.

Thein, R.M. (1990) 'A Guide to Privatisation – A Practical Framework for Policy Makers and Practitioners', Conference paper presented in Singapore, Singapore.

Treedson, R. (1996) 'Corporatisation and Privatisation: In Whose Interest? A Review of Conference', *The Public Interest*, 3, 2: 19–20.

2

GAINING BALANCE ON THE REGULATORY TIGHTROPE

Justin Malbon

Introduction

Government-owned utilities were privatised throughout the world during the 1980s and 1990s partly as a result of perceived regulatory failures caused by government ownership. They were also privatised because of the irresistible financial benefit to the privatising government. The sale of a relatively successful public entity brought huge injections of finance into government treasuries, providing scope to pork-barrel disgruntled electors. The mixed motives of achieving optimum consumer benefit and government financial benefit obscured what should have been the ultimate purpose of privatisation – to ensure consumer and social benefits. Perhaps it was always too much to ask of a process which reassigned ownership of billions of dollars of assets that it be driven by clear public benefit objectives.

To the extent that privatisation was motivated by the desire to deal with regulatory failure, it was usually argued that market discipline would awaken sluggish utilities. In some cases it was argued, most effectively in New Zealand, that the response to regulatory failure should be to 'deregulate' or apply 'light-handed' regulation. That is, privatisation simply involves shifting an entity from public to private ownership and treating it as being little different, for the purpose of regulation, than any other corporation. This is misguided logic. It misses a number of points. First, the logical response to regulatory 'failure' is not necessarily to abandon regulation, but to reform it. Second, the reason that many utilities were government owned was because they were natural monopolies, which would take advantage of, rather than be constrained by, market conditions. Third, the utilities offer essential public services. It has long been recognised that some services are affected by the public interest so as to require the service provider to offer the services to all, without discrimination, at a reasonable price.

The way in which the New Zealand and Australian governments pursued their privatisation and corporatisation agendas offers an interesting study in opposites. The New Zealanders opted for 'light-handed' regulation, which translates as privatisation without the establishment of regulators to address the specific regulatory requirements of utilities. That is not to suggest that New Zealand abandoned its utilities to the market. It has baulked, for example, at full privatisation of the electricity industry because of the electoral implications of doing so. Ironically, the lack of a utility-specific regulator arguably has constrained full privatisation, leaving New Zealand behind in the rush to privatise electricity utilities. Australia, on the other hand, has adopted the UK approach of creating utility-specific regulators, although it has not created a regulator for each particular utility industry. New South Wales, for example, has established the Independent Pricing and Regulatory Tribunal which regulates all the State's 'monopoly services', whereas in the UK industry-specific regulators like Oftel for telecommunications, Ofwat for water and Offer for electricity have been established.

The Australian process has been affected by its federal structure. The States and Territories engaged in differing, and somewhat slower, corporatisation and privatisation programmes than the Federal Government. The State reform process gained its impetus from the commissioning by the Federal and State Governments of an independent inquiry into competitiveness. The inquiry, headed by Professor Hilmer, recommended a wide range of reforms in 1993 which were aimed at improving the competitiveness of State and Territory government utilities and services.

Privatisation was vigorously sold by governments in Australia, the UK and other places to sceptical electorates as the panacea for regulatory failure. Claims were made about market discipline delivering efficient and effective utility services. Utilities were required to compete in the market place and, as a result, were required to be responsive to consumer demand. It was claimed that consumers would benefit from competitive pricing, improved service quality and service delivery. It was also claimed that utility-specific regulators would be required only to manage the transition period between government ownership and full competition. In some cases, experience has proven these claims to be extravagant and self-serving. There have been undoubted benefits in some industries, although assessing the extent and cause of the benefits is no easy task. Empirical evidence of consumer benefit arising from privatisation is extremely difficult to establish, not the least because obtaining sufficient reliable data is itself difficult. Often the only data available for judging success are surveys of consumer satisfaction. These have shown mixed responses, as Meek's chapter in this book illustrates. The cause of apparent success is also difficult to determine. In some cases simply the fear of privatisation and the changed culture in which utilities were required to operate itself improved the efficiency of government-owned utilities.

This chapter claims that unless there are radical technological changes in delivering utility services, the core natural monopoly character of many of the utilities will remain. Consequently the need for continued regulation will remain to prevent abnormal profit taking by the utilities in relation to their monopoly activities. There is, however, a need to improve the regulatory mechanisms to ensure the utilities operate to provide consumer and social benefits. Consumer benefit involves satisfying the individual interests of consumers, that is by providing an efficient, high quality service at a fair price. These are the sorts of benefits a consumer would gain if the utility was operating in a competitive market. Social benefit includes providing universal access to utility services and ensuring they are provided in a way that promotes a sustainable environment. The New South Wales Independent Pricing and Regulatory Tribunal provides an interesting example of an attempt to require consumer and social benefits to be taken into account when fixing utility prices. The US provides useful examples of ways to provide universal access.

The regulatory challenge is to attain a policy mix which promotes social harmony by ensuring universal access to utility services while deploying resources in an economically efficient way. Policy should also promote resource use which best ensures a sustainable environment. Attaining the appropriate policy mix essentially involves matters of political and moral judgement, aided by economic tools for identifying inefficient resource use. This of course is more readily stated than achieved. There is no template policy or scientific formula available for policy makers and legislators. The various experiences and policy mechanisms of nations who engaged in the privatisation process does, however, offer a basis for developing policy. These are briefly canvassed in this chapter.

What is a utility?

Utilities have two characteristics: they supply essential goods or services and their core business is a natural monopoly (Winward 1994: 251–2). The essential nature of the goods or services provided introduces an obligation to provide consumers access to them on a non-discriminatory basis at a fair price. There is nothing new in the concept that some goods and services are of such a nature as to impose an obligation on the provider to offer them on a fair and non-discriminatory basis. It derives from the common law principle of common carriage which date to the Middle Ages. This placed an obligation on businesses with 'public callings' to provide their service on a non-discriminatory basis to members of the public who were willing and able to pay the set price. The public callings included bakers, shipowners, innkeepers and ferrymen. The concept of common callings was further refined by the leading common law jurist Sir Matthew Hale (1606–76) who made a distinction between private and public interests and proposed in his treatise *De Portibus Maris*[1] that a private interest is imposed with different obligations when affected by the public interest. The idea that private interests become affected by public interests to create a public obligation gained judicial recognition in the 1810 English decision of *Allnutt v. Inglis*,[2] which considered whether storage rates imposed by warehouses were unlawfully high. The warehouses were allowed by Treasury to store imported goods which would be exempted from customs duty. The Court held that:

> Here the company's warehouses were invested with the monopoly of public privilege, and therefore they must by law confine themselves to take reasonable rates for the use of them for that purpose . . .

Similar principles were applied to other common callings. According to Lord Sumner in *Hammerton v. Earl of Dysart*[3] the ferryman is obliged to carry all those who wish to be ferried, must have sufficient number of employees and boats, and must charge only reasonable and uniform tolls, without discrimination. These early English decisions influenced the US development of principles regarding common callings, spawned by the 1876 decision of *Munn v. Illinois*,[4] which in turn prompted development of the modern regulatory construct of universal access. It requires that a utility service be provided to as many members of society as possible at a reasonable and non-discriminatory price. In the US it involves regulations requiring the monopoly utility to use some of its profits to support poorer and remote area consumers. The regulatory settings are somewhat eclectic:

> There are inter-carrier transfers such as high access charges paid by inter-exchange and mobile carriers to local exchange companies (LECs). There are high cost funds, toll pools, long-term support agreements, lifeline contributions, and universal service funds. Major inter-customer transfer mechanisms also exist, such as higher prices on business customers and prices that are 'averaged' across geography. And there are some direct governmental contributions, primarily by Rural Electrification Administration loan guarantees.
>
> (Noam 1997: 957)

As mentioned, utilities not only provide goods and services affected by a public interest, their core business is a natural monopoly. A natural monopoly arises where economies of scale exist so that the cost of producing a variety of products is lower than making each product separately (Price 1994: 78). The benefit of economies of scale is undermined by a utility's monopoly position if it takes advantage of its position by realising supernormal prices and profits, that is, by gaining an abnormal benefit by not passing the gains onto consumers. This problem can be overcome by government ownership where the utility is not required to maximise profits, but to achieve allocative efficiency. The problem this in turn creates is that the utility has little incentive to achieve productive efficiency. The apparent answer to the dilemma is to set the regulatory incentives in a way that achieves both allocative efficiency in the form of output price and productive efficiency. Economics assists with achieving productive efficiency but not allocative efficiency or achieving equity. These are essentially policy objectives. The central point remains, as Prosser notes, that 'any adequate form of regulation of public utilities must include some commitment to values which are not encompassed within the economic efficiency objective but which are based on distributive and egalitarian concerns' (1994: 17).

The privatisation debate

The privatisation debate and subsequent implementation of privatisation policies began in earnest in the UK in the early 1980s. According to Prosser and Moran privatisation was not inspired by a single, clear ideological rationale, rather 'it was the result of a shifting mix of motives in which the poor performance of public enterprises, the cutting of public borrowing, the destruction of political constituencies hostile to the Conservative Party and increasing share-ownership all played a part' (1994: 35). Although government policy requiring the sale of public utilities was clearly motivated in part by the financial (and political) benefit to government of obtaining income from asset sales, the rhetorical focus was very much on the need to make the utilities more efficient and responsive to the market. Government ownership and regulation, it was argued, is wasteful and inefficient. The solution was to have utilities regulated by market discipline rather than government regulation. Wildly optimistic claims were made that all utilities would eventually be players within a competitive market – utility monopolies would seemingly disappear for all time. The Littlechild Report of 1983, which apparently forgot about the economic advantages of natural monopolies, claimed that utility regulation was only required for five years, after which ' . . . the extent and strength of competition should have become more apparent' (Winward 1994: 255).

Needless to say, regulation itself was seen to be a bogey, suggesting that the regulatory state itself was a failure. Linking the rhetorical attack on government ownership of utilities with deregulation led at times to policy confusion which became most evident in New Zealand. The policy debate obscured the fact that merely transferring public ownership to private ownership would not deal with the problem, from a market perspective, of monopoly. If anything the potential for abuse of monopoly status is accentuated by private ownership because government ownership arguably carries with it notions of public duty which constrain the aggressive attainment of abnormal profits. Thus privatising a monopoly, if anything, increases the need for regulation to prevent market abuse.

The post-privatisation regulatory system was weakened by the characterisation of regulation as a bogey in itself. The Littlechild Report predicted that post-privatisation regulation would be temporary, which meant that attention was focused on short-term regulatory mechanisms such as RPI $- x$ price capping. This involves the regulator capping utility prices at the retail price index (RPI) minus a mystical factor of '*x*'. The aim of lowering consumer prices was to force a utility to become more economically efficient. This mechanism can only be temporary (unless modified) because continued price cutting will eventually bankrupt the utility. The rhetoric which characterised regulation itself as a bogey also had the effect of marginalising the regulator as being an obstructionist force, which played into the hands of the dominant privatised utilities.

The attack on regulation *per se* was misconceived in that it wrongly assumed that post-privatisation no natural monopolies would exist, and consequently there would be no need for specific regulation of utilities. The attack, however, ignored the positive role that regulation has played in society. Regulation has brought about significant improvements 'in a variety of areas, including the environment, energy conservation, automobile safety, endangered species, and discrimination on the basis of race and sex' (Sunstein 1990: 74).

It cannot be assumed, however, that regulation will necessarily deliver better outcomes for consumers than for industry. A utility industry may actively seek regulation to gain an exclusive licence or entitlement to produce a commodity or service and to maintain a monopoly position. This problem was identified by public choice theory which raised concerns about industry involving itself in rent-seeking behaviour, which mitigates against achieving optimum consumer benefit. But it cannot be assumed that a privatised utility will not engage in rent-seeking behaviour, even those subject to an independent regulator. British Telecom (BT), for example, devoted substantial resources in persuading the public through advertising and publicity campaigns that regulatory constraints which prevented BT from engaging in market abuse practices were somehow un-British. It was suggested that because BT is a British company, limiting its dominant market position would hurt Britain. The Australian Government-owned telephone company Telstra also successfully appealed to patriotism when fending off a regulatory initiative to have consumers 'vote' on whether their primary carrier would be Telstra or new rival Optus.

The old regulatory system was prone to rent-seeking behaviour because the process was not sufficiently transparent and accountable and it did not focus on setting incentives to promote productive efficiency. There was a clear conflict between the government as utility owner and as its regulator. In practice this led to a system which was secretive and idiosyncratic. Winward notes with regard to the UK's pre-privatisation experience of utility price setting that:

> In practice the decisive voice was that of the Treasury. Financial targets and External Financing Limits became the major influences

> on tariff-setting. Mechanisms were developed which allowed the Treasury to extract surpluses from the industries (for example the Gas Levy and the 'negative EFL'). The effect was to create a perverse environment in which government was simultaneously the economic regulator of monopoly undertakings, banker to the same undertakings, and the principal beneficiary of any monopoly profits which they could accrue. Unsurprisingly, this created significant internal conflicts in the agent–principal relationship between the industries and government.
>
> (1994: 253)

The lack of clear mechanisms allowed government to pursue macroeconomic policies unrelated to the utility service delivery. UK gas prices, for example, were kept down during the 1970s in order to reduce inflation, but were doubled between 1980 and 1984. Many governments also influenced pricing to promote their privatisation agendas, often increasing prices before privatisation to increase profitability for the purchasers of the utilities. This has created problems evaluating the benefits of privatisation, because in the relatively short term at least the freezing of utility prices or the imposition of RPI – *x* pricing regulation provided the impression of efficiency gains from privatisation that could have been achieved without privatisation.

Case study: New Zealand

New Zealand provides an interesting contrast to the developments occurring in most other nations with regard to regulation. It equated privatisation with deregulation and light-handed regulation, and thus aimed to treat the privatised utilities as being similar to other commercial organisations. Although New Zealand avoided creating specialist regulators for utilities, it did not simply sell off all the utilities without public interest constraints being imposed. In the case of electricity, it has not sold the generators or transmission lines – which, despite its robust pro-market image, leaves it behind many other nations on this score. The lack of utility-specific regulation has meant that New Zealand has been left with an inefficient and inadequate regulatory regime.

New Zealand began reforming its government-owned businesses after decades of high protection which left its economy in a precarious state. By the early 1980s New Zealand manufacturers had a virtual monopoly on the supply of household goods, price control existed for some goods and services, wage/price freezes existed and industry subsidies were rife, including for farming. Consequently, the national debt mounted and so did unemployment (Russell 1994). The pending economic crises prompted the government to undertake a large agenda of reform at breathtaking speed. Reforms were made to a wide range of government business activities including airlines, airports, banking and finance, telecommunications, postal services and ports. The economy was also reformed by the reduction and removal of import duties and tariffs, reforms to the local government sector and changes to the employment relations through the Employment Contracts Act 1991.

Within a decade New Zealand shifted from being one of the most protected OECD economies to one of the least. Two utilities that were subjected to privatisation (to a greater or lesser extent) which are of interest because of their size and public significance are telecommunications and electricity.

New Zealand is the only country which has moved directly from government monopoly in telecommunications to privatisation without an industry-specific regulator (Janisch 1994: 266). Corporatisation of Telecom was followed by its sale in 1990 to private interests and it is now effectively an American-owned company. Telecom is New Zealand's largest publicly listed company. Competition arrived the following year with Clear Communications, which was majority owned by Television New Zealand, New Zealand Rail and Todd Corporation. It commenced business by focusing on national and international tolls and gained the Justice Department and New Zealand Rail as its first clients (Russell 1994: 3). Despite competition from Clear and a number of mobile-phone operators, by 1994 Telecom was earning 90 per cent of telecommunications market revenue.

The electricity generation and transmission functions of the Ministry of Energy were corporatised in 1987 forming the Electricity Corporation of New Zealand Ltd (ECNZ). The retailing of electricity remained with numerous local power boards, many of which were constituted by local government authorities. These had local monopolies and were corporatised in 1990, which involved the government appointing directors and the board members becoming trustees for the consumers.

The local government authorities have taken different steps regarding their electricity retail operations. Some have sold them and others have constituted them as a community trust. By 1994 the franchises (local monopoly rights) were removed, allowing consumers to choose their electricity source. This remains a theoretical choice for domestic consumers, but a real one for large industrial users. A number of them have entered into contracts with one of the forty-odd retailers who have been aggressively competing for their business. Domestic consumers rely on their local retailer (the former local government-constituted board) for the supply of electricity. The new retailer, however, is not obliged to supply them electricity and is not subject to any explicit price regulation, except for price caps for city domestic consumers until 1997 and a price cap of 15 per cent per annum for rural consumers for a much longer period.

In 1994 responsibility for high voltage transmission was passed to Trans Power, a newly created corporatised body. Its assets on formation were NZ$3 billion and its annual income was NZ$560. It owns the national grid and is involved in transmitting electricity from about forty generators to about fifty grid customers, most of whom are the retailers. It also operates the dispatch functions for the generators. Its charges make up about 25 per cent of the wholesale price.

During 1996, the government required ECNZ to sell a number of its power stations, introduced a wholesale electricity market and removed ECNZ's obligation to supply all customers and provide all generation. ECNZ retains over 60 per cent of the country's electricity generation capacity, which allows the majority of remaining generation to be provided by the new state-owned enterprise, Contact Energy Limited. ECNZ will retain the Waikato, Tongariro, Waitaki and Manapouri hydro systems, together with the thermal stations, Huntly and Marsden A. ECNZ is constrained from building more than half of any new generation capacity until its market share falls to 45 per cent. Eight small hydro stations and two non-operating thermal plants are being offered for sale to power companies and Maori interests. The wholesale market began on 1 October 1996, which offers power on a spot market and futures market basis. Long-term contracts are offered in tranches of up to five years' duration.[5]

Despite New Zealand's deregulation rhetoric, it has sought to regulate the privatised utilities by employing a number of express and implied legislative restraints (temporary price caps, mandatory obligations to provide specified minimal services and the Kiwi share), and by threatening future political intervention if the participants do not play fair and by relying on the general competition law (the Commerce Act and the Fair Trading Act). Where regulation has proved inadequate, new market entrants have resorted to the courts and legal commentators have proposed the revival of old common law remedies to gain entitlement to the provision of essential services.

Legislative prescription

The Government has imposed a number of express legislative restraints upon the telecommunications and electricity markets. Telecom, for example, is required by the Telecommunications (Disclosure) Regulations 1990 to publish separate audited financial statements about its regional operating companies as if they were independent entities. It is also required to fully disclose its prices, terms and conditions. The aim is to provide sufficient information for consumers to make informed choices about the services they wish to use. The problem is that it is left to individual consumers to spend the time and to have sufficient expertise to assess the information. Given the overall cost of telecommunications to a household budget, the time and expense involved in the process is economically inefficient for most households.

Telecommunications remains within the definition of a utility to the extent that there is a general community expectation that it is entitled to universal access to a telephone service. The New Zealand Government has sought to satisfy this expectation through the 'Kiwi share' which is provided for in Telecom's Articles of Association. The Kiwi share provides the government with special voting rights to ensure, amongst other things, that Telecom complies with its residential service pledges:

- to maintain free local calls;
- not to increase the standard residential phone rental beyond the consumer price index unless Telecom's regional operating companies are unreasonably affected;
- to ensure that rural residential customers pay the same costs and receive the same service as city residential customers (Janisch 1994: 267).

Telecom has complained that these restraints introduce 'significant welfare losses by distorting prices and inhibiting the development of efficient competition by making subsidised residential service unattractive to entry' (Janisch 1994: 269).

The Electricity Act 1992 provides for price caps until 1997 for city domestic users and a 15 per cent per annum cap for rural users. The newly privatised distributors are sensitive to consumer perceptions of price. The Canadian-owned distributor for Wellington, Capital Power (which recently 'merged' with neighbouring distributor EnergyDirect, and is now called TransAlta NZ) extensively advertised the fact that it would freeze its prices for two years. It failed to mention in the advertisements that this was being offered after a 28 per cent price increase.

The threat of legislative intervention

The New Zealand Government has been sensitive to its constituency with electricity, particularly its rural constituency. Under the Electricity Act 1992 prices are monitored by the Rural Electrical Reticulation Council and the Ministry of Commerce. The Act allows the Minister for Energy to introduce price controls if a case can be made of market abuse. Price is obviously a sensitive issue for consumers, suppliers and the government, which is answerable to the people. The government has been extremely hesitant in privatising the generation and transmission of electricity because together they account for 97 per cent of an electricity bill. The local distributors are left with playing within a tight margin of 3 per cent. If the generators (power stations) were to be privatised and sold at a high price, the purchasers would reasonably expect a return on their investment which would be recovered through higher generation charges. That is, assuming a fixed rate of return on the investment, it will be tempting for government to keep the valuation of the corporatised power stations relatively low so as to keep the domestic price of electricity low. If the stations are sold at a price higher than the government had valued it when it was corporatised, then (assuming the same rate of return is applied) the private owner will charge a higher price, which will immediately impact on the domestic user, because the local distributor will not have a sufficient margin to absorb the extra cost. A dramatic increase in costs would have political implications for government. The government has obviously decided to tread cautiously in privatising the big ticket items of generation and grid transmission, and maintain the threat of legislative intervention for the privatised distributors.

The Commerce Commission

The problem for generalist regulators like the New Zealand Commerce Commission is that they can only deal with the market as they find it. If the market already has dominant players, then there is no power (as exists in the US) to order divestiture to break up the monopolies, and governments have problems breaking them up because of the political pressure that can be exerted by the self-interest of the dominant players.

Other more specific difficulties face the Commerce Commission when dealing with the existing dominant market player, namely the courts. The New Zealand Court of Appeal ruled in *Telecom Corp. of New Zealand v. Commerce Commission*[6] that the Commerce Commission had no authority to restrain Telecom from maintaining its market dominance. The Commission had refused to allow Telecom to acquire an additional mobile-phone frequency because it believed that potential competitors would be forced to enter into unfavourable interconnection agreements with Telecom, thus strengthening its already dominant market position. Two of the Appeal Court judges stated that Telecom was not dominant in the mobile-phone market and the acquisition would not lead to dominance, and in doing so rejected an economic definition of dominance, preferring the ordinary meaning of the term. The other judge stated that authorisation should be granted despite Telecom being dominant in the market.

The courts

Light-handed regulation has not, as the legislators had forecast, led to a robust market in which competition has flourished. Instead, new entrants into the privatised telecommunications market have faced a monopolist determined not to lose market share. Janisch quotes the new entrant Clear Communications as complaining that 'the whole New Zealand competitive model had become entangled in a net of legal hearings, quasi-judicial actions and protracted negotiations leading to limited competition in an expensive and increasingly adversarial environment' (1994: 270). Electricity has been spared this antagonism largely because generators and grid transmission lines are still owned by the government and the privately owned distributors have effective local monopolies, except with regard to a few large industrial users.

In the case of telecommunications, Clear Communications finally resorted to court action after the failure of prolonged negotiations with Telecom to gain reasonable interconnection charges on the domestic phone lines. The High Court ruled in Clear's favour after making a brave attempt at closely considering an enormous amount of technical and economic data before providing over one hundred pages of detailed reasons (which included maps, diagrams and engineering drawings) for its decision. On appeal, the Court of Appeal complained about the complexity of the High Court's reasons and added that the Court of Appeal was not a regulatory agency.[7] This observation highlights the inappropriateness of having the courts make detailed assessments of economic impacts and technical data on implementing pricing and market access mechanisms. It also confirms the inadequacy of light-handed regulation when privatisation converts a public monopoly into a private monopoly.

The common law

The restructuring in 1996 of the electricity generators included removing the obligation on generators to supply all customers. This constitutes a fundamental reversal of the obligation on utilities to provide universal access to an essential service. The government's move towards removing this obligation for a number of utilities has prompted legal commentators like Professor Michael Taggart to propose the revival of the common law remedies along US lines which require the providers of essential goods and services to supply them to all customers (1995: 214). Taggart argues that corporatisation and privatisation have weakened or abolished public accountability mechanisms that once existed. He proposes in their stead the law of common callings and prime necessity be revived and be developed and applied by the New Zealand courts. The problem with this approach is that it is essentially a response to the lack of sufficient regulatory mechanisms. It relies on an inefficient and expensive regulator (the courts) to undertake the task of protecting consumers.

The New Zealand experience regarding regulating the privatised and partly privatised utilities is probably best summed by Janisch's description of the privatisation of telecommunications:

> Four matters need to be highlighted. First, popular mythology notwithstanding, there has been no flash cut from monopoly to competition and a number of regulatory instruments unique to telecommunications have been put in place. Second, it is not at all evident that New Zealand has arrived at a perfect state of grace in general with respect to the achievement of genuine competition. Third, more specifically, there do not appear to be effective means of preventing the former monopolist from indulging in the abuse of its dominant position. Fourth, the courts, which have been assigned the

principal responsibility of policing the telecommunications market, appear to be making very heavy weather of it and as generalists are institutionally poorly equipped to deal with either the economic principles or technological issues involved.

(1994: 266)

An Australian comparison

The Australian privatisation programme was slowed by its federal structure. Most of the utilities are under State or Territory jurisdiction. The Federal Government has responsibility under the Australian Constitution for a number of services, including telecommunications, airlines and banks (except State banks and airlines that only operate within a State). The States and Territories have responsibility for water, electricity, gas and other utilities. The Federal Government engaged in privatisation at an ambulatory rate. It corporatised the domestic telephone company and merged it with the wholly government-owned overseas telecommunication company. About a decade passed before it sold a third of the corporation in 1997. A competitor, Optus, was allowed into the market, with no non-mobile entrants allowed into the market for the first five years. A regulator, Austel, was established to assist with the development of a competitive market. After initial price competition, the two players appeared to avoid aggressive price competition, partly to allow them to fund the heavy losses sustained by laying fibre-optic cables. The government-owned international airline Qantas was merged with the government-owned domestic carrier Australian Airlines and then sold. Again there was no rush after corporatisation for privatisation. The government-owned Commonwealth Bank was also sold off in stages. In 1991, 30 per cent of the bank was sold, in 1993 the government reduced its shareholding to 50.4 per cent and in 1996 the bank was totally sold off.

By the late 1980s the Federal Government was keen to promote regulatory reform to reduce inefficiencies created by uncoordinated State utility activity. State parochialism meant, for example, that there was an inefficient electricity generation system, partly due to the fact that transmission between the States was not linked. That meant that electricity surpluses in one State could not be used to meet supply shortages in another. In response to perceived productive inefficiencies, the Council of Australian Governments (COAG) commissioned an inquiry in 1992 into Australian competitiveness, which was headed by Professor Fred Hilmer. The Hilmer Report (Hilmer 1993) recommended wide-ranging reforms to improve productive efficiency. These included the familiar mechanisms promoted by the privatisation debate: allowing third-party access to government-owned infrastructure, removing entry costs for potential competitors and introducing price regulation for utility monopolies.

The Federal Government, anxious to maintain public pressure on the States to adopt the Hilmer reforms, touted an Industry Commission report which claimed that the reforms would improve Australia's efficiency by A$23 billion each year. The strategy backfired somewhat because the States refused to sign on to the reform package unless they received a share of the productivity dividend. They argued that they would endure the employment loss and other pain associated with the reforms, while the Federal Government would reap all the benefits through increased tax revenue. The Federal Government eventually agreed to financially reward the States if they introduced the reforms, which led the COAG to agree to the implementation of National Competition Principles in April 1995. As part of the reform package a number of States created an independent regulator to regulate pricing, third-party access and competitive neutrality (equal competitive entry costs).

The States presently have a patchwork quilt of corporatised and privatised utilities. Victoria has sold off electricity generators and distribution franchises, and New South Wales has a corporatised electricity industry. The NSW Government has recently made a controversial announcement that it will privatise the industry. New South Wales has one of the more interesting State regulators, the Independent Pricing and Regulatory Tribunal, which was established before the Hilmer Report. The regulator is responsible for all the State-owned utilities and is required to take into account both consumer and social benefits when fixing utility prices. It seems at this preliminary stage, however, that the regulator places more emphasis on consumer benefits than social benefits. The issue of universal access is not a matter for the regulator, but may be provided for in legislation applying to the particular utility.

Who benefits?

The privatisation trend gained a strong grip on public policy throughout the world during the 1980s and 1990s. In a little more than a decade, assets worth billions of dollars shifted from public to private ownership and thousands of jobs were lost in industry restructuring. It is not altogether clear that governments' enthusiasm for delivering consumer benefit through privatisation was shared by the beneficiaries themselves. Indeed measuring the benefits they have received from the process is no easy task. Pollitt noted the difficulties he faced in an empirical study of the impact of ownership of electricity utilities on their efficiency in a number of countries throughout the world. He found that there are a substantial range of variables involved when making comparisons and noted that a study will usually examine a static situation, which does not account for possible future new technologies (1995: 188).

One of the other problems that confronts an empirical study is that privatisation of a poorly managed utility (because of previous government policy) can result in spectacular improvements in the first few years of privatisation. These improvements are gained by picking at the low branches of easy reforms of poorly managed utilities, which could have been achieved with public ownership had the policy settings been right, for example by corporatisation in which a publicly owned utility is required to operate along commercial lines. Another problem that faces an empirical study is the fact that input prices can vary. Pollitt noted in his study that since privatisation the UK electricity industry has derived substantial benefits from lower coal prices (1995: 189). Another difficulty he noted was that an empirical study is only as good as its data. In addition, productivity and other improvements may arise from the changed culture associated with privatisation rather than directly from privatisation itself. Ramamurti notes, for example, that Mexico's success in privatising its state-owned telephone company Telmex owed a great deal, not to the change from public to private ownership, but to the changed regulatory culture that it introduced. The privatisation debate prompted the introduction of anti-trust legislation and policy, which improved the competitive environment generally (Ramamurti 1996: 102). There are other accounts of government-owned utilities dramatically improving performance because of the privatisation debate. In some cases privatisation occurred at a time during the cultural change which allowed the newly privatised entity to lay claim to the change of ownership as being the cause of success. It seems then that the causes of the productivity improvements are better explained by a sociologist than an economist.

In addition, caution should also be exercised to avoid judging outcomes within too short a time frame. Privatisation in some instances led to the entry of numerous competitors and substantial price fall in the short term, only to have competitors bail out and prices return to pre-privatisation levels in the long term. The short-term effect of removing entry barriers can be misleading. The initial impression can be that it delivers a highly contestable market. After the initial shake-up, however, there will sometimes be a return to the pre-privatisation domination of the original utility. In the UK, express coaches were one of the first industries to be deregulated. This led to substantial fare declines and numerous new entrants. After a decade the National Bus Company's dominant market position was restored and fares in real terms returned to pre-privatisation prices.

Experience suggests, nevertheless, that there are winners and losers from privatisation, despite the difficulty in quantifying those gains and losses. One of the major benefits of privatisation is that there is a great deal more public information about the financial operation of utilities. Prosser (1994: 6) notes, for example, that in the UK the true cost of nuclear power was revealed at the time of attempted privatisation which made it impossible to sell the nuclear stations. Weyman-Jones (1994: 111) notes that by the early 1980s the US airline industry had been completely deregulated, except for safety. Efficiency gains were noticeable in the development of hub-and-spoke route operations, so that small-scale flights fed into the major airports, and in more imaginative and flexible pricing. The losers have been consumers in remote areas. Weyman-Jones (1994: 117) notes that the main losers from transport deregulation are those in small and rural areas who used to have direct routes to several major centres. The gainers are consumers enjoying efficiency improvements and taxpayers relieved of funding public sector investment programmes. But taxpayers also lose the continuing revenue stream from the profitable utilities. In most cases privatisation has involved the selling of profitable utilities and the retention of loss-making utilities, adding a longer-term budgetary burden.

Beesley (1992) claims that there has been an improved use of investment under privatisation:

> There has been a marked speeding up in adoption of available but hitherto neglected technical improvements, related to the removal of capital and constraints on raising capital and purchasing. BT, for example, has chosen to speed up and considerably modify its programme of digitalization of its network, involving among other things substantial change in its previous efforts to pioneer and develop a system which has received virtually no support in export terms.
>
> (1992: 45)

The improved investment environment was discerned in Pollitt's extensive study of electricity utilities, although the extent of the improvement is debatable, depending on the methodologies used. He concluded after an exhaustive empirical study comparing the impact of public and private ownership of electricity utilities on efficiency that the form of ownership had no discernible impact on the costs of electricity transmission and distribution. Privately owned generators were however more efficient, suggesting that they made better investment decisions than public generators. The degree of the efficiency (depending on the methodology used) varied between a negligible 0.02 per cent to a substantial 15.05 per cent (Pollitt 1995: 188).

Regulatory options

The privatisation debate highlighted the failure of the pre-existing regulatory system under government ownership. During the debate extreme claims were made about the failures, possibly to attack and dislodge entrenched interests. Once governments became aware of the short-term value of asset sales, they took little further persuasion about the merits of privatisation. Despite appealing to disingenuous motives, the debate did mount an effective case for reforming the pre-existing system which suffered inefficiency and rent-seeking behaviour. It would be wrong, however, to characterise it as lacking merit. The pre-existing system did ensure reliable utility services at affordable prices to all without discrimination. The challenge that exists is to refine a policy and regulatory mix which attains optimum consumer and social benefits. There is a range of regulatory options and experiences available from nations which have undertaken privatisation, and from the US where regulatory parameters are also undergoing reform. These will be briefly considered under the heads of establishing competitive markets and enabling third-party access, quality control, determining price, universal access and the environment. Competitive markets and quality control tend towards satisfying consumer benefits whilst universal access and the environment relate to social benefit. Price determination relates to both.

Establishing competitive markets and enabling third-party access

Under the pre-existing regulatory system there were numerous formal restrictions on potential competitors delivering services provided by the utilities. This provided the utilities freedom to operate without any fear of loss of market share because of the operations of a more efficient competitor. Requiring a utility to open up its services for third-party access is sometimes thought of as opening contestable markets which do not require special utility regulation. Telephone and electricity transmission lines presently represent natural monopolies, although technological advances may change that position. In a number of countries the utilities must make the lines available for other operators (for example, other telephone companies or electricity generators) so that they can provide their services to consumers. Third-party access may create a competitive market for phone services or electricity generation, but does not, of course, create a lines market. Because of the infrastructure costs of the lines, they remain a natural monopoly requiring continuing regulatory attention.

Removing formal entry barriers has not necessarily led to the entry of numerous competitors. This is because a rational potential competitor will not enter the market unless there is free entry, in the sense of having the same entry costs as other players, and costless exit, in the sense that if the venture fails, the cost of leaving does not exceed the economic depreciation on its capital stock. A potential competitor also needs to be able to offer different (competitive) prices than existed pre-entry (Weyman-Jones 1994: 108). Merely removing entry regulations itself can inhibit a natural monopoly from taking abnormal profits because of the threat of other entrants if prices are too high (Weyman-Jones 1994: 104).

Quality control

Consumers are not merely interested in lower prices in relation to utility services. Indeed, if the cost of the service is relatively low compared to other household expenses, there is a far greater interest in gaining a reliable good quality service. An annual decline in price of a few dollars is usually of less significance than receiving a reliable supply of gas or electricity, and a rapid response if there are breakdowns or faults. Regulating quality is, however, more difficult than regulating price. Indeed, consumers face two problems in the absence of competition:

> First, it is not clear what level of service it is reasonable to expect at any particular price level. Secondly, there is no direct power to influence the industry's level of quality by changing supplier, or to gain personal redress when things go wrong.
>
> (Winward 1994: 258)

The UK has attempted to deal with the issue of standards by introducing Citizen's Charters. The charters were strongly promoted by the then Prime Minister, John Major. The aim of the charters was to have government service providers outline measurable service delivery standards. There was a great deal of public scepticism at the time of the introduction of the charters because they were seen to be unenforceable. Indeed, the two major weaknesses of a charter are the potential for setting meaningless and unmeasurable performance targets and the lack of enforceability. The first weakness can be addressed by management and organisational commitment to taking a charter seriously, the second by introducing a system of reward for compliance or punishment for non-compliance. The UK government took the latter step by introducing the Charter Mark in which the government issues a badge of honour (the Charter Mark) for service providers that successfully applied its charter. A provider with a Charter Mark can advertise the fact that it has been awarded the mark.

Organisational commitment does not come cheaply. An Australian insurance company, AAMI, has taken the unusual step of voluntarily introducing a consumer charter. In doing so it spent two years consulting with government, consumer groups and regulators, as well as researching world practices before it embarked on developing its charter. It then spent a considerable amount of money involving its staff in developing and monitoring the charter. Its research indicated that consumers preferred a limited number of clear, concrete, measurable and achievable promises to a long shopping list of (possibly unattainable) promises. It also introduced a penalty regime in which customers are paid A$50 for breaches. Monthly board meetings are provided with a report on the rate and nature of breaches around the country. That information is then used as the basis for management decisions about improving the company's performance. AAMI claims impressive growth and profit improvements in a flat insurance market since the introduction of the charter. The AAMI case illustrates the point that the mere introduction of a charter in itself achieves nothing; it takes the input of considerable financial resources and organisational commitment before a charter delivers benefits.

Determining price

In the absence of a contestable market, price regulation of some form remains the only viable option to prevent a utility obtaining abnormal profits. Beesley, however, claims that fears about monopoly exploitation have been exaggerated. He argues for example that:

> . . . if one inspects the actual price changes associated with privatization, one has to recognize the possibility that there may, for a considerable time, be a coincidence between raising prices to get more profits and move towards a 'better' set of prices from the welfare viewpoint. . . . Under nationalization [products or services] were typically priced in ways not reflecting respective marginal costs, and with arbitrary requirement to create an overall surplus. More logical, profit-based pricing, reflecting costs *and* exploiting the relative demand elasticities, could well have resulted, so far, in a constellation of process more in line with welfare maxims.
>
> (1992: 45–6)

All this reflects is a more sophisticated exploitation of the monopoly position than had previously existed rather than pricing which is responsive to a competitive market. In other words, it does not provide a rationale for avoiding the regulation of utility prices to avoid unfair exploitation of the monopoly position.

A major problem facing the regulator is information asymmetry. The utility has an enormous information advantage which it can use to manipulate capital costs to increase profits. The regulator is largely dependent on the information provided by the utility. The utility's superior information makes it extremely difficult for the regulator to provide incentives to maximise efficiency. Pollitt (1995: 20) notes that this asymmetry can be reduced, but not eliminated, by *ex post* auditing and learning about the utility in a dynamic setting.

The UK has attempted to overcome the information asymmetry problem by simply fixing price caps using the RPI – x formula, where RPI is the retail price index (in Australia referred to as the consumer price index: CPI) and x is a somewhat arbitrary figure determined by the regulator. This method avoids attempting to locate the complex information requirements and applying the calculations of a rate-of-return method. In addition, although rate of return can prevent monopoly abuse if the allowed rate is close to the cost of borrowing, it does not achieve productive efficiency because there is an incentive to over-capitalise (Price 1994: 82).

The problem with RPI $- x$ is that it was intended as a short-term solution when it was established. Extended use of this mechanism inevitably becomes a rate-of-return regulation when price cap is determined creating a hybrid regulatory mechanism (Price 1994: 82). This may lead an industry seeking to expand its capital base to lower price at peak capacity to increase peak demand causing excessive demand, thus proving to the regulator that more capital is required to cope with peak demand.

If there is little chance of competition and there is little chance of cost reduction, the price cap is obviously of little value; the only regulatory option is rate of return. In any event the price cap has not been consistently applied in the UK. For example, in some industries the price cap has excluded certain input prices, for example the cost of coal for electricity generators over which they arguably have little control. However, passing this cost through to consumers means that there is little incentive for generators to negotiate for lower coal prices.

A policy dilemma arises in relation to the level of public accountability for the regulatory process. In the US the regulatory process involves open hearings and determinations which are subject to judicial review, which creates a more costly process than in the UK in which the regulator conducts confidential negotiations with the regulator and is subject to low review in practice. The UK approach, however, risks the regulator becoming captive of the industry. The UK regulatory system sets few rules and constraints for the regulator leading to an idiosyncratic system which is dependent on the quality and traits of the individual appointed as regulator. The US experience also alerts us to keep the regulatory system simple. There a myriad of state and federal pricing and allocation arrangements have 'created a system of such aggregate complexity that it is barely intelligible, even to specialists' (Noam 1997: 958).

Universal access

The concept of universal access has a long antecedence, as mentioned above. The US has for a substantial time provided for universal access both through common law developments and statutory provision. Illinois' policy as expressed in the Illinois Utilities Act 1921, for example, states that 'no person should be denied essential utility service during the winter months due to financial inability to pay' (Clause 8-201).

There are three principal ways of achieving universal access: through direct budget subsidy (e.g. community service orders or CSOs), licensing requirements in which the universal access costs are spread across all competitive utilities and mandated 'lifeline' services (Carver 1995: 48). The first is mentioned in the previous paragraph. An example of the second appears in Australia's Telecommunications Act 1991 which states that the 'losses that result from supplying loss-making services in the course of fulfilling the universal service obligation should be shared among carriers' (Section 287). The third involves setting minimum standards of service for low-income households at rates less than those payable by other households. California set a 15 per cent discount on utility bills for consumers with an income of less than 130 per cent of the federal poverty guidelines. District of Columbia sets a 25 per cent discount on the first 400 kilowatt-hours of usage (Carver 1995: 51). The US federal Telecommunications Act 1996 mandates universal service in a number of ways. It requires that –

- the absolute level of prices be 'just, reasonable and affordable';
- there be rough equality between rural areas, high-cost areas, and low-income consumers on the one hand and metropolitan customers on the other;
- there be subsidised access to advanced services for schools, hospitals and libraries.

The reason a conservative legislature enacted the universal access provisions was because the representatives of conservative rural states combined with liberal Democrats, who had concern for the poor, and the high-tech Democrats, who wanted phone access for school computers, to enact the legislation (Noam 1997: 961).

The policy response to the allocation–productivity dilemma has led, in the case of corporatisation at least, to a requirement that the utility act along commercial lines to maximise productive efficiency and that it identify the uncommercial costs of meeting government allocative (social) policy objectives. These are referred to as community service obligations (CSOs). The cost of CSOs is drawn from general government revenue rather than from the utility's revenue. Although this makes any cross-subsidisation for allocative purposes transparent, it has been criticised for leaving the CSO recipients as a visible target for future government cost-cutting measures.

Environment

The use and manufacture of utility services like electricity, water and gas has a significant impact on the environment, and is therefore a matter of policy and regulatory concern. One means of reducing environmental impact is to moderate demand for the utility product by using price. The market mechanism pays no heed to environmental concern and can therefore facilitate demand-and-supply patterns which damage the environment. There may, however, be underlying regulatory constraints that restrict consumption or impose conditions on the manufacture and delivery of goods and services which drive up price and reduce demand. The Coase theorem (1960) can be useful in this context in prompting a comprehensive exploration of efficient regulatory mechanisms to reduce environmental detriment.

The New South Wales regulator has express power under Section 14 of the Independent Pricing and Regulatory Tribunal Act when fixing utility prices to take into account 'the need to maintain ecologically sustainable development (within the meaning of Section 6 of the Protection of the Environment Administration Act 1991) by appropriate pricing policies that take account of all the feasible options available to protect the environment'. This factor can be taken into account along with others including:

- the government agency's economic cost of production;
- past, current or future expenditures in relation to the government monopoly service;
- charges for other monopoly services provided by the government agency, economic parameters, such as discount rates, or movements in a general price index;
- a rate of return on the assets of the government agency;
- a valuation of the assets of the government agency;
- the need to promote competition in the supply of the service concerned;
- considerations of demand management (including levels of demand) and least-cost planning (Section 14).

The tribunal has taken environmental issues into account when fixing price, but it appears to attach far greater weight to the more readily measurable consumer benefit factors. Emphasis is therefore placed on price capping and rate-of-return mechanisms, with environmental protection given less attention. In the 1996 Pricing Determination for Electricity, for instance, emphasis was placed on improving efficiency by applying CPI $- x$ price capping to reduce returns for generators (which it considered to be relatively inefficient) and increase them for distributors. The tribunal then added that:

> In its Interim Report, the Tribunal expressed concern about the possible biases against energy efficiency and renewables. However, it considered its proper task was to ensure that prices and the form of regulation did not contribute to this bias. Policies to promote energy efficiency and renewables or to overcome non-price barriers are the domain of the energy and environmental policy agencies.
>
> (1996: 10)

It reasoned that 'setting a cap on overall revenues or margins rather than average prices reduces the link between revenues and sales of electricity'. The tribunal argued as follows:

> This significantly reduces the incentive to promote electricity sales and increases the range of demand management and energy efficiency options which are commercially feasible.
>
> (1996: 10–11)

The tribunal therefore saw itself as playing a supporting role for government departments responsible for regulating the environment and the electricity utility. Specifically, the tribunal claimed it was supporting an industry reform package developed by the other regulators which involves:

- establishing a sustainable energy fund;
- meeting requirements for integrated resource planning prior to construction of transmission lines or supply capacity;
- requiring distributors to develop strategies to meet greenhouse gas reduction targets as a condition of obtaining a retail licence (1996: 11).

Conclusion

The challenge now exists, in light of the privatisation experience, to reform the regulation of utilities to attain optimum consumer and social benefits. Although privatisation, and the surrounding debate, identified efficiency and accountability problems under the previous regulatory system, it does not offer an answer to a range of social concerns. Privatisation does not directly address, for example, universal access and environmental concerns. The privatisation experience has also confirmed that the ambitions of some proponents of privatisation for the abolition of specific utility regulation or the mere application of scientific or quasi-scientific economic formulas cannot be realised without risking serious social disruption. The regulation of utilities remains ultimately a question of moral and political judgement.

Acknowledgements

I thank Professor Stephen Parker for his comments on an earlier draft of this chapter. The section dealing with New Zealand has appeared previously in a slightly different form as a conference paper entitled 'The New Zealand experience of utility price regulation' delivered at a Business Law Education Centre Conference in Sydney and Melbourne, February 1997, and published by BLEC Books, Melbourne, 1997.

Notes

1 F. Hargraves (1787) *Collection of Tracts relative to the Law of England* (London) pp. 77–8.
2 (1810) 12 East 527; 104 ER 206.

3 [1916] AC 57 at 102–3.
4 (1876) 94 US 77. For a detailed account of the law regarding common callings see Taggart (1995).
5 See http://www.ecnz.co.nz/competitive/ and http://www.ecnz.co.nz/what/
6 [1992] 3 NZLR 429.
7 *Clear Communications v. Telecom Corp. of New Zealand* (1993) 4 NZBLC 103,340 per Cooke P.

References

Beesley, M.E. (1992) 'Privatization: Reflections on UK Experience', in M.E. Beesley, *Privatization, Regulation and Deregulation*, London: Routledge.

Beesley, M.E. and Littlechild, S.C. (1992) 'The Regulation of Privatized Monopolies in the United Kingdom', in M.E. Beesley, *Privatization, Regulation and Deregulation*, London: Routledge.

Carver, L. (1995) 'Equity and Pricing in Competitive Markets for Gas, Water and Electricity', paper presented to 'What Price Competition?' conference held at the University of New South Wales, Sydney, June 1995.

Coase, R.H. (1960) 'The Problem of Social Cost', 3 *Journal of Law and Economics* 1.

Hilmer, F. (1993) *The Report of the Independent Committee of Inquiry into National Competition* (the 'Hilmer Report'), Canberra: Australian Government Publishing Service.

Janisch, H.N. (1994) 'From Monopoly Towards Competition in Telecommunications: What Role for Competition Law?', 23 *Canadian Business Law Journal* 239.

New South Wales Independent Pricing and Regulatory Tribunal (1996) *Electricity Prices Determination*, http://www.ipart.nsw.gov.au/

Noam, E.M. (1997) 'Will Universal Service and Common Carriage Survive the Telecommunications Act of 1996?', 97 *Columbia Law Review* 955.

Pollitt, M.G. (1995) *Ownership and Performance in Electric Utilities: The International Evidence on Privatization and Efficiency*, Oxford: Oxford University Press.

Price, C. (1994) 'Economic Regulation of Privatised Monopolies', in P.M. Jackson and C.M. Price, *Privatisation and Regulation: A Review of the Issues*, Harlow: Longman.

Prosser, T. (1994) 'Privatisation, Regulation and Public Services', *The Juridical Review* 3.

Prosser, T. and Moran, M. (1994) 'Privatisation and Regulatory Change: The Case of Great Britain', in M. Moran and T. Prosser (eds), *Privatization and Regulatory Change in Europe*, Buckingham: Open University Press.

Ramamurti, R. (1996) 'Telephone Privatisation in a Large Country: Mexico', in R. Ramamurti (ed.), *Privatizing Monopolies: Lessons from the Telecommunications and Transport Sectors in Latin America*, Baltimore: Johns Hopkins University Press.

Russell, D. (1994) 'The New Zealand Experience and the Consumer Protection Lessons Australia Can Learn From It', conference paper for 'Consumers and the Reform of Australia's Utilities', Sydney, 17–18 March, held by the Trade Practices Commission.

Sunstein, C.R. (1990) *After the Rights Revolution: Reconceiving the Regulatory State*, Cambridge, MA: Harvard University Press.

Taggart, M. (1991) 'Corporatisation, Privatisation and Public Law', 2 *Public Law Review* 77.

—— (1995) 'Public Utilities and Public Law', in P.A. Joseph (ed.) *Essays on the Constitution*, Wellington, New Zealand: Brokers.

Weyman-Jones, T. (1994) 'Deregulation', in P.M. Jackson and C.M. Price, *Privatisation and Regulation: A Review of the Issues*, Harlow: Longman.

Winward, J. (1994) 'Privatization and Domestic Consumers', in M. Bishop, J. Kay and C. Mayer (eds), *Privatization and Economic Performance*, Oxford: Oxford University Press.

3

'PLUS ÇA CHANGE . . .'

The effects of markets and corporate law on the governance of privatised enterprises

Michael J. Whincop and Stuart Rowland

PART ONE: INTRODUCTION

The vast literature on privatisation makes a variety of claims for and against the concept. Acquaintance with that literature leaves a lasting impression that commentators often treat privatisation as a monolithic concept, a process about which generalisations could reliably be made. There has rightly been a great deal of attention paid to the effects of markets on the efficiency of privatised enterprise. One issue that has been rather poorly understood is the relationship between these efficiency (or inefficiency) claims, and the governance of the privatised enterprise. By 'governance', we mean the framework of controls in which the integrity of a related set of transactions is determined (Williamson 1996: 11). Governance is a crucial issue as the ubiquity of the term in discourse on businesses and corporations surely suggests. The ability of a privatised enterprise to achieve efficiencies depends in important ways on the governance processes of that enterprise. This chapter seeks to bridge the gap by clarifying some important theoretical issues relevant to the relationship between the effects of capital and factor markets, the governance of corporations, and corporate law. Corporate law is an essential (but neglected) influence on the governance and, therefore, the efficiency of a privatised corporation. The analysis in this chapter is particularly influenced by the changes that have taken place over the last few years in Australia's corporate law. These changes are significant because they suggest that the structure of corporate law is moving away from the norms by which it historically has been dominated. The claim in this chapter is that it is moving towards norms that are more typical of public (in particular, administrative) law. This finding is of particular significance, because we believe that it undermines, or at least gives cause for reappraisal of, some of the efficiency claims that can be made for privatisation. The transition of corporate law towards a model of active judicial review of managerial discretion works in precisely the opposite direction to the effects of the stronger managerial incentives available to managers, and the liberation of managerial policy from politics and the pork-barrel.

Parts Two and Three of this chapter approach these issues in a complementary way. Part Two studies some issues associated with the effect of markets on the governance of the privatised enterprise. As part of this task, we study some aspects of the efficiency claims made for privatisation. This part introduces some important modern theory concerning the governance of corporations which has been developed by law and economics scholars. The central idea in this theory – that corporations are a process, or a framework, in which conflicting objectives of different claimholders are resolved contractually – is particularly relevant to analysing the effect of markets on the discretion of the senior managers of privatised enterprises. Our analysis represents a critique of a use of the contractual theory of the firm by Farrar and McCabe (1995) to advocate privatisation. Our purpose is not in this analysis to advocate continuing public ownership. Instead, two points are suggested. First, we offer a reminder that there are *agency* problems in both alternative ownership forms, and that contractual theories of the corporation must be used with great caution in the comparison of discrete structural alternatives (cf. Williamson 1996). Second, the analysis clears the way for examination and comparison of the law governing the public enterprise and the private enterprise, and its effect on managerial discretion.

Part Three seeks to offer an analysis of corporate law, and the sensitivity of efficiency claims to changes in the underlying structure of corporate norms. These norms are changing, and Australian courts have played an important part in this change. The changes move away from the concepts of majority rule and non-intervention, in favour of a more active judicial review. Although public law has not been the touchstone of these changes, it is not difficult to recognise that the values which seem to motivate these changes resonate with those underlying public law and policy; likewise, the grounds for judicial intervention are more familiar from administrative law than from contract law and equity. Part Four offers some conclusions.

PART TWO: A THEORETICAL ANALYSIS OF EFFICIENT GOVERNANCE

This part introduces the contractual theory of corporations. The object of doing so is to enable an appreciation of the effect of markets on the governance of the corporations. The conclusion is that, in both public and private enterprises, management will be inclined to use their discretion in a way which does not maximise value. The analysis sets the scene for Part Three which describes the influence of corporate law on the ways in which managerial discretion will be exercised.

An introduction to contractual theory

The key problem in corporations, as in all organisations, is the difficulty of controlling the way in which managers exercise their managerial discretion. Various solutions have been identified: contractual theory emphasises how controls take their place within larger contractual equilibria. The original scholars to identify the problem of separation of ownership and control in corporations were, of course, Berle and Means (1932). This was an important development as it explained why a corporation should not be expected to act as a classical value maximiser. The significance of Berle and Means' theory to scholarship was its profound effect on the perceived relevance of corporate law to corporate management. It sponsored a *managerialist* paradigm, in which management was regarded as the key strategic constituency in corporations. That paradigm has been persistent in its influence on thinking about corporate affairs.

The normative weight of the separation of ownership and control was challenged in the 1970s by economics scholars (Alchian and Demsetz 1972; Jensen and Meckling 1976). The object of their research was the application of the tools of neoclassical microeconomics to 'the firm'. The firm had, shortly after Berle and Means' book, been the subject of analysis by Ronald Coase (1937). Coase demonstrated that markets operated in a costly way. Organising as a firm was a means by which the costs of contracting could be reduced. Between the time of expounding this theory of the firm, and its later reworking by neoclassical economists, Coase had proposed his extraordinarily influential theorem that where transaction costs were nil, efficiency would be independent of any allocation of property rights (Coase 1960). In other words, the initial allocation of property rights would not affect efficiency, because the party valuing resources most highly would contract to acquire those property rights.

Michael Jensen and William Meckling's 1976 article represented an adaptation of neoclassical economic theory, adjusted for Coase's theory of transaction costs, to corporations (Jensen and Meckling 1976). It followed from Coase that the corporation was no more than a network, or a nexus, of contracts between the constituencies of the corporation. One form of contract involved in this 'web' of contracts is between those who manage the production process, and the shareholders who contract for a right to share in its residual risks. The shareholders will often be referred to in this chapter as residual claimants (Klein 1982; Fama and Jensen 1983). This separation of ownership and control leads to the incentive problems that Berle and Means had recognised. Jensen and Meckling subsumed this problem within the larger concept of an agency relationship, in which a *principal* delegates decision-making authority to an *agent* to perform a service. These problems were a function of transaction costs. If transaction costs were nil, the agent would maximise the value of the firm. However, costly contracting precludes any attempt to bring incentives completely into alignment.

The divergence of incentives of the two parties induces the principal to monitor the agent's activities. The agent may seek to bond herself to the principal's interests by making a credible commitment to suffer if she takes actions detrimental to the principal. The parties will seek to trade off the costs of monitoring, bonding and the expected reduction in welfare from residual opportunism so that the sum of these *agency costs* is minimised.

By invoking the contractual themes of consensus and exchange, the new theory implies the efficiency of existing institutional structures (Butler and Ribstein 1995: 4–13). It also redirected attention to the means of controlling agency problems. Three levels of control are identifiable. The first is the process of bonding and monitoring that operates 'within' the corporation. It includes mechanisms such as external audits, compensation committees, 'monitoring' boards of directors, and other corporate governance processes. Second, competition in markets also limits discretion. The effect of markets on the discretion of managers has, as we see below, important implications for the privatised enterprise. While product markets and markets for executive services are significant, two markets are particularly important (Fama 1980; cf. Black 1990: 579). One is the market for corporate control, in which inefficient managers are displaced in takeovers by those who value the control of the corporation more highly than its present owners (Manne 1965). The other is the capital market. Jensen and Meckling argued that a corporation selling securities in an efficient market would only receive the value of the securities net of agency costs. In an efficient market, the implications of information relevant to the risk or cash flows of a corporation are impounded into stock prices in a timely way and without *systematic* underestimation or overestimation. If the pricing process is efficient in this sense, the risk of error can be eliminated by holding a diversified portfolio of securities (Fama 1970, 1991; Gilson and Kraakman 1984; Gordon and Kornhauser 1985; Langevoort 1992). Jensen and Meckling's claim implies that the promoter selling the securities would have an incentive to subject the agent to controls that minimise total agency costs.

The law, especially corporate law, is a third means by which agency costs are controlled. Given the existence of transaction costs, the Coase theorem suggests that corporate law should do three things. It should provide means by which contracting costs can be reduced (for example, by providing a cheap means for incorporation), it should respect and enforce the contracts which are agreed by parties to the corporate nexus of contracts, and it should provide a series of efficient *default* rules to govern corporate contracts (e.g. Easterbrook and Fischel 1991; Macey 1993). Because transaction costs are positive, parties will not bargain their agreements in full. Therefore the law has a role in decreasing transaction costs by supplying rules that fill gaps in the contract. However, the Coase theorem implies that the rule should permit the parties to exclude, vary, or contract around, it; hence, the description of the rule as a default (Ayres and Gertner 1989; Craswell 1989; Johnston 1990; Schwartz 1992). Some of the most interesting questions in corporate and contract law are the properties of an efficient default rule when one of the contracting parties has information another does not possess (Ayres and Gertner 1989; Johnston 1990; Whincop 1997a). Mandatory terms – those which cannot be excluded by the agreement of the parties – can only be justified if the body establishing those terms (the parliament, or a court) is more competent in identifying the parties' interests than the parties are, and if preferences for the specified rule are homogeneous.

Markets, management and privatisation

The case for privatisation has been extensively debated. Economists have been interested in the efficiency of management of assets under private and public ownership. Economists of the 'property rights' school have used their analytical models to predict that public ownership will lead to inefficient management of assets compared to a private ownership regime (e.g. Alchian 1965; Demsetz 1967; cf. Hansmann 1980). This follows from the idea that the more attenuated the property rights of a person in an asset which that person manages, the less incentive that person has to manage it efficiently. Thus, an asset will be used more efficiently if the property rights in the asset are owned by a person who can capture the gains from its efficient use, than in the situation where the property rights are owned by the government which employs the same person to manage the asset. However, a related problem arises when the asset is owned by a corporation managed by persons who do not own significant interests in the corporation's residual claims. Such persons, like public bureaucrats, do not bear a significant part of the wealth effects of their management.[1] To return to the analysis in Part One, the residual claimants in both enterprises – taxpayers in the public enterprise, and shareholders in the private enterprise – must contend with an agency problem. The difference is that in the case of the corporation, its members have unrestricted property rights in shares (Baxter 1978; Hirschman 1970). In contrast, it is very difficult for citizens to trade profitably on their status as taxpayers. If the efficiency claims for privatisation are valid, the incentives created by private ownership of shares in the privatised enterprise must permit the control of the agency problem in a way that surpasses the means available in the public bureaucracy. Shareholding must create the incentive for managers to manage assets more efficiently, and the means to impose discipline and control on managers for failures.

Professors John Farrar and Bernard McCabe use economic analysis (strongly dependent on the contractual theory examined above) to argue that privatisation leads to more efficient management of assets than corporatisation does (Farrar and McCabe 1995). Corporatisation implies that governments retain ownership of residual claims in the enterprise. Farrar and McCabe look specifically at issues of comparative governance, and argue that when ownership becomes private, the governance of the organisation will be more efficiently monitored (1995: 34–6). As a consequence of ownership rights becoming a traded commodity, enterprises obtain access to monitoring effects provided by markets. These are hypothesised to motivate managers to act in the best interests of the residual claimants.[2] The basis of the argument is that a privatised enterprise must compete in more markets than a corporatised enterprise will. These motivate the contracting parties to seek more efficient governance structures, and motivate managers to act more efficiently. Markets and their monitoring effects should motivate managers to act in the best interests of the residual claimants.

Farrar and McCabe argue that competition in product markets compels managers to act in the shareholders' best interests (1995: 32). If a market is not monopolistic, a corporation that cannot supply products and services at a competitive price will exit the market because it will be unable to earn a sufficient return on invested capital. By contrast, a state-owned enterprise is unlikely to be subject to competition. However, the key issue is not the ownership of the enterprise in this respect – it is the competition in, and liberalisation of, the market. If the public enterprise has been a monopolist, privatisation scarcely changes that result (Domberger and Piggott 1986; Foreman-Peck 1989; Howard 1989; Kay and Thompson 1986; King 1995; Starr 1988; cf. Megginson *et al.* 1994). Liberalisation can be pursued either together with or independently of privatisation (Starr 1988). The problem is that a government pursuing a privatisation agenda may have minimal incentives to liberalise. A monopolist ought to be worth more than a firm subject to competition, because it generates monopoly profits by generating artificial scarcity (King 1995). If privatisation is driven by the need to maximise the financial returns from the 'sell-off', the need to preserve the monopoly may be a dominant motive. The usual response to privatised monopolies involves further regulation, for instance, of rate of return (McGrory 1989). However, these forms of regulation involve substantial costs and compromises (Laffont and Tirole 1991; Maddock 1993; Olsen and Torsvik 1993), including the possibility that regulation becomes the means demanded by the regulated firm to transfer wealth to it from the public (Mueller 1989).

If, on the other hand, market reform does take place at the time of privatisation, and the public asset sells for lower than the price it otherwise might, taxpayers suffer. Customers and new suppliers in the liberalised market may gain. However, some customers (often consumers) may lose where they have been charged less than marginal cost as a result of cross-subsidy from other types of customers (Posner 1971). While this may be efficient (Polinsky 1989: 7–10; 1992: 12–16), that only does not necessarily endorse it as a policy (Calabresi 1991). Given the denunciation by classical liberals and economic libertarians of wealth redistribution by governments (Epstein 1995), one notes the tension between liberalisation and privatisation.

Farrar and McCabe's remaining argument concerns capital markets. This conforms with the comments that prefaced this section that the only difference in the allocation of property rights is the ownership of corporate securities. Farrar and McCabe argue that the capital market reduces agency costs. Before dealing with the specifics of the argument, a general problem emerges. There is no doubt that markets play an important role in contractual theory. If parties contract in markets characterised by rational expectations, agents will have incentives to bond themselves to principals and provide for monitoring. However, the theory is not very well adapted to analysing the issue of the increase in allocative efficiency when an enterprise is privatised. Contractual theory explains the evolution of corporate governance within a contractual framework – it is not a theory which offers a great deal of insight into the comparison of discrete structural alternatives (Williamson 1996: 11).

The first argument concerns bonding. Farrar and McCabe assert that the ability to use residual claims as a means by which to compensate managers increases the ability to bond the interests of managers to those of shareholders. The argument ignores the empirical evidence that the observed bonding of managers to the interests of shareholders is minimal (Coffee 1988: 942–50; Jensen and Murphy 1990; Stout 1988: 644–51). This evidence may be consistent with the problem of managerial risk aversion. A manager is inherently risk averse because his or her human capital is already invested in the corporation in a way that does not permit risk reduction by diversification (Coffee 1986; Kraakman 1984). Increasing the amount of compensation that depends on firm performance increases the risk that the manager bears. Thus, one must draw real-world comparisons between the very limited bonding in corporations with the means of motivating the managers of corporatised public enterprises to maximise performance. Contractual theory provides few clues to the answer of this empirical question.

Second, Farrar and McCabe argue that capital markets penalise inefficient governance. If promoters offer shares in efficient capital markets, they should have an incentive to establish an optimal governance structure in order to maximise their return on the shares they sell. Some commentators treat this argument suspiciously. Professor John Coffee has argued that most corporations, especially those making an initial public offering, will find it difficult to differentiate the claims that they make for their governance from suspect ones that other corporations make (Coffee 1988: 935–6; cf. Butler and Ribstein 1995: 33–42). This follows from the extreme uncertainty of the nature of future managerial opportunism and the endogenous nature of this risk. Obviously, if Coffee's argument is correct, the likelihood that the privatised enterprise will be subjected to efficient governance is low. This issue can ultimately be resolved only by empirical evidence. However, there is a more fundamental contradiction in the basic logic, which resides in the government's identity as the promoter.

According to agency theory, the promoter has the incentive to impose an efficient governance structure, because the promoter bears the agency costs in the capital offering. If one accepts that the government is the promoter in a privatisation, the argument suggests that the capital market will give the government incentives to select efficient governance structures. The problem is that such a prediction is inconsistent with the premises of property rights economics. Farrar and McCabe are unwittingly suggesting that a government, when selling the enterprise, can devise an optimal governance structure that it could not devise when the asset was subject to public management. To put it another way, if the government is capable of designing an efficient governance structure, why should it bother privatising (cf. Jackson and Price 1994: 11)? Consider an example. Some of the most important influences on the governance of the privatised enterprise will be decided in the legislation which is enacted by the government to privatise the enterprise. Quite apart from rate-of-return regulations, the legislation may provide for the avenues through which the government influences the enterprise. This may be through mandatory board representation, the ability to block a hostile takeover through golden shares, and the like. The problem is that such legislation is not the product of a market bidding situation. It is the product of parliamentary voting, by representatives with an eye on their prospects at the next election. Public choice theory suggests few reasons for optimism concerning the quality of such decisions (Gillette 1988; Mueller 1989; Priest 1988; Shearmur 1988). One need only consider for confirmation the liberal use of the pork-barrel by the present Australian government to buy off two independent senators in order to secure the passage of legislation privatising Telstra, Australia's telecommunications utility. The advocates of privatisation cannot have it both ways – the government cannot be inefficient except when it privatises.

This process is also apparent in share offerings. The government has political incentives to underprice (Hamilton 1995). Underpricing increases the likelihood of the issue being oversubscribed. Although underpricing represents an opportunity cost to taxpayers, oversubscription is nonetheless desired by politicians as it suggests that the privatisation policy has succeeded (Hamilton 1995; Quiggin 1994; Vickers and Yarrow 1988: Table 7.1). Where information costs in the political process are high, these motivations are likely to prevail. As is true of market liberalisation, privatisation is as much a matter of redistribution as it is of efficiency.

Outside of this initial public offering situation, the influence of share markets on governance is restricted to cases of takeovers and subsequent offerings of shares. We defer the vexed question of takeovers for a moment.

So far as subsequent offerings are concerned, the argument is that the corporation must reform its governance structures to attract new capital. Quite apart from the fact that subsequent offerings are both highly expensive and infrequent, Farrar and McCabe concede that any penalty from a subsequent capital raising is suffered by existing shareholders (Farrar and McCabe 1995: 32; Gordon 1989: 1573–5).

Finally, what of takeovers? While the so-called market for corporate control provides residual discipline (cf. Coffee 1984), it does *not* do so at 'low cost', as Farrar and McCabe maintain (1995: 32, 36). Takeovers are costly, in terms of the premiums bidders pay, the transaction costs of the process, and the potential value-decreasing conduct by incumbent managers who defend their own positions (Black 1989; Coffee 1984; Fischel 1987; Jarrell *et al.* 1988). High transaction costs will therefore mean that only major managerial inefficiency is disciplined. A comparison with public bureaucracies is useful at this point. In general terms, a takeover is really only a matter of the security of managerial tenure. The takeover is the only means by which directors and managers are likely to be ousted where shareholders are many and dispersed. However, the crucial issue is to compare the security of tenure of a public bureaucrat, the likelihood of displacement by political masters, and the effect on managerial efficiency. There is some anecdotal evidence concerning the displacement of inefficient bureaucrats (Wettenhall and Beckett 1991: 222–4)[3] – enough to make the efficiency issue one which can only be resolved by comparison and empirical evidence, rather than *a priori* theorisation. In the context of privatisations, commentators have shown that governments privatising public enterprises have retained powers that thwart the discipline of the market for corporate control (Graham and Prosser 1987; Taggart 1991). The main example is the 'golden' share retained by the government, which enables it to eliminate hostile takeovers it does not favour. The retention of the golden share may reflect naive beliefs amongst the public that 'the people's assets' should stay in the hands of 'the people' (i.e. in the hands of a wide group of shareholders), not those of a single entity. Such a belief fails to acknowledge that dispersed ownership permits real control to remain in management's hands, not 'the people's' hands. This reminds us that even if private is to be preferred to public ownership, one must acknowledge the costs of any attempt to cross the fabled line.

To conclude this part, it is worth repeating that too much attention has been given to markets, and too little to governance. However, as we have seen, markets are only one influence on governance. Others include a more explicit contracting process, and the default and mandatory rules applied by the law. This failure to concentrate on governance issues has perhaps diverted us from studying what really changes in a privatisation. However, a contractual theory makes this study crucially important, since it rejects the proposition that corporations are anything other than a network of contracts. The next part analyses some important changes in the doctrinal structure of

Australian corporate law which further qualify our ability to make efficiency claims for privatisation.

PART THREE: THE LAW AND GOVERNANCE OF CORPORATIONS

Motivation and scope of analysis

Where the costs of contracting are positive, the implication of the Coase theorem for corporate governance is that the law matters (cf. Black 1990). This part therefore analyses the impact of changes in corporate law doctrine on the governance of corporations. Our analysis is directed to Australian law. Although in one sense that limits the extent to which our conclusions can be generalised, the legal issues that we consider are of broad application. Thus, the significance of this part is its normative analysis of the effect on governance of certain types of legal changes, of which the Australian experience represents examples. In this part, we focus on four recent developments of significance to corporate governance. First, we consider the modern content of a director's duty of care. Second, we consider the statutory duty of propriety to which officers are subject. Third, we consider the review of shareholders' entitlements to alter articles of association. Fourth, we consider the standing of shareholders and others to bring litigation on behalf of or against the corporation. The courts have been prime movers in this process. At the time of writing, the government has appointed a programme to review the *Corporations Law* from an economic perspective (Treasurer 1997). The proposals which have appeared at the time of writing do not really propose major changes (Corporate Law Economic Reform Program 1997).

An outline of our argument is as follows. It is arguable that efficiencies may be achieved through privatisation by liberating a company's investment and financing policies from political interference, and in order to limit the extent to which the management of business enterprises is used by governments in the redistribution of wealth. The government's role in redistribution would be limited to the more visible and more acceptable taxation and social welfare systems. In order for privatisation to accomplish these things, the structure of the law to which the privatised entity is subject must afford a substantial region of managerial discretion. Management must be able to manage, to react to markets, and to undertake obligations consistently with the demands of the markets in which the corporation transacts. Even if one could rid oneself of the doubts in respect of these matters that were expressed in Part Two, this part suggests that corporate law, as the general body of rules governing the management of privatised entities, is increasingly taking a shape that is inconsistent with this goal. In the past, corporate law vouchsafed the discretion of corporate management. Judges rarely intervened in the internal management of companies, and reviewed corporate decisions only on the grounds of bad faith or gross negligence. That policy is sometimes described as the internal management rule.[4] However, the developments studied below suggest that courts are exercising an increasingly active form of judicial review, at the instance of a wider range of claimants, on grounds that are more familiar from public than private law (cf. Bottomley 1991).

Therefore, the developments that we study are important for the following reasons. First, they invite analysis of their efficiency as rules applying to corporate contracts. Are these rules consistent with the development of efficient governance structures, or with some other policy object? The grounds for review in the 'new' law seem not to serve, or at least they serve very equivocally, the welfare of shareholders. Second, the rules enable one to understand the scope of managerial discretion which corporate law marks out for corporations in general, and privatised enterprises in particular. Third, the momentum of changes in corporate law reveals a tension between two alternative conceptions of the corporation. One conception is the contractual analysis presented in this chapter; another is a picture of corporations which resonates with romantic ideas of community and involvement (Mitchell 1995). The tension between contractual and communitarian theories of corporate law is a central issue in American scholarship at the moment (Bainbridge 1997). Communitarian theories argue that corporations are not just networks of contracts – they are communities in which a range of people have varied human experiences. The reliance on contract not only discriminates against some of these constituencies, but it diminishes the scope and value of the human experience. While our analysis should not be regarded as lending normative support for communitarian theories (it does not), it suggests communitarian values as an explanation of modern changes in corporate law.

The modern reformulation of the officers' duty of care

Historically, English law imposed a low standard of care on directors. The leading case on that standard of care was *Re City Equitable Fire Insurance Corporation*.[5] That case is authority for two propositions. First, decisions by a director will be negligent only where he or she is cognisant of circumstances of such a plain character that no reasonable person would have made the decision in question. Second, a director is entitled to rely on the information and advice of other managers, unless there is a strong reason to be suspicious of the information or the advice. The standard so established might be described as one of *unreasonableness* – it subjects to liability those decisions, whether substantive or concerning delegation, that have no rational basis (Whincop 1996a). The low positive standard resembles (although it does not completely converge with) the spacious defence in American law known as the business judgment rule.[6] Such a standard reposes a great deal of discretion in management and directors, which is reviewed only in exceptional circumstances.

It is possible to articulate a defence of these rules in Coasean theoretical terms, as the bargain that shareholders and directors would strike if they negotiated the matter (Scott 1983; Whincop 1996a, 1997a). This is because the rules set a standard that minimises the expected cost of judicial errors. A judicially administered standard of care involves two possible error types. A Type I error is a failure to subject a negligent defendant to liability; a Type II error subjects to liability a defendant who exercised reasonable care (Davis 1985). The object is to minimise the costs of the two types of errors, plus the cost of administering the standard. An unreasonableness standard offers the advantage of predictability – only very clear cases are negligent. A rule generating a predictable outcome will result in less opportunistic litigation. Its low obligations virtually eliminated the cost of Type II errors. Obviously, the possibility of Type I error was comparatively high. Given the clarity of the standard, however, any additional losses from negligence might be anticipated in capital markets characterised by rational expectations.

More onerous standards increase the risk the director bears. Executive directors, in particular, are inefficient bearers of such risk. Because they tend to work for one corporation at a time, they inevitably 'overinvest' their human capital given the difficulty to them of diversifying the risk of that investment (Coffee 1986; Kraakman 1984). Unable to diversify, the manager can only reduce that risk by an insurance policy, or by making more risk-averse decisions. The latter course is unlikely to be in shareholders' interests. The cost of an insurance premium is often borne by the shareholders in any case.[7] Thus, other influences on management and governance (operating within firms and across markets) are more likely to achieve good quality management and board decisions than increasing the risk the director bears.

These principles have been comprehensively eroded in the last decade. The major development is that directors are expected to take reasonable steps to be informed of matters relevant to the corporation and the director's office. This principle originally emanated from cases under provisions in companies legislation which subject directors to personal liability for debts contracted in insolvency.[8] These cases provided an oblique opportunity for reviewing directors' standards of care.[9] Courts considered that directors were required to be aware of the corporation's financial position, and to be informed of the implications of matters to which a reasonably prudent director would attend.[10] In Australia's historic *AWA* litigation,[11] these principles were affirmed by the New South Wales Court of Appeal, which held that directors have an onerous duty to be informed, which is incapable of delegation.[12]

The most obvious problem with the rules is that they greatly increase the likelihood of Type II errors, and they increase the cost of administering the standard. The likelihood that a court, sitting in hindsight judgment, and relying on evidence produced through the notoriously distorted adversarial process (Posner 1990: 203–19), will be able to judge whether a director was right not to acquire a certain piece of information is not very high. Moreover, the costs of putting a court into a position to make such a judgment are likely to be much higher than under an unreasonableness standard.

This more demanding standard creates a more intrusive process of the judicial review of managerial discretion. In this respect, the restriction on delegation is particularly important. The principles underlying this restriction seem to be predicated on an implicit model of corporate decision making, in which directors are monitors, and their monitoring function must be performed personally. A requirement that decision-making power and monitoring responsibilities be exercised at the board level constrains the private ordering of governance structures. The revised duty of care prevents directors attributing blame for mistakes to lower levels of the organisation.[13] In this sense, the principle resonates with the much asserted, but often vacuous, populist demands for 'accountability' by senior executives in public and private organisations.

A public law perspective is also discernible in the fact that the duty to be informed has an inherent procedural quality. An unreasonableness standard rarely has occasion to review decision-making processes. The articulation of standards of informed decision making departs from this approach. When a breach of the duty to be informed is pleaded, the court must review the decision process itself. It must review the information a director relied on in making a decision. The emphasis on procedure and on *relevant considerations* resembles judicial review in administrative law.[14] This point is confirmed when one examines the analysis of causation of damage. A recent case, *Permanent Building Society v. Wheeler*,[15] suggests that it is possible to breach the duty to be informed even when the decision actually taken would not have been changed by the discharge of the duty.[16] This suggests that judicial conceptions of propriety in decision making can reach a long way. The existence of a cause of action which reviews the procedure of decision making is unlikely to be consistent with the region of managerial discretion essential to efficiency claims for privatisation.

Whose interests are served by the new law? One might assert that the duty serves shareholders by compelling greater diligence from directors. However, if one can breach the duty to be informed, notwithstanding that the 'negligent' act would have been taken anyway, the duty seems to have little to do with the interests of shareholders. It is much easier to believe that the duty merely results in an inefficient transfer of risk to directors. In contrast, the duty to be informed might advance communitarian goals. While shareholders are able to decrease or eliminate the risk associated with an individual corporation, the adverse consequences of a corporate decision on a local community or on workers, for example, are not similarly susceptible to mitigation (Coffee 1986; Mitchell 1995). While few cases are in point, the duty of care could protect such external interests by compelling the collection of relevant information regarding the interests of external constituencies affected by the corporation. This resembles a natural justice requirement. This issue is obviously relevant to a privatised corporation, given that privatisation usually implies substantial changes to the distribution of goods and services to the community.

The officer's duty of propriety

Contractarians regard fiduciary duties as a response to the difficulties of contracting between shareholders and officers. The scope for managerial opportunism in corporate governance structures is great. However, the inability to foresee specific forms of opportunism limits the ability to protect residual claimants against opportunism by a better specified and more explicit contract. Hence, fiduciary duties operate as a standard applying to future exercises of discretionary power (Easterbrook and Fischel 1991, 1993). The fiduciary duty thus fills gaps in contracts. Contractarians generally consider that fiduciary duties, being contractual, can be excluded by contract (Butler and Ribstein 1995; Romano 1989; cf. Brudney 1985), although precisely what is required to do that is unclear. The better view is that if fiduciary duties are default rules, they are a very persistent sort, which are excludable only in a very specific way (Coffee 1989; Whincop 1997a).

Given the difficulties, both theoretical and doctrinal, in excluding fiduciary duties, the normative question of the proper content of a fiduciary duty is exceptionally difficult. Finn has argued that a fiduciary standard requires selflessness (Finn 1989). Transferring such a standard, developed in the relatively stable context of trustees' duties, to the director of a company is difficult for several reasons. Unlike the normal trust situation, the interests of shareholders can be sharply antagonistic to those of directors. The two constituencies have fundamentally different attitudes to risk (Coffee 1988: 950). A director who takes entrepreneurial risks is endangering an undiversifiable investment in the corporation. The director has an inevitably intrusive self-interest that fiduciary rhetoric cannot disguise (Coffee 1989: 1626–7). That situation has no parallel in the trust, because the trustee is constrained from adopting risky strategies by conservative prudential standards. Moreover, the director's tenure is much less secure than a trustee's. Judging director actions taken in the context of hostile takeovers and contests for control is therefore difficult to resolve in fiduciary terms. One of us has suggested elsewhere that the fiduciary duty applies to contests for control in a way that is fundamentally different to their proscription of self-dealing transactions (Whincop 1997a). In the former situation, judicial method resembles a process of comparing and balancing merits that seems to concede some scope for director self-interest.[17]

In Australia, the corporate fiduciary duty is supplemented by various statutory provisions, the most important of which is a prohibition on improper use of office. That duty is found in s. 232(6) of the *Corporations Law*. It provides that officers and employees must not make improper use of their positions, intending[18] to gain an advantage for themselves or any other person, or to cause detriment to the corporation (Whincop 1996b). The section subjects contraventions to various penalties, and also confers a cause of action on the corporation. Impropriety refers to conduct inconsistent with the proper discharge of the officer's duties.[19] The cases confirm that these duties include fiduciary duties. The problem is that 'fiduciary' duties do not have a single, determinate meaning. As noted above, they vary between an inflexible formulation and a lower good faith standard (Whincop 1996c, 1997a). Some clarity has been obtained as a result of the substantial extension of the impropriety concept by the High Court decision in *R v. Byrnes; R v. Hopwood*.[20] That case, however, is problematic for a number of reasons. The High Court considered that a belief by an officer that a transaction is beneficial or even necessary cannot be admitted if other evidence establishes impropriety. Impropriety can be established by any breach of standards reasonably expected from the officer, including fiduciary duties. The High Court also said that an officer who knows that he or she has no authority for the actions alleged to be improper makes improper use of position.[21]

The use of a statutory duty with penal consequences is an obvious example of the increasing infiltration of corporate law by public law concepts. The statutory duty makes the Commonwealth a party to contracts that establish corporate governance structures. The Commonwealth can use the civil penalty regime in Part 9.4B of the *Corporations Law*, of which the statutory duty in s. 232(6) is part, to enforce standards 'reasonably expected' of the defendant. The key issue for the future is determining the content of those standards. We would argue that the approach foreshadowed in *Byrnes* has the scope to emphasise procedure and judicial norms of propriety in decision making, just as the modern duty to be informed does. This is most obvious in the way the court stripped the section of 'business judgment' elements (the justifiability, or the desirability, of a transaction), while at the same time concentrating on objective formulation of standards, and introducing limitations on authority as a relevant issue.

The use of strict standards in blatant cases of self-dealing is not a matter of great concern. However, as noted above, some of the most important cases on the concept of the exercise of a fiduciary power for an improper purpose are best explained by a balancing process between these very issues of business judgment. Courts have inquired into the opinion held by management concerning certain actions, the ability of reasonable persons to hold that view, the substantive merits of the transaction, and its effect on shareholders (Whincop 1997a). When directors have to determine how to act in a situation not directly of their making (such as a competition for control) in which they have an interest, one ceases to be able to use the motivations for a fiduciary duty to justify dogmatic enforcement of that duty. Enforcing a duty as in *Byrnes* tends to treat accountability as an end in itself, rather than as a means. Accountability becomes a matter of procedure and process, rather than a part of a governance structure in a contractual equilibrium. The key element in this procedural review is the existence of some conflict of interest, which invalidates conduct by the director. The fiduciary standard's character is altered from a proscriptive standard (Finn 1989) to a prescriptive standard, which compels obedience to a set of judicially specified norms.

The procedural quality of the s. 232(6) is reinforced by the potential of the civil penalty provisions of the *Corporations Law*. A court can make a declaration that s. 232(6) was breached in the absence of harm to the corporation.[22] Given this remedial structure a great deal turns on how prosecutorial authorities choose to rely on s. 232(6). In this regard it is noteworthy that the section has been contravened by conduct that prejudiced a prospective creditor.[23] Although this is not directly an expansive communitarian interpretation of impropriety, it indicates that the section can be used to protect parties affected by managerial decisions outside of a narrow shareholder constituency. The section can achieve great width because of the cases' emphasis on the 'standards reasonably expected' of a director. Fiduciary duties form only part of those standards. A director might contravene the section where the alleged impropriety involves causing the corporation not to comply with a law. A provocative question explored in the law and economics literature is whether corporations are obliged to comply with laws which it is gainful for them to contravene (Buxbaum 1996; Easterbrook and Fischel 1982). This 'rational illegality' is a paradigm problem where corporate law might be required to mediate between the interests of shareholders and other constituencies protected by the statute. By reference to standards reasonably expected of an officer, s. 232(6) is an obvious means by which such mediation can take place.

The procedural qualities of the prohibition are underlined by the equation in *Byrnes* of impropriety with knowingly engaging in unauthorised conduct.[24] Like the use of the duty to be informed as a means to procure accountability at a corporation's 'top end', this development has strong public law overtones. Authority in corporate law is an outgrowth of agency principles. It is used to determine whether a principal (the corporation) is bound by the actions of its agent (Whincop 1997b). An agent who acts without authority is not liable to her principal, unless there is some contract to that effect or the agent has breached another duty. The use of authority in s. 232(6) therefore becomes a means by which the State can enforce limitations on grants of power to corporate officers. It is analogous to the *ultra vires* doctrine in administrative law,[25] and emphasises procedural accountability as an end in itself.

The implied limitations on alterations of articles

This section deals not with constraints on managerial decisions, but on the decisions of shareholders. The particular issue concerns the rights of shareholders to vary the articles of association, but it could extend to other decisions taken by shareholders. The High Court has recently changed the substantive law in this area, so restricting the exercise of discretions reposed in shareholders. The traditional principle in this area is the famous dictum of Lindley MR in *Allen v. Gold Reefs of West Africa Ltd*, that the power to alter articles was to be exercised 'bona fide for the benefit of the company as a whole, and it must not be exceeded'.[26] This principle, together with the non-interventionist indoor management rule, underwrites the majority rule norm which has dominated corporate law. That norm allows shareholders to decide, amongst other things, whether an alteration of the articles was for the benefit of the corporation. Courts interfered only if the alteration *could* not be regarded by honest shareholders as being for the corporation's benefit.[27] The use of the term 'bona fide' is not gratuitous; a standard of good faith preserves, but in some cases, restrains, self-interest (Finn 1989).

The High Court adopted and further explained the rule in *Allen*'s case in *Peters' American Delicacy Co. Ltd v. Heath*.[28] In that case, Dixon J rejected the notion that one could strike down an alteration by applying a test that assumed the permanence of shareholders' rights. A resolution that merely adjusts and balances shareholders' rights cannot be tested by examining benefit of the corporation as a whole.[29] In these cases, one must examine whether there is a fraud on the power having regard to the alteration's effect on prevailing rights.

These principles were reconsidered in the High Court's controversial decision, *Gambotto v. WCP Ltd*.[30] That case involved an attempt by a majority to confer on itself a power to compulsorily acquire the shares of minority shareholders on terms of fair compensation. The primary motivation of the majority shareholder was the acquisition of tax benefits from losses available in the corporate group. The plaintiff, a minority shareholder, contended the alteration was beyond the scope of the power to alter the articles. Such facts scarcely reveal any abuse of power or lack of good faith. First, the corporation benefited because the expropriation allowed it to take advantage of tax benefits. Second, the price paid to shareholders seemed fair. However, the High Court held the alteration was invalid. Mason CJ, Brennan, Deane and Dawson JJ rejected the application of *Allen*'s case. They held that an alteration to create an expropriation provision would only be valid if it was for a proper purpose and its exercise would not operate oppressively in relation to minority shareholders. Additionally, the expropriation must make provision for both a 'fair' procedure, and a fair price.[31]

The case demonstrates how corporate discretions and procedures are increasingly being exposed to judicial review. In Anglo-Australian law, majority shareholders have never been regarded as exercising their voting rights subject to fiduciary duties to other shareholders.[32] While the High Court did not disturb this rule, its decision constrains the exercise of a majority's property rights. In particular, it foreshadows that courts may review majority changes to the corporation and its governance structure. This is relevant to privatisations, as the ability of governance structures to change is important in a dynamic environment (Gilson 1996).

The case also demonstrates that these corporate discretions will be reviewed according to legal principles familiar from public law. This trend is evident in the dual requirements that the expropriation is for a proper purpose; and that the expropriation is not oppressive either in dealing or price. It is a general principle of liberalism that the actions of private individuals are generally unrestricted unless they have been expressly forbidden (Raz 1979; Sampford 1991). A requirement of proper purpose for altering the articles seems precisely the opposite of this norm: alterations are forbidden unless permitted. It is true that equity limits the exercise of legal rights through such doctrines as unconscionability. However, it does this in ways that are the opposite of using propriety of purpose as a precondition to validity. Thus, under the doctrine of unconscionability, an exercise of legal rights is invalidated if there is an unconscientious use of a superior position;[33] under fiduciary doctrine, the exercise of legal rights is invalidated if the fiduciary has a personal interest or an inconsistent duty to a third party.[34] The test in *Allen*'s case is analogous. These limitations are prohibitory exceptions to a permissive rule. The use of proper purpose as a test of expropriation therefore has stronger resemblances to judicial review in administrative law.[35] The impropriety of purpose for which a power is exercised is a long-standing ground of judicial review in administrative law. This change is more than semantic, because the court ceases to be an arbiter of invalidity, but replaces the shareholder as the judge of the appropriateness of the resolution.

The requirement that there be no oppression also resembles a natural justice requirement from public law. The party seeking to expropriate must demonstrate the fairness of the price paid for the shares, the procedures followed and disclosures made. In his separate judgment, McHugh J held that the alteration was oppressive for lack of fair procedure. He considered the dealings were not fair, because the majority failed to show that they had disclosed all relevant information. This conclusion was not changed by the fact that the price seemed fair;[36] or that objections to disclosure were not taken in the courts below. McHugh J implied that there is a procedure to be followed in expropriations; a failure to follow it is fatal. The requirement is like procedural *ultra vires*[37] in administrative law (Evans 1981), since its effect is to provide for formal accountability by the majority to the minority. As with the duty to be informed and the duty of propriety, the courts seem here to think of accountability as an end in itself, rather than being instrumental to some goal.

There is a risk of exaggerating the significance of this case. As yet, the rule applies only to alterations conferring expropriation power on a majority shareholder (Legal Committee of the Companies & Securities Advisory Committee 1995: 7–10; cf. Bird 1996: 57–9). It is not difficult, however, to imagine the principles extending to cases where the alteration adversely affects some shareholders, or where a majority shareholder votes in favour of some alteration. The first of these possibilities is evident in the High Court's decision in *Bailey v. New South Wales Medical Defence Union Ltd.*[38] That case involved the effect of a change to an article that provided for the availability of professional indemnity insurance. The change eventually proved adverse to the interests of the personal representative of a member of the company. The High Court evaded the adverse consequences of the change by constructing a 'special' contract between the member individually and the company, the terms of which remained the same as the articles *before* the change. Although the decision did not rely on *Gambotto v. WCP Ltd*, it exhibits a similar propensity to freeze the status quo (Whincop 1997c). Returning to the theme of efficiency and discretion, the case is undesirable because it implies a norm that constrains the primary source of flexibility and efficiency in corporations – the principles of majority rule and non-intervention.

Perhaps the most important matter is identifying the interests that the principles in *Gambotto v. WCP Ltd* protect. Does the decision implicate corporate law in balancing wider interests than those of shareholders? At surface level, the court seems to be championing the rights of individual shareholders. However, because the case involves competing individual interests, one cannot say that it resolves matters in favour of the individual. The historical position of the law in relation to this conflict was to intervene only in cases of bad faith. What is interesting about the High Court's new law is that while the rule may apply in a way that favours an individual shareholder, the rule nonetheless lacks a strong individualistic basis. The High Court clearly accepts that a shareholder *can* be expropriated if the purpose for doing so is proper. Various interests may enter into the calculus of propriety, perhaps including some interests external to traditional corporate law norms. We have already indicated that propriety in s. 232(6) can accommodate broader interests. That conclusion may also apply here, because the High Court's preference for a test of proper purpose, rather than the narrower 'benefit of the corporation' used in *Allen*'s case is presumably more than semantic.

Standing in corporate law

The argument so far pursued in this article is that while greater managerial discretion might be regarded as a key advantage of privatisation, the law can significantly constrain that discretion. Corporate law can permit the interests of a number of external constituencies to limit the pursuit of managerial policies. While corporate law has no historically imposed constraints, the preceding three sections of this part demonstrate that corporate law is undergoing change. It is becoming less private and more public. Managerial discretion is being limited in various respects, most significantly by a judicial review model that relies on new grounds of review. We have argued that the formulation of these grounds may provide scope to accommodate the interests of constituencies other than shareholders. Although other constituencies have not previously had a recognised claim to the attention of corporate law, their lack of standing to enforce the duties imposed on decision makers prevented the conception of the corporation from changing. Moreover, as can be seen from the exegesis of traditional formulations of duty, it was difficult even for *shareholders* to succeed in enforcing recognised duties. The effect of deferential standards was greatly intensified by the so-called proper plaintiff rule in *Foss v. Harbottle*.[39] Closely related to the internal management rule, it restricted the ability of shareholders to sue to enforce these duties. The corporation rather than shareholders was regarded as the beneficiary of duties owed by directors. Only where a majority wrongfully prevented an action from being brought would a shareholder be entitled to bring a derivative action. This exception is, like the rule in *Allen*'s case, underpinned by the primacy of majority judgments regarding corporate litigation, subject to an exception embodying a good-faith standard (Whincop 1997d).

We have seen above that substantive corporate duties have changed greatly in a short time. These duties demonstrate potential for expansion. However, the fulfilment of that potential depends on rules of standing. First, the ability to sue to enforce duties determines whether this potential expansion is considered by courts, or falls into desuetude. Second, if rules of standing permit non-shareholder constituencies to be represented, the substantive law is more likely to develop in a way that incorporates the interests of these constituencies in the doctrine. Constituencies that lack standing will remain external to the formulation of doctrine. It is with these considerations in mind that we turn to consider the revisions of standing in corporate law. Four matters are of interest to us. These are: (i) standing under the civil penalty regime; (ii) injunctive relief under s. 1324 of the Corporations Law; (iii) the revision of the rule in *Foss v. Harbottle*; and (iv) the proposed derivative action procedures.

(1) **Civil penalty regime.** It was noted in the third section of this part that the civil penalty regime of the *Corporations Law* is a significant development in corporate law. By converting directors' duties into obligations with penal consequences for breach, corporate governance is brought into a public sphere. Of the substantive law developments discussed in this article, the officer's duty of propriety is a civil penalty provision. While the discussion of the duty of care has referred to common law authorities, the statutory duty of care in s. 232(4) should probably have a similar substantive content. Thus,

the two key changes to the judicial review of officers' discretions are integral to the civil penalty regime. The regime serves the dual purpose of compensating corporations and deterring and punishing contraventions (Whincop 1996c). The first purpose is served by conferring a cause of action on the corporation under s. 1317HD to recover loss for breach of the provision. This provision denies standing to shareholders or other constituencies. Deterrence is accomplished by subjecting the defendant who contravenes the section to such orders as requiring the defendant to pay a pecuniary penalty, or banning the defendant from managing a corporation.[40] Because the deterrence function relies on public prosecutions, shareholder and non-shareholder interests can be represented. Although these constituencies do not have a right to compensation under the civil penalty regime, the use of penalties can deter officers' behaviour that injures these constituencies.[41] It follows that the interests that the Australian Securities Commission (Australia's corporate regulator) represents are pivotal to the development of this potential. Australian evidence suggests that private enforcement of corporate rights and duties is dominated by public enforcement by the ASC (Ramsay 1995). Therefore, if the ASC chooses to represent a wider cross-section of interests than shareholders, this potential may be actualised (cf. Millon 1993: 1376). The ASC's enabling legislation, the Australian Securities Commission Act 1989 (C'th), can be read as permitting the ASC to represent wider interests. Section 1(2) requires, *inter alia*, that the ASC strive to maintain and improve the 'performance' of corporations in the interests of 'reducing business costs, and the efficiency and development of the economy'. The reference to performance seems deliberately broader than the narrower calculus of 'profit' or 'value'. The invocation of the interests of the economy gives sufficient scope for the corporate regulator to represent non-shareholder constituencies. The ability of the ASC to represent public interests is confirmed by the ASC's power under section 50 of the same Act to bring representative public interest actions. Such actions involve the ASC itself litigating in the name of a company where it believes it is in the public interest to do so. This power was recently considered by the Full Federal Court in *ASC v. Deloitte Touche Tohmatsu*.[42] In a confirmation of the arguments pursued in this chapter, the court held that the public interest should be interpreted widely. The ASC was not required to consider the opposition of the directors of the corporation to the bringing of any action.

(2) **Injunctive relief.** Whereas the representation of non-shareholder constituencies under the civil penalty regime relies on public enforcement by the ASC, the injunction provision in the *Corporations Law*, s. 1324, creates scope for private enforcement by injunction. An injunction can be sought for any contravention of the Law, including breach of the civil penalty provisions. The injunction can be mandatory or prohibitory. Section 1324 permits a person to apply for an injunction if his or her 'interests have been, are or would be affected by' the contravention. Some authors have suggested that

the section represents a considerable expansion of standing rights in corporate law (Baxt 1989; cf. Kluver 1993; Ramsay 1992). The authorities on the section are not wholly consistent. Its predecessor in the Companies Act 1981, s. 574, was regarded by one judge as being part of a legislative scheme designed to protect the public in respect of the commercial activities of the corporation.[43] In consequence, it should be interpreted broadly. An applicant did not need to prove a proprietary right. It has been suggested that the applicant's interest must exceed that of a member of the public interested in seeing the law enforced.[44] If, however, a *section* of the public could demonstrate that the conduct of the corporation had external effects on it, standing could probably be established. A problem, of course, with injunctive relief is that the plaintiff may have insufficient economic incentives to litigate. These problems may be partially resolved by s. 1324(10). It provides that where a court has power to order an injunction, it also has power to order the payment of damages by the person who is the subject of the injunction. The provision potentially permits the assertion of rights by non-shareholder constituencies, although it has not been the subject of judicial interpretation. A non-shareholder constituency might sue a director who, for example, has contravened s. 232(6) by engaging in conduct deleterious to that constituency. Such personal liability on the part of the director would be valuable if the corporation was insolvent. Recent cases suggest a conflict as to the interpretation of the provision. One judgment held that a company shareholder may not rely on s. 1324 when alleging a breach of a civil penalty provision.[45] The judge acknowledged the expansive trend of earlier cases on the section and its predecessor. However, he rejected the notion that the section, used in conjunction with provisions such as s. 232 that restated general law obligations, swept away the policy considerations underlying the rule in *Foss v. Harbottle*.[46] Accordingly, only the ASC might litigate under s. 1324 for an injunction restraining the breach of s. 232. While the decision represents, in its own terms, a substantial restraint on the opportunities afforded by s. 1324, its analysis of the civil penalty provisions and their interaction with sections such as s. 232, raises questions and doubts (Bird 1997). A subsequent case regards these restrictions as being incorrect,[47] so the position remains unclear.

(3) **Revision of the rule in *Foss v. Harbottle*.** The key historical exception to the rule in *Foss v. Harbottle* was the fraud on the minority exception. Under this exception, it is necessary to demonstrate that a majority opposes the bringing of an action to enforce a corporate right. However, in large corporations, the problems shareholders encounter in taking the collective action required by the rule (such as convening a meeting to consider the matter) could rule out the possibility of an action, even in the absence of a 'majority' as such. The possibility of a further exception 'when the interests of justice require' has therefore long been a subject of speculation. One recent case has upheld the existence of this exception.[48] The judge relied on the

change in the nature of companies since the articulation of the rule in *Foss v. Harbottle*: shareholders have become larger in number and more dispersed. This development clears the way for shareholders who seek the judicial review of the exercise of director and manager discretions. The interesting question remains as to whether it will ever be in the interests of justice for other constituencies to be able to sue.

(4) **Proposed derivative action procedures.** The final liberalisation of standing rules that we discuss are proposed provisions that entitle shareholders to bring proceedings on behalf of corporations (Attorney-General 1995). At the time of writing, these provisions have not been introduced, but they have been on the law reform agenda for some years (Companies and Securities Law Review Committee 1990). The proposed provisions for statutory derivative actions aim to destroy the rule in *Foss v. Harbottle*.[49] Under section 245A of the proposed provisions, proceedings may be brought on behalf of the corporation either by a member or an officer of the corporation, a member of a related body corporate, or the ASC. As has already been suggested in the context of the civil penalty regime, the fact that the ASC is permitted *as of right* to bring actions on behalf of a company may allow constituencies other than members and officers to litigate on behalf of the corporation. Persons besides the ASC may only bring proceedings if granted leave by a court.[50] The court must grant leave under proposed section 245B(2) if it is satisfied that:

a it is probable that the company will not itself bring the proceedings or properly take responsibility for them . . . ; and
b the applicant is acting in good faith; and
c it is in the best interests of the company that the applicant be granted leave; and
d if the applicant is applying for leave to bring proceedings – there is a serious question to be tried . . .

The new provisions are significant in two respects. First, they provide a means by which shareholders can obtain standing to review managerial exercises of discretion. Second, that means of review gives courts an unprecedented centrality in corporate governance. The quoted section requires a judge to determine that it is in the corporation's best interests for leave to be granted. This represents the subjection of decisions by the board concerning litigation – whether against corporate insiders or not – to judicial review. If one compares the ground of review to 'unreasonableness' in administrative law, the breadth of the ground becomes apparent. The court is not instructed to ask whether the decision of the board not to litigate was such that no reasonable board could make it.[51] Instead it asks: would this court's decision to bring proceedings be in the corporation's interests? The procedure approximates a review of merits in corporate litigation. While the report suggests that a corporation may have sound business reasons for not bringing proceedings (Attorney-General 1995: 6), a court is not obliged by the provisions to respect such a judgment.[52]

The provisions carry a significant risk of Type I error; that is, where a judge mistakenly believes litigation is in the best interests of the corporation. The provisions are also likely to be highly costly given the need to place a judge in a position of being able to make an informed decision. These costs must be incurred even if leave is not granted. Generally, the costs of placing a judge in a sufficiently informed position will be inversely related to the probability of Type I and Type II errors. It is also important to understand that these costs are likely to be borne by shareholders generally, because a court is able to order the corporation to bear the plaintiff's legal costs before any decision on the merits is made.[53] An individual shareholder may not bear a sufficiently large proportion of those costs in order to make optimal decisions concerning applications for leave to bring a derivative action (Dooley and Veasey 1989; Fischel 1982; Fischel and Bradley 1986; Romano 1991).

The provisions concerning shareholder ratification further extend the jurisdiction of courts in corporate governance matters. Proposed section 245D provides that ratification of conduct the subject of proceedings does not estop applications for leave, nor the bringing of proceedings once leave is granted. Ratification also does not conclude proceedings in favour of the party whose conduct has been ratified. Instead, the court may take the ratification into account, but must consider the disclosures made to shareholders when they were asked to ratify, and the propriety of purposes of those voting to ratify. Judicial review thus extends beyond the judgment of the board to the expressed will of a majority of shareholders. The first consideration regarding disclosure is familiar from the case law concerning ratification of fiduciary breaches.[54] However, the proper purposes requirement is notable. It conforms to the trends of the new corporate law as evident in *Gambotto v. WCP Ltd* and the duty of propriety. As noted above, shareholders – even majority shareholders – are not fiduciaries in Australian law. Yet, the requirement of 'proper purposes' suggests that shareholders must exercise their power for the benefit of some other person. However, a model of self-interested owners is integral to advocacy of privatisation.

The doctrinal issues associated with proper purposes in this context are complex. What purposes are improper? It is not clear from the section whether it is proper to have regard only to shareholders who also happen to hold a fiduciary office, and their associates. If there are both sound and 'improper' reasons to vote in a particular way, it is not obvious why the latter should not be counted. As is inherent in Justice Ipp's judgment in *Biala Pty Ltd v. Mallina Holdings Ltd*, the application of such a test in publicly listed corporations with widely spread shareholdings is difficult. Many shareholders to whom full disclosure is made may simply vote for management because they have no reason to trust the insurgent shareholder. Apathy could induce such a result. Does that invalidate the vote? It is also unclear who bears the onus of proving propriety. Because the rules are handicapped by the problems of aggregating the purposes of a majority of shareholders, judges will be forced to substitute their own judgment, in place of the shareholders' judgment, on the question for ratification. As in *Gambotto v. WCP Ltd*, the new directions of corporate law evident in this proposal limit self-interested exercises of discretion by shareholders.

Although empowering shareholders to litigate on behalf of the company might seem strongly individualistic, the ultimate question is whether derivative actions significantly reduce agency costs. Our impression based on the existing evidence is that these proposals will not reduce agency costs (Fischel and Bradley 1986; Romano 1991). The procedures are inherently expensive; the costs indemnity can be seen to encourage inefficient litigation; and they reserve an inefficient and unclear jurisdiction for judicial review. Finally, the limitations on ability to ratify and the centrality of courts in these governance issues seem to violate individualistic and pluralist values without obvious benefit.

PART FOUR: CONCLUSION

The purpose of this chapter has been to examine issues related to the governance of the privatised entity. Claims for and against privatisation depend on issues of governance, and the control of managerial discretion. Part Two argued that the exposure of the privatised entity to markets of various forms does not provide a particularly convincing reason to believe that the privatised enterprise will be governed more efficiently. Markets are undeniably important, and the achievement of product competition will frequently be beneficial to society as a whole. However, product competition does not depend on private ownership, but on liberalised market structure. Markets for corporate control and capital are also relevant to issues of governance. But the conversion of a positive theory of the impact of these markets on governance into a normative prescription that the government should privatise is highly doubtful. The theory contradicts itself, as well as failing to take into consideration the effects of rent seeking by interest groups, and commonly observed phenomena such as constraints on the free transfer of shares.

Part Three has analysed the effects of corporate law on corporate governance, and the relevance of the changing structure of Australian corporate law to managerial discretion. At a positive level, it is possible to detect an increasing infiltration of the leitmotivs of public law into corporate law – an analysis of procedure, the treatment of accountability as an end rather than as a means, the increased use of non-substantive grounds of review, and the liberalisation and expansion of standing rights for shareholders and, perhaps, others. It is impossible to justify such rules as the hypothetical bargains that shareholders and managers would strike if the process of corporate contracting was costless. They substitute inefficient judicial review for contract and pricing. Accordingly, managerial discretion is increasingly constrained by a process with much the same defects and inefficiencies as the public law system from which privatisation was supposed to permit an escape. We concede that much of our forward-looking analysis and predictions are contestable. However, the important point is that increasing transitions of enterprise from public to private management are likely to exacerbate these inefficiencies, and the transformation of corporate law's function of maximisation to one of redistribution.

Notes

1 In the corporation, the manager may capture some of the wealth effects of his or her management by holding shares. Nonetheless, in most cases the fraction of the corporation the manager holds will be small and may be confounded by the imperfectly positively correlated wealth effects produced by other managers over whom she has no power to control (e.g., Easterbrook and Fischel 1981: 1172). Also, financial economists have demonstrated the inefficiency of significant shareholdings by managers in their corporations. This is because they already have significant investments of human capital in their corporation which cannot be diversified. The manager will therefore be more risk averse than shareholders (who manifest their willingness to bear risks by acquiring shares) would rationally prefer (Fama and Jensen 1983). Empirical research casts doubt on the ability to 'bond' a manager to the interests of shareholders (Jensen and Murphy 1990).

2 Farrar and McCabe (1995: 34) also assert that governments will be more closely monitored than entities in the private sector, and assume that the 'excess' is necessarily inefficient. However, much less will be expended to monitor government organisations because opportunities to profit from expenditure on information are minimal. There is no market in the residual claims of the entity (Downes 1957; Hirschman 1970; Baxter 1978; Cass 1988).

3 See also Government-Owned Corporations Act 1993 (Qld), s. 94; State Owned Enterprises Act 1992 (Vic), s. 30. The termination of public officials' appointments depends on a number of issues, including whether the employee is the holder of an 'office', the legislation governing the appointment, and the terms of the contract of employment (Campbell 1996).

4 *Burland v. Earle* [1902] AC 83, 93.

5 [1925] Ch 407, 428–9.

6 See, e.g., *Graham v. Allis Chalmers*, 188 A 2d 125 (1963); *Sinclair Oil Co. v. Levien*, 280 A 2d 717 (1971); *Aronson v. Lewis*, 473 A 2d 805 (1984); *Cede & Co v. Technicolor*, 634 A 2d 345 (1994). Although articulated in cases involving breaches of the duty to act in the best interests of the corporation, Anglo-Australian courts have similarly held that they are not tribunals for the review of bona fide business judgments: *Harlowe's Nominees Pty Ltd v. Woodside (Lakes Entrance) Oil Co. NL* (1968) 121 CLR 483; *Howard Smith Ltd v Ampol Petroleum Ltd* [1974] AC 821.

7 *Corporations Law* (C'th) 1991, s. 241A (hereafter referred to as the *Corporations Law*).

8 *Corporations Law*, ss 588G and 592; *Companies Act* 1981 (C'th), s. 556 (hereafter referred to as *Companies Act*).

9 *Corporations Law*, ss 592(1)(b), 592(2)(b); *Companies Acts*, ss 556(1)(b), 556(2)(b).

10 *Metal Manufacturers Ltd v. Lewis* (1986) 11 ACLR 122, 129–31; *Statewide Tobacco Services Ltd v. Morley* (1990) 2 ACSR 405, 431–2 (affirmed on appeal (1992) 10 ACLC 1233, 1245–7); *Commonwealth Bank of Australia v. Friedrich* (1991) 5 ACSR 115, 125–6; *Group Four Industries Pty Ltd v. Brosnan* (1992) 8 ACSR 463, 497–8, 509, 513.

11 *Daniels v. Anderson* (1995) 16 ACSR 607 *sub nom AWA Ltd v. Daniels* (1992) 7 ACSR 759.

12 (1995) 16 ACSR 607, 666–7. Although the duty seems more imposing than the one envisaged by the trial judge, the revision may not be as great as it appears (Whincop 1996a: 80–1).

13 Conversely, the law seems to be expanding towards the bureaucracy itself. The statutory duty of care in s. 232(4), and other duties in the Corporations Law, apply to a wider group than directors. The term 'director' is defined expansively in s. 60 to include anybody, within or outside of the corporation, who gives directions or instructions according to which the board is accustomed to act. The term can include a corporation: *Standard Chartered Bank of Australia Pty Ltd v. Antico* (1995) 18 ACSR 1. It can also include a professional adviser or a bank (Koh 1996). The public law parallel is interesting: in administrative law, decision makers must not act on dictation. The so-called shadow director provision achieves a similar end by imposing all of the director's duties on such a person.

14 See, e.g., *Administrative Decisions (Judicial Review) Act* 1977 (C'th) ('ADJR Act') ss 5(1)(e), (h), 5(2)(a), (b) (cf. s. 5(3)); *Padfield v. Minister of Agriculture, Fisheries & Food* [1968] AC 997; *Murphyores Inc. Pty Ltd v. Commonwealth* (1976) 136 CLR 1. In contrast, see *Minister for Aboriginal Affairs v. Peko-Wallsend Ltd* (1986) 66 ALR 299, 310.

15 (1994) 14 ACSR 109.

16 Ibid., 167.

17 See *Australia Metropolitan Life Assurance Co. Ltd v. Ure* (1923) 33 CLR 199; *Teck Corporation v. Millar* (1972) 33 DLR 3d 288; *Mills v. Mills* (1938) 60 CLR 150; *Harlowe's Nominees Pty Ltd v. Woodside (Lakes Entrance) Oil Co. NL* (1968) 121 CLR 483; *Howard Smith Ltd v. Ampol Petroleum Ltd* [1974] 1 NSWLR 68.

18 *Chew v. R* (1992) 10 ACLC 816 and *Edwards v. R* (1992) 10 ACLC 859.

19 *Grove v. Flavel* (1986) 4 ACLC 654, 659. Cited with approval in *McNamara v. Flavel* (1988) 6 ACLC 802, 807; *Jeffree v. NCSC* (1989) 7 ACLC 556, 564–5; *Southern Resources Ltd v. Residues Treatment & Trading Company Ltd* (1990) 8 ACLC 1151, 1168; *Castrisios v. McManus* (1991) 9 ACLC 287, 293–4; *Chew v. R* (1992) 10 ACLC 816, 823, 827; *R v. Yuill* (1994) 15 ACSR 95, 108; *ASC v. Matthews* (1995) 16 ACSR 313, 317; *R v. Byrnes* (1995) 17 ACSR 551, 560.

20 (1995) 183 CLR 501.

21 Ibid., 515, 517.

22 Section 1317EA. The standard of proof is the balance of probabilities: s. 1332.

23 *Jeffree v. NCSC* (1989) 7 ACLC 556. A sibling provision, s. 232(5), which prohibits the improper use of information acquired by virtue of position, has been similarly applied: *Grove v. Flavel* (1986) 4 ACLC 654; *McNamara v. Flavel* (1988) 6 ACLC 802; *Castrisios v. McManus* (1991) 9 ACLC 287.

24 See also *R v. Cook; ex parte Commonwealth Director of Public Prosecutions* (1996) 20 ACSR 618.

25 See, e.g., *Attorney-General v. Fulham Corporation* [1921] 1 Ch 440.

26 [1900] 1 Ch 656, 671.

27 *Sidebottom v. Kershaw Leese & Company* [1920] 2 Ch 124, 136; *Shuttleworth v. Cox Brothers & Company (Maidenhead)* [1927] 2 KB 9, 22, 26. The attentive reader will note the reference to the corporation as a whole, rather than to shareholders. For analysis that the concept of the corporation as a whole refers to shareholders, rather than to the corporation as a separate legal entity, see Whincop (1995, 1997c, 1997d).
28 (1939) 61 CLR 457.
29 Ibid., 507–12.
30 (1995) 182 CLR 432. For analysis of the decision, see Bird (1996); Ramsay (1996); Whincop (1995).
31 Ibid., 445–7. See also per McHugh J, 456–7.
32 *Peters'* case (1939) 61 CLR 457, 504; *Pender v. Lushington* (1877) 6 Ch D 70, 75–6.
33 *Commercial Bank of Australia Ltd v. Amadio* (1983) 151 CLR 447, 461.
34 *Chan v. Zacharia* (1984) 154 CLR 178, 198–9 per Deane J.
35 See, e.g., *Sydney Municipal Council v. Campbell* [1925] AC 338; ADJR Act ss 5(1)(e), 5(2)(c); but cf. *Arthur Yates and Company Pty Ltd v. Vegetable Seeds Committee* (1945) 72 CLR 37, 68.
36 (1995) 182 CLR 432, 459.
37 See, e.g., *Victoria v. Commonwealth* (1975) 134 CLR 81, 180 per Stephen J.
38 (1995) 18 ACSR 521.
39 (1843) 2 Hare 461; 67 ER 189.
40 Section 1317EA. Under aggravated circumstances set out in s. 1317FA, an offence will be committed. The offence can be punished by imprisonment.
41 On an application for a civil penalty order, a court can order compensation be paid *to the corporation* in the event of finding a civil penalty provision has been contravened: s. 1317HA. Thus, shareholders can be compensated in these suits.
42 (1996) 21 ACSR 332, 364–5.
43 *Broken Hill Pty Co. Ltd v. Bell Resources Ltd* (1984) 8 ACLC 609, 613.
44 *QIW Retailers Ltd v. Davids Holdings Pty Ltd (No. 2)* (1992) 10 ACLC 1162, 1165; *Allen v. Atalay* (1993) 11 ACSR 753, 757–8.
45 *Mesenberg v. Cord Industrial Recruiters Pty Ltd* (1996) 19 ACSR 483.
46 Ibid., 488–9.
47 *Airpeak Pty Ltd v. Jetstream Aircraft Ltd* (1997) 23 ACSR 715 (holding a creditor had standing).
48 *Biala Pty Ltd v. Mallina Holdings Ltd* (1993) 11 ACSR 785, 847–8. See also *Mesenberg v. Cord Industrial Recruiters Pty Ltd (Nos 1 & 2)* (1996) 19 ACSR 483; *Ruralcorp Consulting Pty Ltd v. Pynery Pty Ltd* (1996) 21 ACSR 161.
49 See proposed section 245A(3) in the draft legislation contained in the report (Attorney-General 1995).
50 Proposed s. 245B(1).
51 *Associated Picture Houses Ltd v. Wednesbury Corporation* [1948] 1 KB 233; *Paramatta City Council v. Pestell* (1972) 128 CLR 305, 327; *Australian Broadcasting Tribunal v. Bond* (1990) 170 CLR 321, 356; *Grech v. Minister for Immigration, Local Government and Ethnic Affairs (No. 2)* (1991) 26 ALD 197, 201–2. For an application of such a standard in modern corporate law, see *Wayde v. New South Wales Rugby League* (1985) 3 ACLC 79.
52 In United States jurisdictions, a board decision (usually made by a litigation subcommittee) to terminate a derivative suit is generally assessed with reference to the business judgment rule: see *Auerbach v. Bennett*, 393 NE 2d 994 (1979), *Roberts Alabama Power Co.*, 404 So 2d 629 (1981). Cf. *Zapata Corp. v. Maldonado*, 430 A 2d 779 (1981).
53 Proposed s. 245G. Compare the American common fund doctrine where, in

general, all shareholders bear the plaintiff's costs, but only where the plaintiff succeeds in creating a common fund: *Boeing Co. v. Van Gemert,* 444 US 472 (1980).

54 *Winthrop Investments Ltd v. Winns Ltd* [1975] 2 NSWLR 666, 684 (per Samuels JA), 706 (per Mahoney JA).

References

Alchian, A. (1965) 'Some Economics of Property Rights', *Il Politico* 30: 816–29.

Alchian, A. and Demsetz, H. (1972) 'Production, Information Costs and Economic Organization', *American Economic Review* 62: 777–95.

Attorney-General (Cth) (1995) *Proceedings on Behalf of a Company (Statutory Derivative Action) Draft Provisions and Commentary*, Canberra: Australian Government Publishing Service.

Ayres, I. and Gertner, R. (1989) 'Filling Gaps in Incomplete Contracts: An Economic Theory of Default Rules', *Yale Law Journal* 99: 87–130.

Bainbridge, S. (1997) 'Community and Statism: A Conservative Contractarian Critique of Progressive Corporate Law Scholarship', *Cornell Law Review* 82: 856–904.

Baxt, R. (1989) 'Will Section 574 of the Companies Code Please Stand Up (And Will Section 1324 of the Corporations Act Follow Suit)', *Company & Securities Law Journal* 7: 388–400.

Baxter, W. (1978) 'Enterprise Liability, Public and Private', *Law & Contemporary Problems* 42: 45–52.

Berle, A. and Means, G. (1932) *The Modern Corporation and Private Property*, New York: Macmillan.

Bird, H. (1996) 'What's in a Publicly Listed Share? One Analysis of the Conflict Between the Contractual and Proprietary Models of Share Entitlements Following *Gambotto v. WCP Ltd*', unpublished conference paper presented at the Sixth National Corporate Law Teachers' Conference, Bond University.

—— (1997) 'A Spanner in the Works: The Impact of *Mesenberg v. Cord Industrial Recruiters Pty Ltd* on Enforcement Rights under the Corporations Law', *Australian Business Law Review* 25: 179–89.

Black, B. (1989) 'Bidder Overpayment in Takeovers', *Stanford Law Review* 41: 597–660.

—— (1990) 'Is Corporate Law Trivial: A Political and Economic Analysis', *Northwestern University Law Review* 84: 542–97.

Bottomley, S. (1991) 'Shareholder Derivative Actions and Public Interest Suits: Two Versions of the Same Story?', *University of New South Wales Law Journal* 15: 127–48.

Brudney, V. (1985) 'Corporate Governance, Agency Costs, and the Rhetoric of Contract', *Columbia Law Review* 85: 1403–44.

Butler, H. and Ribstein, L. (1995) *The Corporation and the Constitution*, Washington: AEI Press.

Buxbaum, R. (1996) 'Responsibilities of Transnational Corporations to Host Nations', in L. Heng (ed.), *Current Legal Issues in the Internationalisation of Business Enterprises*, Singapore: Butterworths.

Calabresi, G. (1991) 'The Pointlessness of Pareto: Carrying Coase Further', *Yale Law Journal* 100: 1211–37.

Campbell, E. (1996) 'Termination of Appointments to Public Offices', *Federal Law Review* 24: 1–41.

Cass, R. (1988) 'Privatisation: Politics, Law and Theory', *Marquette Law Review* 71: 449–523.

Coase, R. (1937) 'The Nature of the Firm', *Economica* 4: 386–405.

—— (1960) 'The Problem of Social Cost', *Journal of Law & Economics* 3: 1–44.

Coffee, J. (1984) 'Regulating the Market for Corporate Control: A Critical Assessment of the Tender Offer's Role in Corporate Governance', *Columbia Law Review* 84: 1145–296.

—— (1986) 'Shareholders Versus Managers: The Strain in the Corporate Web', *Michigan Law Review* 85: 1–109.

—— (1988) 'No Exit?: Opting Out, the Contractual Theory of the Corporation, and the Special Case of Remedies', *Brooklyn Law Review* 53: 919–74.

—— (1989) 'The Mandatory/Enabling Balance in Corporate Law: An Essay on the Judicial Role', *Columbia Law Review* 89: 1618–91.

Companies and Securities Law Review Committee (1990) *Report No. 12: Enforcement of the Duties of Directors and Officers of a Company by Means of a Statutory Derivative Action*, Canberra: Australian Government Publishing Service.

Corporate Law Economic Reform Program (1997) *Directors' Duties and Corporate Governance: Proposals for Reform Paper No. 3*, Canberra.

Craswell, R. (1989) 'Contract Law, Default Rules, and the Philosophy of Promising', *Michigan Law Review* 88: 489–529.

Davis, K. (1985) 'Judicial Review of Fiduciary Decision-Making – Some Theoretical Perspectives', *Northwestern University Law Review* 80: 1–99.

Demsetz, H. (1967) 'Towards a Theory of Property Rights', *American Economic Review* 57: 347–59.

Domberger, S. and Piggott, J. (1986) 'Privatisation Policies and Public Enterprise: A Survey', *Economic Record* 62: 145–62.

Dooley, M. and Veasey, E. (1989) 'The Role of the Board in Derivative Litigation: Delaware Law and the Current ALI Proposals Compared', *Business Lawyer* 44: 503–42.

Downes, A. (1957) *An Economic Theory of Democracy*, New York: Harper.

Easterbrook, F. and Fischel, D. (1981) 'The Proper Role of a Target Management in Responding to a Tender Offer', *Harvard Law Review* 94: 1161–204.

—— (1982) 'Antitrust Suits by Targets of Takeover Offers', *Michigan Law Review* 80: 1155–78.

—— (1991) *The Economic Structure of Corporate Law*, Cambridge, MA: Harvard University Press.

—— (1993) 'Contract and Fiduciary Duty', *Journal of Law & Economics* 36: 425–51.

Epstein, R. (1995) *Simple Rules for a Complex World*, Cambridge, MA: Harvard University Press.

Evans, J. (1981) 'Mandatory and Directory Rules', *Legal Studies* 1: 227–46.

Fama, E. (1970) 'Efficient Capital Markets: A Review of Theory and Empirical Work', *Journal of Finance* 25: 383–417.

—— (1980) 'Agency Problems and the Theory of the Firm', *Journal of Political Economy* 88: 288–307.

—— (1991) 'Efficient Capital Markets II', *Journal of Finance* 46: 1575–617.

Fama, E. and Jensen, M. (1983) 'Separation of Ownership and Control', *Journal of Law & Economics* 26: 301–25.

Farrar, J. and McCabe, B. (1995) 'Corporatisation, Corporate Governance and the Deregulation of the Public Sector Economy', *Public Law Review* 6: 24–43.

Finn, F. and Higham, R. (1988) 'The Performance of Unseasoned New Equity Issues-cum-Stock Exchange Listings in Australia', *Journal of Banking & Finance* 12: 333–51.

Finn, P. (1989) 'The Fiduciary Principle', in T. Youdan (ed.), *Equity, Fiduciaries and Trusts*, Toronto: Carswell.

Fischel, D. (1982) 'The Corporate Governance Movement', *Vanderbilt Law Review* 35: 1259–292.

—— (1987) 'Efficient Capital Market Theory, the Market for Corporate Control and the Regulation of Cash Tenders', *Texas Law Review* 57: 1–46.

Fischel, D. and Bradley, M. (1986) 'The Role of Liability Rules and the Derivative Suit in Corporate Law: A Theoretical and Empirical Analysis', *Cornell Law Review* 71: 261–97.

Foreman-Peck, J. (1989) 'The Privatisation of Industry in Historical Perspective', *Journal of Law & Society* 16: 129–48.

Gillette, C. (1988) 'Who Puts the Public in Public Good?: A Comment on Cass', *Marquette Law Review* 71: 534–50.

Gilson, R. (1996) 'Corporate Governance and Economic Efficiency: When do Institutions Matter?', *Washington University Law Quarterly* 74: 327–46.

Gilson, R. and Kraakman, R. (1984) 'The Mechanisms of Market Efficiency', *Virginia Law Review* 70: 549–644.

Gordon, J. (1989) 'The Mandatory Structure of Corporate Law', *Columbia Law Review* 89: 1549–98.

Gordon, J. and Kornhauser, L. (1985) 'Efficient Markets, Costly Information and Securities Research', *New York University Law Review* 60: 761–849.

Graham, C. and Prosser, T. (1987) 'Privatising Nationalised Industries: Constitutional Issues and New Legal Techniques', *Modern Law Review* 50: 16–51.

Hamilton, C. (1995) 'Assessing the Arguments for Privatisation', *Current Affairs Bulletin* 72 (3): 14–21.

Hansmann, H. (1980) 'The Role of Nonprofit Enterprise', *Yale Law Journal* 89: 835–901.

Hirschman, A. (1970) *Exit Voice and Loyalty*, Cambridge, MA: Harvard University Press.

Howard, W. (1989) 'Privatisation and Management', *Australian Quarterly* 3: 87–106.

Jackson, P. and Price, C. (1994) *Privatisation and Regulation: A Review of the Issues*, London: Longman.

Jarrell, G., Brickley, J. and Netter, J. (1988) 'The Market for Corporate Control: The Empirical Evidence since 1980', *Journal of Economic Perspectives* 1: 49–68.

Jensen, M. and Meckling, W. (1976) 'Theory of the Firm: Managerial Behaviour, Agency Costs and Ownership Structure', *Journal of Financial Economics* 3: 305–60.

Jensen, M. and Murphy, K. (1990) 'Performance Pay and Top Management Incentives', *Journal of Political Economy* 98: 225–64.

Johnston, J. (1990) 'Strategic Bargaining and the Economic Theory of Contract Default Rules', *Yale Law Journal* 100: 615–64.

Kay, J. and Thompson, D. (1986) 'Privatisation: A Policy in Search of a Rationale', *Economic Journal* 96: 18–32.

King, S. (1995) 'Competition: The Missing Link in Australia's Privatisation Program', *Policy* 10 (4): 12–16.

Klein, W. (1982) 'The Modern Business Organization: Bargaining Under Constraints', *Yale Law Journal* 91: 1521–64.

Kluver, J. (1993) 'Derivative Actions and the Rule in *Foss v. Harbottle*: Do We Need a Statutory Remedy?', *Company & Securities Law Journal* 11: 7–25.

Koh, P. (1996) 'Shadow Director, Shadow Director, Who Art Thou?', *Company & Securities Law Journal* 14: 340–51.

Kraakman, R. (1984) 'Corporate Liability Strategies and the Costs of Legal Controls', *Yale Law Journal* 93: 857–98.

Laffont, J. and Tirole, J. (1991) 'Privatisation and Incentives', *Journal of Law Economics & Organization* 7: 84–105.

Langevoort, D. (1992) 'Theories, Assumptions, and Securities Regulation: Market Efficiency Revisited', *University of Pennsylvania Law Review* 140: 851–920.

Legal Committee of the Companies & Securities Advisory Committee (1995) *Compulsory Acquisitions Report*, Canberra: Australian Government Publishing Service.

Macey, J. (1993) 'Corporate Law and Corporate Governance: A Contractual Perspective', *Journal of Corporation Law* 18: 185–212.

McGrory, D. (1989) 'Privatisation in the United Kingdom and Economic Regulation in the United States: Lessons in Administrative Law', *Liverpool Law Review* 11: 117–36.

Maddock, R. (1993) 'Reforming Australia's Utilities: Deregulation and Regulation', *Policy* 9 (2): 14–17.

Manne, H. (1965) 'Mergers and the Market for Corporate Control', *Journal of Political Economy* 73: 110–20.

Megginson, W., Nash, R. and Van Randenborgh, M. (1994) 'The Financial and Operating Performance of Newly Privatised Firms: An International Empirical Analysis', *Journal of Finance* 49: 403–52.

Millon, D. (1993) 'Communitarians, Contractarians and the Crisis in Corporate Law', *Washington & Lee Law Review* 50: 1373–93.

Mitchell, L. (ed.) (1995) *Progressive Corporate Law*, Boulder: Westview.

Mueller, D. (1989) *Public Choice II*, New York: Cambridge University Press.

Olsen, T. and Torsvik, G. (1993) 'The Ratchet Effect in Common Agency: Implications for Regulation and Privatisation', *Journal of Law, Economics & Organization* 9: 136–58.

Polinsky, M. (1989) *An Introduction to Law and Economics*, Boston: Little, Brown.

Posner, R. (1971) 'Taxation by Regulation', *Bell Journal of Economics* 2: 22–50.

—— (1990) *The Problems of Jurisprudence*, Cambridge, MA: Harvard University Press.

—— (1992) *Economic Analysis of Law* (4th edn), Boston: Little, Brown.

Priest, G. (1988) 'The Aims of Privatisation', *Yale Law & Policy Review* 6: 1–5.

Quiggin, J. (1994) *Does Privatisation Pay?*, Discussion Paper Number 2, Canberra: The Australian Institute.

Ramsay, I. (1992) 'Corporate Governance, Shareholder Litigation and the Prospects for a Statutory Derivative Action', *University of New South Wales Law Journal* 15: 149–76.

—— (1995) 'Enforcement of Corporate Rights and Duties by Shareholders and the Australian Securities Commission: Evidence and Analysis', *Australian Business Law Review* 23: 174–83.

—— (ed.) (1996) *Gambotto v. WCP Ltd: Its Implications for Corporate Regulation*, Melbourne: Centre for Corporate Law and Securities Regulation.

Ramsay, I. and Sidhu, B. (1995) 'Underpricing of Initial Public Offerings and Due Diligence Costs: An Empirical Examination', *Company & Securities Law Journal* 13: 186–201.

Raz, J. (1979) *The Authority of Law: Essays on Law and Morality*, Oxford: Clarendon Press.

Romano, R. (1989) 'Answering the Wrong Question: The Tenuous Case for Mandatory Corporate Laws', *Columbia Law Review* 89: 1599–617.

—— (1991) 'The Shareholder Suit: Litigation without Foundation?', *Journal of Law Economics & Organization* 7: 55–87.

Sampford, C. (1991) 'Law, Institutions and the Public/Private Divide', *Federal Law Review* 20: 185–222.

Schwartz, A. (1992) 'Relational Contracts in the Courts: An Analysis of Incomplete Agreements and Judicial Strategies', *Journal of Legal Studies* 21: 271–318.

Scott, K. (1983) 'Corporation Law and the American Law Institute Corporate Governance Project', *Stanford Law Review* 35: 927–48.

Shearmur, J. (1988) 'Public Choice, Contracting Out and Contractarianism', *Marquette Law Review* 71: 445–7.

Starr, P. (1988) 'The Meaning of Privatisation', *Yale Law and Policy Review* 6: 6–41.

Stout, L. (1988) 'The Unimportance of Being Efficient: An Economic Analysis of Stock Market Pricing and Securities Regulation', *Michigan Law Review* 87: 613–709.

Taggart, M. (1991) 'Corporatisation, Privatisation and Public Law', *Public Law Review* 2: 77–108.

The Treasurer, Commonwealth of Australia (1997) *New Focus for Corporate Law*, Press Release No. 15, March 1997, Canberra.

Vickers, J. and Yarrow, G. (1988) *Privatisation: An Economic Analysis*, Cambridge, MA: MIT Press.

Wettenhall, R. and Beckett, I. (1991) 'Movement in the Public Enterprises and Statutory Authority Sector', in J. Halligan and R. Wettenhall (eds), *Hawke's Third Government*, Canberra: Royal Australian Institute of Public Administration.

Williamson, O. (1996) *The Mechanisms of Governance*, New York: Oxford University Press.

Whincop, M. (1995) '*Gambotto v. WCP Ltd*: An Economic Analysis of Alterations to Articles and Expropriation Articles', *Australian Business Law Review* 23: 276–92.

—— (1996a) 'A Theoretical and Policy Critique of the Modern Reformulation of Directors' Duties of Care', *Australian Journal of Corporate Law* 6: 72–92.

—— (1996b) 'Developments in Directors' Statutory Duties of Honesty and Propriety', *Company & Securities Law Journal* 14: 157–73.

—— (1996c) 'An Economic Analysis of the Criminalisation and Content of Directors' Duties', *Australian Business Law Review* 24: 273–92.

—— (1997a) 'Of Fault and Default: Contractarianism as a Theory of Anglo-Australian Corporate Law', *Melbourne University Law Review* 21: 187–234.

—— (1997b) 'Nexuses of Contracts, the Authority of Corporate Agents, and the

Doctrinal Indeterminacy: From Formalism to Law and Economics', *University of New South Wales Law Journal* 20: 274–310.
—— (1997c) 'A Relational and Doctrinal Critique of Shareholders' Special Contracts', *Sydney Law Review* 19: 314–35.
—— (1997d) 'Overcoming Corporate Law: Instrumentalism, Pragmatism and the Separate Legal Entity Concept', *Company and Securities Law Journal* 15: 411–33.

4

THE ECONOMICS OF PRIVATISATION

Case study of Australian telecommunications

يصور هذا
الفصل بالكامل

Allan Brown

Introduction

Although telecommunications corporations have traditionally been owned by private interests in some countries, for example, the US and the Philippines, until the 1980s telecommunications operations in most countries have been public enterprises. There is now, however, an international trend towards the privatisation of telecommunications companies. The current wave of major privatisations in the industry began in the UK with Cable and Wireless in 1981, and since then many countries have followed suit, including Japan, Canada, Argentina, Singapore and, more recently, Germany. Table 4.1 lists nineteen major telecommunications privatisations in sixteen countries, both developed and developing, between 1981 and 1996. Although in a number of countries the government has privatised a portion only of their telecommunications corporation, many of these are likely in the future to sell part or all of their remaining equity interests.

Because a policy is widely adopted, however, does not mean that it is necessarily beneficial, either economically or socially. A comparison of a range of economic indicators in telecommunications, carried out in Australia by the Bureau of Industry Economics (BIE 1995), found that the US, where the industry is entirely privately owned, had the lowest-priced fixed charges for business customers, but that Iceland, operating under a state telecommunications monopoly, had the world's lowest prices for a national basket of call charges. Similarly, the US was top of the league table for multifactor productivity, but another state monopoly, Switzerland, was the international leader in terms of both 'revenue per employee' and 'revenue per line'. The point is that in telecommunications there is no apparent association between the type of ownership and economic performance.

Table 4.1 Major privatisations of telecommunications companies: 1981–96

Year(s)	*Country*	*Company*	*Private (%)*
1981, 83	UK	Cable and Wireless	100
1984, 91, 93	UK	British Telecom	100
1986, 87, 88	Japan	Nippon Telephone & Telegraph Corp. (NTT)	37
1987	Canada	Teleglobe	100
1988	Chile	Compania de Telefonos de Chile (CTC)	100
1988	Chile	Empresa Nacional de Telecomunicaciones (ENTEL)	100
1990	Argentina	Telefonica Argentina	60
1990	Argentina	Telecom Argentina	60
1990	Malaysia	Telekom Malaysia Berhad	27
1990, 91, 92	Mexico	Telefonos de Mexico (TELMEX)	20
1990	New Zealand	Telecom New Zealand	100
1991	Venezuela	Compania de Telefonos de Venezuela (CANTV)	40
1992	Puerto Rico	Telefonica Larga Distancia de Puerto Rico	79
1993	Hungary	Hungarian Telecommunications Company (MATAV)	70
1993	Korea (South)	Dacom	100
1993	Latvia	Lattelkom	49
1993	Singapore	Singapore Telecom	10
1996	South Africa	Telkom	30
1996	Germany	Deutsche Telekom	25

Source: International Telecommunications Union, ITU World Telecommunication Development Report 1994; Australian federal *Department of Communications and the Arts.*

The purpose of this chapter is to identify and examine the economic issues relating to privatisation in general, and as they relate in particular to Telstra Corporation Limited, the Australian publicly owned telecommunications carrier. The sections next consider respectively the economic theory concerning privatisation of government business enterprises (GBEs), the effects of privatisation on the finances of the public sector, the structure and regulation of the Australian telecommunications industry, the major economic issues concerning the Telstra privatisation proposal, and finally draw some conclusions.

Privatisation and economic efficiency

Property rights and public choice theories

Traditional neoclassical economic theory is generally silent in relation to the relative efficiency of privately owned firms and public enterprises. All firms, irrespective of ownership, are assumed to maximise profits and hence productive efficiency. Allocative efficiency is determined by the extent of competition, which in turn is related to the structure of markets in which firms operate (Nellis and Kikeri 1989). Nevertheless, there exists an important argument, derived from the property rights (Coase 1937; Alchian and Demsetz 1972; Williamson 1975) and public choice (Tullock 1965; Downs 1967; Niskanen 1971) theorists, that GBEs will in practice not be cost minimisers. Their economic performance in terms both of productive efficiency and profitability will thus be inferior to that of privately owned firms.

According to the property rights and public choice schools, the essential problems concern the objectives of GBEs and the system of incentives facing their managers. Property rights in a private sector firm are clearly defined by shareholdings: the amount paid as dividends to equity holders is related to profits earned by the firm and the number of shares owned by individual shareholders. These arrangements are conducive to the pursuit by the firm of the single objective of profit maximisation as self-interested shareholders judge managers by their success or failure to achieve this goal. This process is also supported by the functioning of capital markets whereby rises in actual or prospective profits increase the market value of shares and, conversely, falling profits deflate share prices. In contrast, GBEs are generally given a range of different and sometimes conflicting objectives by their government owners, amongst which cost minimisation might have low priority. Moreover, GBEs will typically be assigned certain non-commercial objectives, or community service obligations (CSOs), which by their nature will be 'inefficient' and thus involve GBEs in costs not usually incurred by private firms. The rational response of public sector managers is to endeavour to maximise a weighted average of those objectives with which they are confronted. The pursuit of profit will usually be one, but not the sole, objective of GBEs (Haskel and Szymanski 1994).

The property rights literature suggests that, because of information asymmetries, governments (the principals) face difficulties in providing appropriate incentives to public sector managers (their agents). Managers of GBEs are therefore given less discretion than private sector managers and so choose a relatively quiet life. They will perform only to the level necessary to meet the standards set for them, and these may be modest compared with the potential of the firms they manage (Hemming and Mansoor 1988). In contrast, the owners of private firms can establish a system of incentives for their managers and employees in the form of bonuses, shares and/or stock options. Again the capital market reinforces this mechanism. Privately owned corporations are subject to threats of bankruptcy and takeover. There are thus both positive and negative incentives for managers and employees to maximise the profits of the firm and the value of its shares. Further, the remuneration a private sector manager can command from a current or prospective employer may well be influenced by movements in the value of the firm as represented by its share price. GBEs, on the other hand, cannot be taken over, and implicit or explicit government backing relieves public sector managers of the threat of bankruptcy. The nature of GBEs also inhibits the benefits of co-ownership, since the stake of an employee in a GBE, as a taxpayer, is too small to be of significance (Rees 1986). Moreover, because the government is the sole shareholder and managers cannot be given shares or share options, GBEs are restricted in their ability to link managerial compensation to financial performance. Salary levels of GBE managers may also be tied to other public sector positions and/or subject to politically acceptable upper limits (Zeckhauser and Horn 1989).

This line of argument is complemented by the approach of the public choice theories which claim that state enterprise managers pursue, not the 'public interest', but their own self-interest. They can secure higher salaries and more power and prestige than their private sector counterparts by forming coalitions with public servants leading to increased departmental and enterprise budgets. Without the degree of monitoring to which private firms are subject by their shareholders, GBEs also provide favourable conditions for employees to pursue their self-interest in the form of generous wage levels, fringe benefits (feather-bedding) and over staffing. Politicians too engage in self-interested behaviour in their attempt to maximise votes. This can result in political interference in the operations of a GBE which can contribute to the diversification of its objectives as well as economic inefficiency (Hartley and Parker 1991).

The implication of the property rights/public choice analysis is that public enterprise is inherently less efficient than private enterprise, and countries wishing to improve the overall efficiency of their economies should transfer the maximum possible amount of economic activity from the public to the private sector. The property rights and public choice theorists have been highly successful in propagating their teachings, and belief in the superior performance of private over public ownership is now widespread among private and public sector decision makers as well as academic economists. The past two decades have witnessed a massive shift to private sector activity and reliance on market forces largely in deference to the new ideology, which has been given further impetus and apparent confirmation by the collapse in the late 1980s of all but a few of the centrally planned economies. The privatisation of GBEs yielded US$64 billion worldwide in 1994, US$73 billion in 1995, and US$88 billion in 1996 (*Australian Financial Review* 1996, 1997).

The property rights/public choice arguments should not be accepted at face value, however. In large private firms with widely dispersed equity holdings there is likely to be a principal–agent problem with managers largely free of effective monitoring by shareholders. This will create conditions for sub-optimal productive efficiency in the form of managerial slack ('X-inefficiency'), especially where product markets are not highly competitive (Leibenstein 1966). Capital markets also have deficiencies as a check on the performance of large private corporations. Large firms can sustain a greater fall in their performance indicators than smaller firms before becoming candidates for takeover, and most very large firms are practically immune from hostile takeover (Mayer and Meadowcroft 1985; Domberger and Piggott 1986; Bishop and Kay 1989). In principle, a large firm can go bankrupt, but in practice, if it is subject to regulation and its insolvency is likely to disrupt a key industry, it is likely to be saved by favourable price regulation which will ensure that it earns sufficient revenues to cover its finance and investment needs (Bishop *et al.* 1994).

Another shortcoming of the property rights and public choice theories is that they are largely static and hold out little prospect for improved economic performance by public sector organisations. Part of the response by governments in many countries to the property rights/public choice analysis, however, has been a comprehensive attempt to reform their public sectors, including their GBEs. 'Corporatisation' essentially involves the introduction of approaches and practices of private enterprise into the operations of GBEs, and to a significant extent addresses the traditional shortcomings of GBEs identified by the property rights and public choice theorists. The principles of corporatisation include: clarity of objectives to provide focus for decision making; increased managerial autonomy (and a corresponding reduced role by government); performance monitoring and assessment of outcomes; and the introduction of rewards and sanctions to enhance incentives (Economic Planning Advisory Council 1987; Allan 1989; Forsyth 1992; Waterman 1993).

Empirical evidence

An obvious way to test the property rights/public choice theories is by empirical analysis. Notwithstanding the numerous methodological and technical difficulties involved in comparing the relative efficiency of public and private enterprises, the economics literature now contains a large number of such studies. In a non-exhaustive compilation, Vining and Boardman (1992) list ninety-five studies dating from 1965. Of these, sixty-eight produced results showing that private corporations were more efficient than public corporations, seven concluded that public corporations were more efficient, and the remaining twenty found there to be no difference between public and private firms. A few years earlier, in 1989, the Industry Commission in Australia (then Industries Assistance Commission [IAC]) carried out an extensive review of the literature comparing the economic performance of public and private firms. It concluded that the weight of empirical evidence to that time supported the view that *under competitive conditions* private firms were generally more efficient than public firms. Where natural monopoly elements were present, however, or where competition was restricted by government regulation, the IAC found the evidence to be *inconclusive* (IAC 1989: Vol. 3, Appendix H).

Vining and Boardman (1992: 216) point out that one problem with the empirical studies conducted up to the late 1980s was that most were concerned with 'somewhat idiosyncratic' industry sectors with special structural and/or regulatory characteristics. In particular, many of the firms examined had geographic monopolies (for example, electricity and water utilities), and the performance of firms in the same industries was compared even though the firms did not compete with one other. To remedy these perceived deficiencies Vining and Boardman carried out two major studies. In both, they narrowed the focus of the comparison by concentrating only on firms operating in *competitive* markets. The first (Boardman and Vining 1989) used 1983 data to compare the performance of 500 non-US industrial firms, both privately owned and GBEs, all in international markets. The second (Vining and Boardman 1992) adopted a similar methodology, this time using 1986 data in relation to 380 large Canadian private and public industrial firms. They controlled for firm size, economies of scale, market structure, market share and industrial sector. The results of the two studies were highly consistent. Deriving several measures of profitability and efficiency, Vining and Boardman found 'robust evidence' (they used the term in both studies) that publicly owned enterprises were less profitable and less efficient than private corporations.

The studies prior to those of Vining and Boardman did not attempt to measure, or to control for, the achievement of socio-political goals (CSOs) which may have been imposed on public sector enterprises. If GBEs but not their privately owned competitors are charged with CSOs, they will be at a relative disadvantage in terms of productive efficiency. Vining and Boardman also did not control for CSOs in their studies, but assumed that GBEs in competitive markets would not have significant non-economic objectives.

Vining and Boardman used profitability as a proxy for allocative efficiency. They justified this on the basis that their sample firms were all operating in competitive markets and that, therefore, '. . . normatively appropriate deviations from profit maximization . . . will be minimal' (Boardman and Vining 1989: 9). This assumption is questionable, however. Profitability will be an appropriate proxy for allocative efficiency only where markets are highly competitive. But many markets will be oligopolistic with firms enjoying varying degrees of market power. If any of the privately owned firms in the Vining and Boardman studies exercised market power in their respective markets, their greater profitability may be an indication of *inferior* rather than superior allocative efficiency (and the converse will apply if any GBEs enjoy market power). Although the privately owned firms in the Vining and Boardman studies were more profitable than GBEs, it cannot be accepted that they were more allocatively efficient in the sense of exhibiting a closer correspondence between price and cost.

There are two other limitations of the Vining and Boardman studies as indicators of the relative efficiency of public and private firms. The first is that they adopt less than optimal proxies for productive efficiency. In another paper, Vining acknowledges that the 'most technically sophisticated' measure of productive efficiency is total factor productivity (TFP) which measures both labour and capital productivity (Vining 1989: 16). Nevertheless, presumably for analytical convenience, Vining and Boardman adopt as proxies for productive efficiency the inferior measures of sales per employee and sales per asset which they describe as 'two measures that relate to aspects of X-efficiency' (Boardman and Vining 1989: 12).

The other limitation is that they are based on data for 1983 and 1986 when the current worldwide emphasis on public sector reform was at a very early stage. Thus the full effect of corporatisation, which can be expected to enhance the productive efficiency of public sector relative to private sector firms, is unlikely to have been captured by the Vining and Boardman studies. The Australian Economic Planning Advisory Commission (formerly the Economic Planning Advisory Council) has found that, over the fifteen-year period to 1993–4, Australian federal and state GBEs experienced an average annual growth in TFP of 4.4 per cent, compared with only 0.3 per cent for the private sector (Economic Planning Advisory Commission 1995; Clare and Johnston 1992). It is likely that a major factor contributing to these results is that the productivity of Australian GBEs was particularly poor in the 1970s, so they began from a low base. Nevertheless, the Economic Planning Advisory Commission study shows that corporatisation can have a substantial impact on the productive efficiency of publicly owned enterprises.

Megginson *et al.* (1994) examines sixty-one companies in eighteen countries and thirty-two industries, all sixty-one companies being fully or partly privatised between 1961 and 1991 (but most between 1985 and 1990). The study compares the performance of each of the sample firms for the three-year period immediately prior to its privatisation, with that for the three years immediately after privatisation. The main finding of the study is that '. . . after being privatized, firms increase real sales, become more profitable, increase their capital investment spending, improve their operating efficiency, and increase their work forces' (Megginson *et al.* 1994: 403).

Like Vining and Boardman, Megginson *et al.* employ a suboptimal proxy for evaluating productive efficiency, namely sales income per employee. However, the Megginson study has an additional, fundamental, defect. In evaluating changes in the performance of the sample firms when they are relocated from the public to the private sector it fails to separate the effects of privatisation from other changes that may have been imposed upon the operations of the firms during either the three years prior or three years following privatisation. In the words of the authors:

> Our data do not allow us to precisely document the causes of these performance improvements after divestiture . . . the very pervasive-

> ness of these improvements and the fact that most share sales did not raise cash for the firm suggest that privatization itself – the involvement of private investors in a firm's ownership structure – critically impacts a firm's operating and financial performance.
>
> (Megginson *et al.* 1994: 448)

All of the measured improvements in the sample firms' operations are thus attributed solely to the privatisation process. Implicit in this approach is the assumption that enterprises cannot improve their economic performance while they operate under government ownership. This assumption not only pre-empts the central issue but, as the Economic Planning Advisory Commission studies show, is unrealistic.

The conclusions of a World Bank study (Galal *et al.* 1994) are similarly flawed. This study employs a sophisticated technique to analyse the post-privatisation performance of twelve companies privatised between 1982 and 1990 (mostly airlines and regulated utilities, including telecommunications corporations) in the UK, Chile, Malaysia and Mexico. In each case it estimates the social value of the enterprise under private ownership, which it compares with an estimate of its social value under the counterfactual scenario of what it would have been under continued government ownership. The study concludes that privatisation resulted in net welfare gains in eleven of the twelve cases and, on average, the value of the gains was equal to 26 per cent of a firm's pre-privatisation sales revenue.

The authors acknowledge that their methodology necessitates subjective judgements regarding the counterfactual outcomes. However, like Megginson *et al.*, they are too eager to attribute the post-privatisation gains to privatisation itself. For example, in estimating post-privatisation welfare gains for British Telecom they take account of the labour improvements resulting from the company significantly reducing its work force, but for the counterfactual case of continued operation as a GBE they ' . . . assume that no corresponding work force reduction would have taken place' (p. 94) (see also 'Productive efficiency' section, below). And in the case of Mexico, the authors note that privatisation was part of a much wider, comprehensive programme of economic reform, but proceed to credit the benefits of the whole policy package entirely to privatisation: ' . . . our contention . . . is that the divestiture program was so integrated into the overall reform that it is risky at best to try to separate the effects of divestiture from those of other economic reforms' (p. 516). The conclusions of the Galal study cannot therefore be accepted as a reliable indication of the welfare effects of privatisation.

Recent analysis of public and private enterprises in the UK has produced results that sit uneasily with those of the Vining and Boardman, Megginson *et al.* and Galal studies, but which are consistent with the Economic Planning Advisory Commission findings. Hutchinson (1991) evaluated the performance of seventeen firms in five competitive industries, each industry group containing at least one firm that was privatised between 1974 and 1986. He compared the profitability and labour productivity, first, of public and private enterprises in each industry prior to the privatisation of the GBEs and, second, of the privatised enterprises both before and after privatisation. He found in his sample that privately owned firms were more profitable than GBEs, but that higher levels of growth in labour productivity were recorded by the firms in public ownership.

Bishop and Thompson (1992) examined productivity in nine UK firms which were in the public sector in the 1970s, six of which were privatised in the 1980s. They measured labour productivity and total factor productivity for each enterprise and compared the performance for the 1970s with that of the 1980s. They found that productivity growth for all nine enterprises was higher in the 1980s than in the 1970s. The highest upturn in productivity performance was by British Steel which was privatised in 1988, but the next three highest increases were recorded by enterprises which remained under state ownership. They conclude that '. . . the changes in the regulation of enterprises in public ownership has had an impact upon performance which is distinct from that resulting from, or anticipating, changes in ownership' (Bishop and Thompson 1992: 1189).

Although a detailed examination of the large number of empirical studies on the comparative efficiency of public and private enterprises is not carried out here, a few general points can be made on the basis of the preceding analysis. The empirical evidence strongly suggests that *historically* private firms have outperformed public firms where both have operated in competitive markets. Traditionally, GBEs have had multiple objectives among which has been profit making, but usually not profit maximisation. Corporatisation has addressed many of the apparent causes of public sector inefficiency, and there is evidence from both Australia and the UK that the productive efficiency of GBEs has greatly improved since the early 1980s. It is still not clear, however, whether it has yet achieved the level of the private sector, or, indeed, whether it ever will. The fundamental question as to whether or not private firms are inherently superior to public enterprises in terms of productive efficiency is, therefore, yet to be conclusively answered. If, in time, it is found that in fact they are, it is likely that the difference between their levels of productive efficiency will be less than traditionally assumed.

The empirical studies examined in this section raise questions regarding the measure of economic efficiency. The major works examined do not estimate the total factor productivity of their sample firms although it is a superior measure of productive efficiency. Nor do they control for any non-commercial obligations imposed on GBEs by their government owners. Where GBEs, but not their private counterparts, have CSOs they will be at a disadvantage in terms of costs. Profitability is an inadequate indication of allocative efficiency. As most GBEs operate in imperfectly competitive markets there can be no presumption that their privatisation will enhance allocative efficiency. In fact, to the extent that privatised firms inherit under-exploited market power their privatisation can be expected to worsen allocative efficiency. This problem is recognised by the frequent establishment of elaborate procedures by governments to regulate the pricing behaviour of former GBEs. In turn, one of the main operating strategies of privatised firms is to endeavour to minimise the effects of price regulation (Bishop *et al.* 1994; Haskel and Szymanski 1994). In the absence of an effective regime of price regulation in imperfectly competitive markets, privatisation is likely to involve a trade-off between increased productive efficiency on the one hand and decreased allocative efficiency on the other.

Where a GBE is subject to full and effective competition there is no strong economic case against privatisation – provided that the sale generates sufficient net proceeds (see below). Where, however, a GBE faces little product market competition – for example, because of the presence of natural monopoly – the empirical evidence regarding the benefits of privatisation is inconclusive. The case for the transfer of ownership is weakest in these circumstances (Industry Commission 1994). Where feasible, monopoly and highly concentrated industries in which GBEs are operating should be opened to greater competition. This can be expected to improve the productive efficiency of the GBE (Domberger and Piggott 1986; Hensher 1986; Rees 1986; Zeckhauser and Horn 1989). The empirical studies of the performance of UK firms privatised during the 1980s strongly support this point (Bishop and Kay 1988, 1989; Bishop and Green 1995). Because of the practical difficulties in introducing new competition after a GBE has been privatised, however, there are considerable advantages in liberalising the market before rather than after privatisation. In the words of Hemming and Mansoor (1988: 14), '. . . as a general rule, where privatization and liberalization come into conflict, the latter should be preferred since privatization can more readily follow liberalization than vice versa'.

Privatisation and public finances

Budget deficits and the PSBR

In the public debate privatisation is frequently supported on the grounds that the sale of a GBE will improve the government's financial position in terms of reducing the size of its budget deficit (or increasing its budget surplus) and the public sector borrowing requirement (PSBR). For example, in 1994, Kim Beazley, the then Australian Minister for Finance, nominated these goals as principal reasons for the Labor government's disposal of public assets (Beazley 1994). This argument is questionable, however.

There is no inherent macroeconomic virtue in lower budget deficits. They may well be desirable to dampen an overheated economy, or if in previous years slack financial management has resulted in public expenditures outpacing revenues. However, lower budget deficits will exacerbate economic problems during business downturns. Generally, governments should aim to balance their budgets over the course of the business cycle and preserve the flexibility to pursue counter-cyclical fiscal policy as economic conditions warrant.

In relation to borrowings, governments are in a different position to private firms when debt becomes due for repayment. The privatisation of a GBE by a government is essentially the conversion of a real asset into cash. While a private firm may be forced to dispose of some of its assets if it faces a liquidity problem, governments have considerably more discretion in relation to public borrowings. They can either refinance public debt as it becomes due for repayment – that is, to sell new bonds and use the proceeds to pay off the holders of maturing bonds – or increase taxation to obtain the funds required. Moreover, because of their taxing power, the risk of governments being unable to repay their borrowings is very much less than that of private firms. This is not to imply that the public debt is irrelevant. Governments may have large amounts of debt becoming due for refinancing at the one time, or may face political difficulties in increasing taxation (Forsyth 1993).

A related issue concerns the funds required by GBEs to enable them to expand and/or improve their productive efficiency. It is commonly argued that governments are not able to make further capital advances to GBEs as this necessitates further public borrowings. Hamilton (1995) points out that this is an ideological assertion based on the assumption that increased public debt is economically harmful. As explained above, however, governments are well placed to raise funds to invest in public enterprises. The criterion for such decisions should be whether or not particular capital injections to GBEs have net economic and social benefits.

An important factor in this issue is that when a GBE is privatised accounting problems arise in recording the transaction which obscure its net effect upon public finances. Privatisation involves the disposal by government of a *capital* asset, whereas government budgets and the PSBR include both *current* and *capital* transactions. The accounting conventions adopted by private firms differ from those generally used by governments in that private firms make a clear separation between current and capital transactions. The sale of an asset by a private firm for less than its book value will show up in the firm's accounts as a capital loss and thus reduce the firm's net worth, while a sale for *more* than book value will produce a capital *gain* and *increase* the firm's net worth. (The amount of the capital loss or gain recorded on sale will be determined by the method of asset valuation adopted in the firm's accounts.) Because neither the government budget nor the PSBR records the value of GBEs, however, they cannot reveal an equivalent effect upon the net worth of the public sector when they are privatised. Changes to the budget outcome and/or the PSBR, therefore, do not provide an appropriate measure of the consequence of privatisation for the public sector.

Because the net budget outcome in any year measures the difference between government expenditure and revenue, the change in the deficit (or surplus) from one year to the next is usually regarded as an indication of whether the government's demand management policy has become more expansionary or contractionary. If budget revenue includes proceeds from asset sales, however, changes in the net budget outcome no longer reflect the fiscal stance of the government and need to be adjusted accordingly.

Post-privatisation profitability

With the sale of any GBE the government disposes of its entitlement to the future flow of profits of the enterprise. The government budget will record the proceeds from the privatisation in the year of sale and, in future years, budget revenues will no longer include the dividend previously received from the GBE. To the extent that the proceeds are directed towards the retirement of government debt, however, future years' budget outlays will be reduced by savings in public debt interest. If any part of the privatisation proceeds are used for current expenditure rather than retirement of debt there will be a lower level of savings in public debt interest and a corresponding reduction in the net worth of the public sector. This practice has been likened to 'selling the family silver to pay for the groceries'.

Consider a situation where the privatisation of a GBE does *not* affect its economic performance in any way: its profitability as well as productive and allocative efficiency are the same under private as under government ownership. In this case there will be no change in the net worth of the public sector resulting from the privatisation if, but only if, three conditions are met, namely: (a) the sale price is precisely equal to the present value of the discounted stream of net earnings of the GBE, (b) the discount rate embodied in the sale price accurately reflects financial opportunity costs, and (c) total privatisation proceeds are used to reduce public debt. Under these conditions the increase in budget revenues in the year of sale would be exactly offset by the net reduction in future years' budget revenues and expenditures (Hemming and Mansoor 1988). For this outcome to occur, however, there would need to be no underpricing of shares and no transaction costs, which both reduce net sale proceeds received by a vendor government and erode public sector net worth. But all privatisations will involve transaction costs and almost all will be underpriced (see below). If a corporation does not improve its economic performance when it is sold to the private sector, therefore, its privatisation can be expected to *reduce* the net worth of the public sector.

Assume now that the profitability of the enterprise is greater following privatisation than it would have been had it remained under public ownership. The government will now be selling a more valuable stream of future profits than would have accrued to the public sector if the GBE were not privatised, and public finances will be affected in two ways: the achievable sale price for the enterprise will be increased; and greater future year profits will increase company income tax payments to the government. Even in this case the net effect on public finances is not entirely clear cut. If the higher sale price and (discounted) taxation payments resulting from increased future profits are not sufficient to cover the combined underpricing and transaction costs, privatisation will still involve a net cost to the public sector. If the increase in sale price and tax revenues exceed the underpricing and transaction costs, however, the net worth of the public sector will be enhanced by privatisation. Underpricing and transaction costs are incurred only once, of course, whereas profitability improvements can be expected to be ongoing.

If the increased profitability of the privatised firm is brought about by a reduction in its level of costs, the increase to public sector finances from privatisation will be accompanied by an improvement in the productive efficiency of the economy generally. Efficiency effects will complement the financial effects. If higher profitability is achieved through greater exploitation of market power, however, there will be a conflict between financial and efficiency objectives. The privatisation will improve the net worth of the public sector, but will impair allocative efficiency in the overall economy because of higher prices to consumers of the firm's products (Vickers and Yarrow 1988; Forsyth 1993).

Apart from the effects of underpricing and transaction costs, the sale proceeds from privatisation are likely to fall short of the present value of the firm's profits. Because private companies pay higher rates of interest on borrowings than governments, the present value of future profits to be derived from a privatised GBE will be worth less to potential private purchasers than to its government owner. In other words, the discount rate used by private investors in evaluating the expected flow of returns from a privatised GBE will be higher than the government's opportunity cost of funds. It follows that, other things being equal, the privatisation of a profitable GBE and the use of the proceeds to reduce government debt will cause a *reduction* in the net worth of the public sector (Walker 1994). In his analysis of several privatisations in Australia, the United Kingdom and New Zealand, Quiggin (1995) concluded that the loss in public sector net worth was greater than the privatisation proceeds received by the vendor governments.

Underpricing

To provide an incentive for investors, the issue price of shares in public floats is generally set at a level somewhat below the price at which they are expected to trade when listed on the stock exchange. Some investors will engage in 'stagging'; that is, they will sell their shares immediately they are listed with the view of realising a quick capital gain. In some cases, however, the market price of the shares upon listing will be less than the issue price, causing the 'stags' to lose money and other investors to incur at least short-term 'paper' losses. The valuation of a newly listed company is difficult and subject to unpredictable influences, and investors will seek a premium for risk taking in an uncertain environment. In addition, the price of a new issue may be further discounted to make allowance for a possible downward movement in the overall level of the stock market between the announcement of the issue price and close of applications.

There are reasons, however, why underpricing may be greater for privatisations than for standard private company floats. Because it will suffer political embarrassment if applications fall short of the available number of shares and/or if individual investors or financial institutions sustain capital losses, a government will have an incentive for each privatisation to be 'successful' (Vickers and Yarrow 1988; Hamilton 1995). An unsuccessful outcome will cause added difficulties for any planned future privatisations. The government may also underprice shares to encourage subscriptions from those who do not usually invest in shares ('mums and dads'), and may offer a special discount to company employees. If a GBE is to be subject to regulation following privatisation there may also be a 'sovereign risk problem' whereby uncertainty concerning the effects of regulation upon the future profits of the enterprise may increase the premium demanded by subscribers (Quiggin 1995).

The UK experience during the 1980s suggests that the percentage underpricing tends to be greater the higher the value of the privatisation share issue (Foster 1992). The imposition of maximum limitations upon the proportion of equity that can be acquired by individual shareholders or class of shareholders will narrow potential sources of funds available for investment in the company and act further to drive down the achievable issue price. Limitations on the proportion of foreign ownership in a privatised enterprise, therefore, will tend to reduce sale proceeds. Where foreign participation in a privatisation is permitted, however, the premium on the shares purchased by overseas investors will represent a direct loss of national wealth by the vendor country (Mayer and Meadowcroft 1985).

Governments can, nevertheless, take steps to reduce underpricing on privatisations. There are different methods for making an initial share issue, and the incorporation of some kind of tender process to determine the issue price may have the effect of reducing the extent of underpricing compared with the sale of shares at a fixed, predetermined price. A tender will also reflect movements in the general share market during the bidding period (Kay and Thompson 1986; Domberger 1995). For its recent privatisation of CSL Limited and Qantas Airlines, for example, the Australian government employed the 'constrained open pricing' method to determine the sale price of shares. Under this procedure the government announces a price range for the shares – a minimum ('floor') and maximum ('cap') issue price – and financial investors bid, over a number of days, on the basis of both price and volume. As allotments of shares to financial investors are based upon their bidding behaviour, they have an incentive to bid up the share price. The government determines the share price for institutional and retail investors following, and on the basis of, the outcome of the auction process.

Where there are special difficulties in valuing an enterprise – for example, if there are no other companies in the same industry listed on the domestic stock exchange – the government may decide to sell the shares in tranches. Sale by tranches may also be favoured for the privatisation of a GBE with a large equity value relative to the size of the domestic equity market. Secondary trading in the shares sold in the first tranche will set the market price and the government can then dispose of subsequent tranches at a discount to that price (Jenkinson and Mayer 1994). Sale in tranches will also allow the government to benefit from any increase in the share value of a privatised firm subsequent to the initial public issue (but will carry the risk of reduced proceeds if the share value falls). With the privatisation in Australia of the Commonwealth Bank, the issue price of shares for the first tranche in August 1991 was $5.40; for the second tranche in November 1993, $9.35; and for the third and final tranche in July 1995, $10.45.

Underpricing also involves efficiency costs in the form of unproductive rent-seeking activity by prospective purchasers of shares in a privatised firm. If there is a strong possibility that the sale price of a GBE is less than its real value – that is, the issue price of shares is less than their subsequent market price – aspiring shareholders will expend resources in their attempt to be issued with shares. Further efficiency costs will arise following the issue of shares as some successful shareholders employ additional resources and incur expenses while engaging in stagging. Selling a GBE for less than its market price also involves a deadweight cost to the economy as additional taxation will need to be raised in future years to cover the revenue shortfall caused by privatisation. There will be an efficiency loss because it costs more than a dollar to raise a dollar of government revenues; the marginal cost of every additional dollar of income tax collected in Australia has been estimated to be between $1.20 and $1.25 (Findlay and Jones 1982). Underpricing of privatisation issues also involves a redistribution of wealth in favour of successful applicants for shares at the expense of taxpayers generally (Forsyth 1993).

Transaction costs involved with a privatisation by public float will include the costs of preparing and printing the prospectus, advertising, processing applications for shares, and payments to lawyers, accountants, bankers, advertising and marketing consultants and other intermediaries. There are likely to be some economies of scale in relation to transaction costs; the larger the value of the share issue, the lower the level of costs as a percentage of gross proceeds (Walker 1994). If the government decides to have the share issue underwritten it will also incur underwriting fees. Privatisation in the form of a 'trade sale', that is, a direct sale of an enterprise to a private entity or consortium of interests, will usually involve considerable savings in transaction costs. A trade sale to, say, a foreign investor seeking a strategic advantage from investment in a privatised firm may also produce a higher sale price than a public float.

In summary, the implications of privatisation are complex and depend upon a number of factors including whether or not the enterprise will be more profitable under private than continued public ownership, and the amount of underpricing and transaction costs. Privatisation will increase the net worth of the public sector and the economy generally only if post-privatisation profits are greater than they would have been under continued public ownership, and if the increased profitability is a result of improved productive efficiency. If the increase in profits results from the privatised firm charging higher prices, allocative efficiency in the economy generally will decline. Underpricing and transaction costs will reduce the proceeds to the government from privatisation. Underpricing is likely to increase proportionally with the size of a public float, restrictions on eligibility for shares and the perceived sovereign risk facing the privatised firm, but will be minimised by the use of a tender process and/or the sale of shares in tranches. There will be a direct loss of national wealth to the extent of the premium on shares sold to foreign investors.

Australian telecommunications industry

Industry reform and regulation

Telecommunications in Australia has been subject to a series of reform measures over the past two decades. In 1975 the Australian Telecommunications Commission (Telecom) was established as a separate statutory authority to take over the telecommunications functions of the former Postmaster-General's Department. This was accompanied by the relaxation of government control over day-to-day decision making and the gradual shift to management of accountability for performance in accordance with specifically defined objectives. In the early 1980s competition was introduced by the licensing of 'service providers' in the value-added services and customer premises equipment segments of the telecommunications market, and in 1989 industry regulatory functions were taken from Telecom and placed with a new independent body, the Australian Telecommunications Authority (Austel). At about the same time the markets for value-added services and the installation and supply of customer equipment were further liberalised, and new price-capping arrangements for Telecom and the publicly owned international operator, Overseas Telecommunications Corporation (OTC), were implemented.

More fundamental changes were introduced with the Telecommunications

Act 1991. Telecom was merged with OTC to form the Australian and Overseas Telecommunications Corporation (AOTC, renamed Telstra in 1993). The government-owned satellite system, Aussat, was privatised and became the basis for a second general telecommunications carrier, the licence for which was granted to Optus Communications. Optus was also licensed to provide mobile services, and a third mobile licence was granted to Vodafone. The transitional framework of a network duopoly and a mobile triopoly was set in place until July 1997.

A detailed regulatory structure has been adopted for the industry. There is open competition for the sale, installation and servicing of customer equipment, and for the lease of telephone capacity from the general carriers for repackaging and resale to large private and public organisations. Competition in the industry is far from even, however. Telstra enjoys considerable market power by virtue of its ownership and control of the local customer access network (CAN) which presents special problems for regulation. In the early 1990s the government had the option of instituting structural arrangements conducive to more evenly matched competition, but by merging OTC and Telecom it ensured that Telstra would occupy a dominant position in the industry for at least the early years of competition (Maddock 1992). Telecommunications policy since 1991 has largely been directed to bringing about 'sustainable competition' in the industry, which has required the imposition of restraints on Telstra in the exercise of its market power.

Austel has declared Telstra to be dominant in all major segments of the telecommunications market except mobile telephony (Austel 1995). The main implication of this is that Telstra is inhibited in its ability to exercise selective price discrimination. Whereas, in general, Telstra must make its price reductions available to all subscribers, Optus is granted much more freedom by Austel to enter into special discounting arrangements for long-distance calls with individual large-volume business customers which provide a large proportion of its revenues. Current regulatory arrangements, therefore, prevent full price competition in the industry.

In August 1995 Optus claimed to account for 14 per cent of the STD and IDD markets (measured by minutes of traffic), and 30 and 37 per cent of the mobile analogue and mobile digital markets, respectively (Optus Communications 1995). Because of Telstra's ownership of the CAN, however, Optus has been constrained from competing in the local call market which provides over a third of Telstra's revenues. Optus has addressed this deficiency by commencing the construction of its own local network. Although probably not economically feasible for the carriage of telephony only, Optus is installing a broadband network capable of carrying telephone calls, pay TV and interactive services along the same cable. It plans for its local network to be accessible to 50 per cent of the Australian population by 1998. Telstra, too, is upgrading its network for the carriage of broadband, but if Optus achieves its ambitions regarding cable roll-out, it will be able to offer what only

Telstra can currently provide, namely, a complete range of services, including local calls. It will then be able to win market share from Telstra in the local call market and increase its share of the long-distance markets. Under changes to the regulatory arrangements for the industry which came into effect in July 1997, there is now no limit to the number of carrier licences issued and no regulatory restriction on the number of service providers. Both Telstra and Optus are required to interconnect all other carriers and service providers and to guarantee them access to customer equipment.

In most industries economic efficiency can be best achieved by allowing prices to be determined by market forces, subject only to general competition and consumer protection safeguards. In telecommunications, however, there are severe limits to the number of general carriers which a single market can support. Notwithstanding the removal of regulatory barriers to entry from July 1997, therefore, it may well be that the current regulated duopoly will become a permanent feature of the Australian telecommunications industry (Brown 1996). Proposed new arrangements facilitating access to Telstra's network and lower service provider interconnection charges, however, should ensure stronger competition to the general carriers from service providers from July 1997.

Table 4.2 provides data on the telecommunications market in Australia for the four financial years to 1995–6. It shows that Telstra accounted for a substantial 81.3 per cent of the market in 1995–6, but this was 10.5 per cent down on three years earlier. Of this loss in market share, most was picked up by Optus, and the rest by service providers. Although Telstra's market share declined over the three years its total revenue increased significantly, by 24 per cent in nominal terms, by virtue of growth in the total market of approximately $5.3 billion (40.3 per cent).

Table 4.2 Australian telecommunications market: 1992–3 to 1995–6[a]

	1992–3		*1993–4*		*1994–5*		*1995–6*[b]	
	Revenue ($m)	*%*	*Revenue ($m)*	*%*	*Revenue ($m)*	*%*	*Revenue ($m)*	*%*
Telstra	12,140	91.8	12,800	88.2	13,600	84.9	15,080	81.3
Optus[c]	100	0.8	550	3.8	1,005	6.3	1,640	8.8
Service providers	978	7.4	1,170	8.0	1,408	8.8	1,832	9.9
Totals	13,218	100.0	14,520	100.0	16,013	100.0	18,552	100.0

Source: Paul Budde Communication, *Superhighway News,* 1996.

Notes:
a Excludes equipment industry.
b Estimated.
c Figures are net of interconnection costs.

Telstra Corporation Limited

'Corporatisation' has been extensively adopted by the national carrier since the mid-1980s when government concern shifted from the day-to-day decisions of the company to monitoring its performance. Internally, Telstra is organised into separately accountable business units, and from 1991–2 has been fully subject to the principles of 'competitive neutrality' for GBEs, including the payment of state and local government taxes and charges, customs duties, corporate taxes and dividends to the Commonwealth government. The financial results of the national carrier for the five financial years to 1995–6 are set out in Table 4.3. (The 1991–2 results include those for both Telecom and OTC as single entities up to their merger on 1 February 1992. Telstra's total revenue figures differ between Tables 4.2 and 4.3 due to the exclusion from Table 4.2 of interconnection charges paid to Telstra.) In the face of increased competition, Telstra's total revenues grew steadily over the four years from $12.2 to $15.2 billion (in nominal dollars), while after-tax profit increased substantially from $0.3 to $2.3 billion. The dividend paid to the government as sole shareholder increased from $0.48 billion in 1991–2 (representing 159.4 per cent of net profit, and coinciding with the government converting $2.0 billion of Commonwealth loans from debt to equity) to $1.37 billion in 1995–6 (59.4 per cent of net profit). The basic financial ratios – return on assets, return on investment and return on equity – all increased substantially between 1991–2 and 1995–6.

The national carrier is a leading performer among Australian GBEs in terms of productivity growth. For the period 1980 to 1994, Telstra (to 1991, Telecom and OTC combined) achieved an average annual growth in TFP of 6.3 per cent, and for 1991 to 1994, 11.9 per cent (BIE 1995: Table A3.7, p. 166). It is likely that one factor affecting the extent of these improvements is

Table 4.3 Telstra Corporation Limited: selected financial data 1991–2 to 1995–6

	1991–2	*1992–3*	*1993–4*	*1994–5*	*1995–6*
Financial statement items ($million)					
Revenues	12,228.5	12,656.0	13,362.5	14,081.4	15,238.6
Expenses	11,570.3	10,661.8	10,834.6	11,676.3	11,791.9
Operating profit (before tax)	658.2	1,994.2	2,527.9	2,405.1	3,446.7
Operating profit (after tax)	313.5	904.3	1,704.8	1,755.5	2,302.1
Dividend	478.0	674.0	738.0	944.0	1,368.0
Dividend as % of after-tax profit	152.5	74.5	43.3	53.8	59.4
Financial ratios (percentages)					
Return on assets	7.7	13.2	15.4	13.5	17.4
Return on investment	9.3	16.4	19.7	18.2	24.2
Return on equity	2.9	8.7	15.7	15.6	18.9

Source: Telstra Corporation, Annual Report 1995–6.

that Telecom started from a particularly low level of productivity in 1980. Staffing levels have been progressively reduced (without involuntary retrenchments) since 1986 when they reached a peak (for Telecom and OTC combined) of almost 97,000 (see Table 4.6). Employment was reduced by 11,000 in 1991–2 alone, and by 30 June 1995 Telstra's total full-time staffing level stood at around 72,000. (The sharp jump of 7,000 in 1994–5 was due mainly to rapid growth in mobile sales and additional staff employed on Telstra's cable roll-out.) Significant productivity gains by Telstra have also been reflected in the number of 'lines per employee' which increased between 1990 and 1993 by 49 per cent (from 92 to 137) (BIE 1995: Table 5.3, p. 118).

As impressive as these results are, Telstra's productivity performance lags well behind world best practice. The most recent international comparison places Australia eighth out of eleven comparable countries in terms of TFP, and twenty-sixth out of thirty for lines per employee (a position unchanged from 1990). In fact, Australia has less than half the number of lines per employee as the two leading countries, South Korea and Italy (BIE 1995: Table 1, p. xiv; p. 118). Although there are difficulties involved with international comparisons, and Australia performed better in terms of capital than labour productivity, the BIE study concludes (1995: 138) that:

> . . . some concern must remain as to the rate of change relative to our international counterparts and competitors, and the distance between Australia's recent public telecommunications infrastructure operating performance and international best practice. The clear message is that labour productivity in telecommunications in Australia remained low by international standards up to and including 1992–3.

In the same study Australia rated somewhat better in comparisons in the prices of calls. Australian prices compared relatively favourably for mobile and international call charges, but were higher than the OECD average for the costs to business of local and STD calls and fixed charges. When all call and service charges are combined in a composite business basket, Australia ranks slightly better than average at eleventh out of twenty-four OECD countries. This ranking, however, has remained unchanged since 1989 (BIE 1995: xiii).

The issues of privatisation

Options

The fundamental options involved with any proposed privatisation are to privatise or not to privatise. A decision to privatise opens up a new range of options concerning the disposal of shares in the enterprise. The main options available to the Australian government in relation to the privatisation of Telstra are set out in Table 4.4.

The first concerns the percentage of equity to be sold by the government to private shareholders. The sale of all shares will essentially transfer Telstra out of government control (although the company would remain subject to regulation). With a total sell-off, however, it is possible for the government to retain the ownership of one special share in the company giving it specified veto rights regarding operation and/or the composition of ownership. The UK and Malaysian governments each hold a so-called 'golden share' in their privatised telecommunications corporations, and the New Zealand government maintains a 'kiwi share' in Telecom New Zealand (Mustafa 1993). Alternatively, over 50 per cent of Telstra's equity could be sold with the government holding a minority interest, or it could decide to dispose of a minority equity interest and maintain a majority shareholding. If the government sold a minority interest in a first tranche it would then have the option to sell further tranches thus moving from majority to minority ownership, and subsequently to the disposal of its entire shareholding.

The second set of options involves the types of investors to allow in a privatised Telstra. The government's choice of investors and the maximum equity holding allowed to each category is likely to affect the control of the privatised firm. For example, if a foreign telecommunications company were to hold the largest single shareholding it might be in a position to exercise effective control, whereas a widely dispersed shareholding would be likely to leave control in the hands of Telstra's management.

The decision regarding the types of investors will largely determine the method to be adopted for the sale of shares. A trade sale would be favoured for the sale of a sizeable shareholding to a single entity or consortium, whereas a public offering is more suitable for the disposal of relatively small individual shareholdings to institutional and/or private investors.

Table 4.4 Options for privatisation

Percentage of equity to sell	*Types of investors*	*Methods of sale*
1. 100	1. Foreign telecommunications corporations	1. Trade sale
2. 50–99.9	2. Domestic institutional investors	2. Public offering
3. <50	3. International institutional investors	3. Combination of (1) and (2)
	4. Domestic private investors	
	5. International private investors	
	6. Any combination of (1)–(5)	

What is Telstra worth?

Predicting the achievable privatisation value of Telstra is a popular activity in Australian financial and political circles. The average price/earnings ratio for all companies listed on the Australian Stock Exchange (ASX) during June 1996 was 18.7, and for all industrial companies, 15.5. The price/earnings ratio at end June 1996 for Telecom New Zealand, a privatised telecommunications company which also has a dominant position in its market, was 15.4. Applying these price/earnings ratios to Telstra's 1995–6 after-tax profit places a market capitalised value on the company of between $35 and $43 billion.

It should be emphasised that the estimate of the market value of Telstra by this method is a rough approximation only and is likely to vary significantly over time. Each financial year produces a different profit result as a new base for calculation, and each month provides a different multiplier in the form of a new price/earnings ratio depending upon stock market fluctuations. Moreover, expectations regarding Telstra's future profitability may be affected by the prospect of privatisation. For example, the company might be considered to be able to achieve greater cost savings as a private than as a public enterprise (see below).

The value of companies in industries subject to detailed price regulation will be significantly influenced by the effect of regulation upon their earnings and profits, and assessments of the likely future behaviour of regulators. Similarly, movements in the share prices for listed corporations will largely reflect the market's response to regulatory decisions and announcements rather than changes in the 'intrinsic value' of their assets (Bishop *et al.* 1994). For the privatisation of Telstra, therefore, a key determinant of its realisable value will be expectations concerning the form and effect of the future regulation of its pricing, and the extent and nature of competition in the telecommunications market. More liberal regulation would enhance potential profits and valuation of the corporation, while more restrictive regulation would reduce its value.

Savings in public debt interest

It was explained earlier that the effect of any privatisation upon public finances was best considered in terms of its consequences for the net worth of the public sector. If all proceeds from the privatisation of a GBE were directed towards the retirement of public debt, future years' budget outlays would be reduced by the resultant savings in public debt interest. It follows that for any privatisation to be financially beneficial to the public sector the savings in public debt must exceed the profits foregone from the sale of the GBE. Conversely, if the savings in public debt interest are less than the profits of the enterprise would be under continued public ownership, privatisation will have an adverse effect on public finances.

This test can be applied to the proposed privatisation of Telstra to ascertain the minimum net sale proceeds necessary to avoid a loss to the public sector. When the public debt is reduced the public sector is saved the equivalent of the real interest rate on government bonds, which over recent years in Australia has averaged around 5 per cent (Quiggin 1995). If this rate is applied to Telstra's 1995–6 after-tax profits of $2.3 billion it is found that the required minimum net sale proceeds necessary to avoid a loss of public sector net worth is around $46 billion ($2.3 billion × 100/5). This is $3 billion more than the higher limit of the range for the estimated market value based on price/earnings ratios.

It was seen above that Telstra's after-tax profits increased substantially in the four years to 1995–6 (from $0.3 to $2.3 billion). The company obviously cannot maintain this rate of profit improvement, and the telecommunications market is becoming more competitive. Under continued public ownership, however, Telstra's profitability for at least the 1996–7 financial year seems more likely to rise than to fall. In this case, the $46 billion valuation based on 1995–6 profits will be an *underestimate* of the required minimum net sale proceeds necessary to avoid a loss to public sector net worth.

The analysis here is subject to possible changes to government taxation revenues after privatisation. If the company's profitability is higher following privatisation than it would have been under continued public ownership, and if the proportion of its profits on which it is liable to pay taxation is unchanged (that is, no greater tax minimisation), public finances will benefit from higher taxation revenues as a direct result of privatisation. These increased revenues would then need to be offset against any loss of public sector net worth.

Depending upon its post-privatisation profitability performance, therefore, the value to the public sector of Telstra remaining under government ownership may be in excess of the estimated $35–43 billion market value of the company. Furthermore, the net sale proceeds received by the government will be less than this amount by the total of 'underpricing' and transaction costs (see below). For the sale of the company to generate overall economic benefits, the improvements in productive efficiency subsequent to, and as a direct consequence of, privatisation would need to be sufficient to outweigh this loss.

Underpricing and transaction costs

It was explained earlier that most new public share issues are deliberately underpriced, but that there are several reasons why underpricing may be greater for privatisations than for private company floats. The cost of underpricing in the sale of a GBE represents a transfer of public wealth to private investors, and the extent of underpricing may vary proportionally with the size of the privatisation. If Telstra were to be fully privatised by public share issue it would be by far the largest public float in Australian corporate history. The market capitalisation value of domestic companies listed on the ASX at 30 June 1996 was approximately $341 billion. If the capitalised value of a privatised Telstra fell between $35 and $43 billion it would be the largest listed company on the exchange and would represent some 10 to 12.5 per cent of total market capitalisation. The sale of Telstra would also be of substantial size relative to recent Australian public share issues. In the six years to 1996 there were only four domestic share issues in excess of $1 billion, namely: the Commonwealth Bank second tranche in 1993 for $1.69 billion; Woolworths, 1993, $2.45 billion; Qantas, 1995, $1.45 billion; and Commonwealth Bank third tranche, 1996, $2.8 billion.

Because of Telstra's size, its privatisation would place heavy demands on the capacity of the Australian capital market. The total amount of new equity raised in Australia varies considerably from year to year, and averaged around $8.7 billion over the period 1991–2 to 1994–5 (McIntosh 1995). It is clear, therefore, that if Telstra is privatised it should be done in tranches. The sale of all government equity in the corporation in, say, three tranches of equal size would involve individual tranches of around $10–13 billion – each several times that of the Qantas, Woolworths and Commonwealth Bank floats. Of course, the average size of a smaller number of tranches would be greater (and smaller for a greater number of tranches), and tranches need not be of equal size.

The five Australian federal government privatisations since 1993 and the share premium on each issue are set out in Table 4.5. The calculation of the share premium follows the method used by Jenkinson and Mayer (1994) and is measured as the difference between the issue price and the stock exchange listed price at the end of five days' trading. With the four issues since 1993 the share premiums have ranged from negative 1.8 per cent for the Commonwealth Bank third tranche (this issue coinciding with a significant fall in the stock market), to 9.5 per cent to the retail investors in Qantas. (Because the issue of the first tranche of the Commonwealth Bank was the first major federal government privatisation and was at a fixed price, its share premium can probably be dismissed as an indication of future underpricing.)

The size of the share premium in relation to any initial share issue is determined by the eventual market price upon listing, and cannot be exactly prescribed by the vendor. Nevertheless, considering the results of recent privatisations, and taking account of the size of Telstra, it may be that an anticipated premium of 6 per cent or more will be required for the 'successful' sale of the first tranche of shares in the company. The issue price of shares in subsequent tranches could then be set at a more modest discount to their prevailing market price.

Transaction costs reduce the proceeds received by the government from any privatisation. For 1994–5 transaction costs for Australian public floats averaged 4.1 per cent of the total amount raised. The average for the float of

Table 4.5 Share premium on federal government privatisations: 1991–6

Company	*Date of privatisation*	*Share premium (%)*[a]
Commonwealth Bank: tranche no. 1	August 1991	17.8
Commonwealth Bank: tranche no. 2	November 1993	
retail investors		3.7
institutional investors		1.0
CSL Limited	May 1994	4.3
Qantas Limited	July 1995	
retail investors		9.5
institutional investors		4.0
Commonwealth Bank: tranche no. 3	July 1996	−1.8

Note:
a Calculated as difference between issue price and ASX listed price five days after listing.

industrial companies was 3.2 per cent, and the float of Qantas (which was not underwritten) cost 3.4 per cent of gross proceeds (McIntosh 1995). Transaction costs for the first tranche of Telstra would be likely to be about the same percentage as that for Qantas (but higher if it were underwritten), with a lower level of costs for subsequent tranches.

Foreign investment

The issue of foreign investment presents a dilemma in relation to the privatisation of Telstra. Imposing restrictions on the level of foreign ownership narrows the source of potential investable funds and is likely to reduce the achievable sale proceeds. Alternatively, a trade sale of a sizeable equity holding to foreign interests could be expected to yield a higher price than a public float and hence reduce the loss from underpricing. A number of large foreign telecommunications companies would certainly be interested in obtaining a strategic shareholding in Telstra, and would support their bids to the government by emphasising the benefits to the company of importing their managerial, technical and marketing expertise. The government may thus be tempted to consider a trade sale of a majority or significant minority interest to an overseas telecommunications company which, in one transaction, would yield substantial proceeds and dispose of a large proportion of Telstra shares.

There is likely, however, to be significant public opposition to foreign interests obtaining a controlling or sizeable equity interest in Telstra, as this may be construed as a loss of sovereignty over a major national asset. Control of Telstra by a foreign telecommunications company may also create a conflict between its own interests and that of Telstra's, especially in relation to tendering for contracts in Asia and elsewhere (Shires 1995). The premium on shares sold offshore represents a direct transfer of public wealth to foreign investors. Overseas participation in the privatisation of Telstra also has the usual implications for the country's external account, with an immediate inflow of funds set against the outflow of dividend payments on equity obligations in future years.

Productive efficiency

It was noted earlier that although Telstra has achieved substantial productivity gains since 1980 it continues to rank poorly in comparison with its overseas counterparts, especially in terms of labour productivity. This suggests that there is scope for further reductions in employment within Telstra.

Specific comparisons with British Telecom and Telecom New Zealand further suggest the possibility of significant labour productivity gains by Telstra. Table 4.6 sets out Telstra's staffing levels for the fifteen years from 1980–1 to 1994–5, together with those of British Telecom (BT, which was privatised in November 1984) and Telecom New Zealand (Telecom NZ, privatised in September 1990). Staff numbers for Telstra reached a peak in 1986 and have since declined considerably. By comparing staffing levels for the three corporations from 1987 to 1995, however, it can be seen that while the reduction for Telstra was 25.0 per cent (from 95,934 to 71,961), the reduction over the same period for BT was 40.7 per cent (from 223,084 to 132,351) and for Telecom NZ a massive 65.8 per cent (from 25,040 to 8,568).

International comparisons should always be treated with caution. Nevertheless, it is clear that the two privatised companies have reduced their staffing levels by a much greater extent than Telstra. More significantly, Telecom NZ, in the four years *prior* to its privatisation (1987–90), reduced its staffing by 32.5 per cent (from 25,040 to 16,900), a greater proportion than the total reduction of 25.6 per cent for Telstra in the nine years from its peak in 1986 (96,672) to 1995 (71,961).

Telstra announced in September 1996 that within three years its staff levels were to be reduced by 22,000 – about 30 per cent of the June 1995 level. While it is possible that staff numbers may be cut further under private ownership resulting in increased cost savings, the scope for this has been substantially reduced. The greater the staff reductions made while Telstra remains government owned, the smaller the cost efficiencies available from privatisation.

Allocative efficiency

While savings in staffing costs will increase the scope for price reductions, the extent to which the benefits from such cost efficiencies are passed on to consumers is not clear. As indicated earlier, the pricing of Telstra's calls and other services is subject to detailed regulation, and price regulation will continue under privatisation. For as long as Telstra is considered by the

Table 4.6 Total staffing for Telstra, British Telecom and Telecom New Zealand: 1981–95

Year[a]	*Telstra*[b]	*British Telecom*	*Telecom NZ*
1981	92,114	253,102	na
1982	92,410	251,647	na
1983	91,819	245,976	na
1984	91,600	241,124	na
1985	93,887	235,178[c]	na
1986	96,672	230,184	na
1987	95,934	223,084	25,040[d]
1988	91,207	225,132	21,763
1989	86,204	231,982	17,505
1990	88,883	231,523	16,900
1991	86,109	215,366	14,925[e]
1992	75,291	199,325	13,562
1993	68,180	165,210	12,338
1994	65,102	150,374	9,257
1995	71,961	132,351	8,568

Sources: Telstra Corporation; Telecom New Zealand; Communication Workers Union (UK).

Notes:

a Telstra as at 30 June; British Telecom and Telecom NZ as at 31 March.

b Telecom and OTC merged in February 1992. Data are for combined Telecom and OTC for 1981 to 1991, and for Telstra 1992 to 1995.

c British Telecom privatised November 1984.

d As at 1 April 1987, date Telecom NZ was separated from NZ Post Office.

e Telecom NZ privatised September 1990.

na = not available

regulatory authority to be dominant in the non-mobile call markets it will continue to be restrained in its pricing behaviour, especially in relation to long-distance calls. The whole thrust of the government's policy of sustainable competition in telecommunications is to limit short-term benefits to consumers for the purpose of achieving a more competitive industry in the medium to long term (Brown 1996). If the present restraints on Telstra's pricing remain in place its competitors can be expected to continue to increase their market shares, while most of the benefits of improvements in productive efficiency achieved by a privatised Telstra are likely to flow through to its shareholders in increased profits rather than to consumers by way of lower prices.

Even if in the future Telstra is declared to be no longer dominant and the industry achieves a higher level of competition among carriers, price regulation will continue to take account of the cost to carriers of their past and future investment (Nightingale 1995). Recent estimates of the combined cost to Telstra and Optus of their cable roll-outs are around $8 billion (over 40 per cent of total 1995–6 industry revenues) which ultimately will be borne by telecommunication consumers. Under current policy, therefore, allocative efficiency in the industry will be determined largely by regulation, and prices will remain well above marginal cost – whether or not Telstra is privatised.

Telecommunications industry policy

There is a tension between maximising sale proceeds from the privatisation of Telstra and maximising competition in the telecommunications industry. As mentioned, the current policy of promoting sustainable competition in telecommunications involves tilting the playing field against Telstra to assist its existing competitors and to encourage new entrants into the market. This is a delicate process but is likely to be less difficult to achieve when it is in the interest of the government, as manager of the microeconomic reform process and as ultimate decision maker in telecommunications, for the policy to succeed. It will certainly be against the interest of Telstra's new shareholders under privatisation.

There is general agreement among economists that the market in which a GBE operates should be made as competitive as possible before privatisation. The danger of premature sale is that it will generate pressures to tilt the playing field back in Telstra's favour too soon, especially if disappointing financial results and the share price under privatisation cause disaffection among its large number of shareholders (most of whom will also be voters).

Another problem with privatisation before the telecommunications market attains optimal efficiency is that it denies the government the opportunity to make structural changes to Telstra – for example, by breaking up the corporation into smaller units – which may better promote industry competition. The separation of network provision from service provision is receiving serious examination in the UK (Solomon and Walker 1995), and has been canvassed for Australia (Stokes 1994). The privatisation of Telstra would entrench the existing situation of greatly uneven competition in Australian telecommunications with Telstra the dominant player.

Conclusions

It is clear that privatisation is not a necessary condition for improved productive efficiency of publicly owned enterprises. The dual effect of the corporatisation of GBEs and the introduction of increased competition to the markets in which they operate is mainly responsible for their improved economic performance. Telstra has been subject to both of these influences and has made significant productivity improvements in recent years. These gains, and those it is still to make as a GBE, will have the effect of reducing the scope for additional productivity improvements under privatisation. If a public enterprise is already run well the potential for further efficiency gains is quite small.

The privatisation of a government asset has political appeal because it can improve the government's budget position in the year of sale. Using any part of the proceeds from privatisation to finance current expenditure (or to reduce taxation), however, will tend to increase the government's revenue needs in future years.

Privatisation will reduce the net worth of the public sector if the net proceeds accruing from the sale are less than what the value of the GBE would be if it were retained under public ownership. By estimating the market value of Telstra based on its 1995–6 after-tax profits, and comparing it with the net sale proceeds required to generate similar savings in public debt interest, it is concluded that the privatisation of Telstra may result in a loss to the public sector, depending upon its profitability performance post-privatisation. For its sale to yield net economic benefits for the economy, Telstra would need to achieve sizeable improvements in productive efficiency under privatisation that are not available to it under continued public ownership.

The high value of Telstra in comparison with the absorptive capacity of the Australian financial market poses special problems to a government endeavouring to obtain sufficient net proceeds to make its privatisation an economically sound proposition. The obvious solution, namely for the government to seek offshore investment funds, compounds rather than solves the problem. The share premium on equity sold to foreign interests constitutes a direct transfer of national wealth outside the country, and control of Telstra by a major foreign telecommunications carrier poses a threat to its independence.

From an economic perspective there is little sense in supporting or opposing the proposition of privatising Telstra *per se*. The economic issues are complex and privatisation involves potential benefits as well as costs. The balance of benefits and costs of privatising Telstra depends crucially on the timing of the proposed sale and the terms and conditions on which it might proceed, especially in relation to industry regulation, the level of foreign ownership and the achievable net sale proceeds.

Postscript

This chapter was written prior to December 1996 when the Australian parliament, with a newly elected Liberal–National party coalition government in office, passed legislation providing for the partial privatisation of Telstra. One-third of the Commonwealth's equity in the corporation is to be sold by public float in November 1997. The issue price for Telstra shares is yet to be announced. Total foreign investment is to be limited to 35 per cent of the one-third interest to be sold (that is, to 11.67 per cent of total Telstra equity), and shareholdings by individual foreign investors are to be limited to 5 per cent of the one-third (1.67 per cent). The Minister of

Communications has stated that he considers the full privatisation of Telstra to be 'inevitable' and 'highly desirable' (Lewis 1996). It is likely that the government will move towards that end should it be returned to office at the next general election scheduled for early 1999.

References

Alchian, A. and Demsetz, H. (1972) 'Production, Information Costs and Economic Organisations', *American Economic Review* 62: 777–95.

Allan, P. (1989) 'Corporatisation: The NSW Experience', *Economic Papers* 8(3), September: 34–43.

Austel (1995) *Review of Telstra's Dominance in the International Telecommunications Services Market: Final Report*, August.

Australian Financial Review (1996) 'The Nerve to Tackle Telstra', 26 January, p. 14.

—— (1997) 'Privatisations Expected to Reach $125bn', 18 March, p. 10.

Beazley, K. (1994) 'Paying for our Future: The Changing Role of Public Investment', Address to the National Press Club, 24 August.

Bishop, M. and Green, M. (1995) 'Privatisation and Recession: The Miracle Tested', Discussion Paper 10, Centre for the Study of Regulated Industries, London.

Bishop, M. and Kay, J. (1988) *Does Privatization Work? Lessons from the UK*, London: London Business School.

—— (1989) 'Privatization in the United Kingdom: Lessons from Experience', *World Development* 17(5): 643–57.

Bishop, M. and Thompson, D.J. (1992) 'Regulatory Reform and Productivity Growth in the UK's Public Utilities', *Applied Economics* 24: 1181–90.

Bishop, M., Kay, J. and Mayer, C. (1994) 'Introduction: Privatisation in Performance', in M. Bishop, J. Kay and C. Mayer (eds), *Privatisation and Economic Performance*, London/Oxford: Oxford University Press, pp. 1–14.

Boardman, A.E. and Vining, A.R. (1989) 'Ownership and Performance in Competitive Environments: A Comparison of the Performance of Private, Mixed, and State-owned Enterprises', *Journal of Law and Economics* 32, April: 1–33.

Brown, A. (1996) 'Reform and Regulation of Australian Telecommunications', *Economic Papers* 15(3), September: 38–56.

BIE (Bureau of Industry Economics) (1995) *International Performance Indicators: Telecommunications 1995*, Research Report No. 65, March.

Clare, R. and Johnston, K. (1992) *Profitability and Productivity of Government Business Enterprises*, EPAC Research Paper No. 2, August.

Coase, R.H. (1937) 'The Nature of the Firm', *Econometrica* 4, November: 386–405.

Domberger, S. (1995) 'What Does Privatisation Achieve? – A Comment on Quiggin', *The Australian Economic Review* 110, 2nd Quarter: 43–7.

Domberger, S. and Piggott, J. (1986) 'Privatization Policies and Public Enterprise: A Survey', *The Economic Record* 62(177), June: 145–62.

Downs, A. (1967) *Inside Bureaucracy*, Boston: Little, Brown.

Economic Planning Advisory Commission (1995) 'Microeconomic Reform Paying Off for Government Business Enterprises and the Economy Generally', Media Release 7/95, 14 September.

Economic Planning Advisory Council (1987) *Efficiency in Public Trading Enterprises*, Council Paper No. 24, January.

Findlay, C. and Jones, R. (1982) 'The Marginal Cost of Australian Income Taxation', *The Economic Record* 58(162), September: 253–62.

Forsyth, P. (1992) 'Public Enterprises: A Success Story of Microeconomic Reform?', Discussion Paper No. 278, Centre for Economic Policy Research, The Australian National University, November.

—— (1993) 'Privatisation: Private Finances and Public Policy', in K. Davis and I. Harper (eds), *Privatisation: The Financial Implications*, St Leonards: Allen & Unwin, pp. 8–22.

Foster, C.D. (1992) *Privatization, Public Ownership and the Regulation of Natural Monopoly*, Oxford: Blackwell.

Galal, A., Jones, L., Tandon, P. and Vogelsang, I. (1994), *Welfare Consequences of Selling Public Enterprises: An Empirical Analysis*, Oxford: Oxford University Press.

Hamilton, C. (1995) 'Assessing the Arguments for Privatisation', *Current Affairs Bulletin* 72(3), October/November: 14–21.

Hartley, K. and Parker, D. (1991) 'Privatization: A Conceptual Framework', in A.F. Ott and K. Hartley (eds), *Privatization and Economic Efficiency*, Aldershot: Edward Elgar, pp. 11–25.

Haskel, J. and Szymanski, S. (1994) 'Privatization and the Labour Market: Facts, Theory and Evidence', in M. Bishop, J. Kay and C. Mayer (eds), *Privatization and Economic Performance*, Oxford: Oxford University Press, pp. 336–51.

Hemming, R. and Mansoor, A.M. (1988) 'Privatisation and Public Enterprises', Occasional Paper No. 56, International Monetary Fund, January.

Hensher, D.A. (1986) 'Privatisation: An Interpretative Essay', *Australian Economic Papers* 25(47), December: 147–74.

Hutchinson, G. (1991) 'Efficiency Gains Through Privatization of UK Industries', in A.F. Ott and K. Hartley (eds), *Privatization and Economic Efficiency*, Aldershot: Edward Elgar, pp. 87–107.

IAC (Industries Assistance Commission) (1989) *Government (Non-Tax) Charges*, Report No. 422 (4 vols), AGPS, 29 September.

Industry Commission (1994) *Improving the Efficiency of GBEs*, Information Paper, May.

Jenkinson, T. and Mayer, C. (1994) 'The Costs of Privatization in the UK and France', in M. Bishop, J. Kay and C. Mayer (eds), *Privatization and Economic Performance*, Oxford: Oxford University Press, pp. 290–8.

Kay, J.A. and Thompson, D.J. (1986) 'Privatisation: A Policy in Search of a Rationale', *The Economic Journal* 96, March: 18–32.

Leibenstein, H. (1966) 'Allocative Efficiency vs "X"-Efficiency', *American Economic Review* 56: 392–415.

Lewis, S. (1996) 'Telstra: It's All Got to Go', *Australian Financial Review*, 2 September, p. 1.

McIntosh Corporate Limited (1995) *Australian Equities Markets: Capital Raising Activity 1994–95*, August.

Maddock, R. (1992) 'Microeconomic Reform of Telecommunications: The Long March from Duopoly to Duopoly', in P. Forsyth (ed.), *Microeconomic Reform in Australia*, St Leonards: Allen & Unwin, pp. 243–59.

Mayer, C.P. and Meadowcroft, S.A. (1985) 'Selling Public Assets: Techniques and Financial Implications', *Fiscal Studies* 6(4): 42–56.

Megginson, W.L., Nash, R.C. and Van Randenborgh, M. (1994) 'The Financial and

Operating Performance of Newly Privatized Firms: An International Empirical Analysis', *The Journal of Finance* 49(2): 403–52.

Mustafa, M.A. (1993) 'Methods of Sale of State-owned Telecommunications Enterprises', *Telecommunication Journal* 60(9): 345–53.

Nellis, J. and Kikeri, S. (1989) 'Public Enterprise Reform: Privatization and the World Bank', *World Development* 17(5): 659–72.

Nightingale, J. (1995) 'The Regulation of Unnatural Oligopoly: Appropriate Criteria for Regulators Where the Goals of Regulation are Economic Progress', in D.M. Lamberton (ed.), *Beyond Competition in Telecommunications*, Amsterdam: Elsevier, pp. 249–76.

Niskanen, W.A. (1971) *Bureaucracy and Representative Government*, Chicago: Aldine Atherton.

Optus Communications Limited (1995) 'Optus Revenue up 71 per cent in 1994–95', Media Release, 28 August.

Quiggin, J. (1995) 'Does Privatisation Pay?', *The Australian Economic Review* 110, 2nd Quarter: 23–42.

Rees, R. (1986) 'Is There an Economic Case for Privatisation?', *Public Money* 5(4), March: 19–26.

Shires, D. (1995) 'Privatisation Threat to Telstra Control: Blout', *Australian Financial Review*, 23 August, p. 9.

Solomon, J. and Walker, D. (1995) 'Separating Infrastructure and Service Provision: The Broadband Imperative', *Telecommunications Policy* 19(2): 83–9.

Stokes, K. (1994) *Advance Australia Where? 1994 Boyer Lectures*, Sydney: ABC Books.

Tullock, G. (1965) *The Politics of Bureaucracy*, Lanham: University of America Press.

Vickers, J. and Yarrow, G. (1988) *Privatization: An Economic Analysis*, London: MIT Press.

Vining, A. (1989) 'Performance Measures for Government Business Enterprises', *Economic Papers* 8(3), September: 13–19.

Vining, A.R. and Boardman, A.E. (1992) 'Ownership Versus Competition: Efficiency in Public Enterprise', *Public Choice* 73: 205–39.

Walker, R.G. (1994) 'Privatisation: A Reassessment', *Journal of Australian Political Economy* 34, December: 27–52.

Waterman, E. (1993) 'Privatisation and Corporatisation in the Public Sector', in K. Davis and I. Harper (eds), *Privatisation: The Financial Implications*, St Leonards: Allen & Unwin, pp. 23–33.

Williamson, O.E. (1975) *Markets and Hierarchies: A Study in the Economics of Internal Organization*, New York: Free Press.

Zeckhauser, R. and Horn, M. (1989) 'The Control and Performance of State-owned Enterprises', in P. Macavoy, W. Stanbury, G. Yarrow and R. Zeckhauser (eds), *Privatization and State-owned Enterprises*, Boston: Kluwer, pp. 7–57.

5

PRIVATISATION DOESN'T NECESSARILY EQUAL COMPETITION

The UK experience

Colin Meek

Introduction

The UK consumer was promised a great deal from privatisation. The government raised the spectre of the 'dead hand' of state control and stressed the need to release companies to allow them to fulfil their potential. It was argued that private control of these stagnating publicly owned industries would make the companies responsive and efficient. Most importantly competition from new, dynamic and imaginative market entrants would force prices down.

Consumers' Association (CA) thoroughly endorses the view that real competition brings benefits to consumers. Competition brings choice, it promotes efficiency within companies and provides the strongest possible incentive to keep retail prices as low as possible.

However, while it is clear that an overhaul of the old nationalised companies was a central policy objective for the Thatcher administration from 1979 onwards, it is also clear that the goal of competition was either relegated or abandoned entirely due to priority given to other policy objectives.

In fact, competition in the domestic market was actually prohibited in the gas, water and electricity industries when they were privatised. Domestic consumers saw only limited competition in the telephony sector at the outset. In the absence of competition the government turned to regulators. These bodies were given statutory powers to impose price controls on the monopolies and were expected to wither away if or when competition developed. In reality, real competition has only developed for business users.

The privatisation process undertaken by the government was woven into the fabric of a wider policy programme which included dramatically increasing the number of individuals who owned shares. Each new privatisation was characterised by multi-million pound campaigns inviting the public to buy stakes. Further, privatisation was also a useful weapon against the government's political opponents. The concept unpicked a key Labour Party policy plank and undermined a strong trade union presence in industries where it was traditionally strong.

In addition to serving all these purposes privatisation also raised a staggering amount of money – the total is unlikely to be less than £40 billion. Privatisation also released the government from its responsibility for funding massive future investment programmes such as those necessary in the water and telecoms industries.

It can be argued that there was a conflict of interests when the plans for privatisation were being drawn up. On the one hand, an efficient competitive environment was desirable, but, on the other hand, a privatised industry can obviously be sold for a much higher price if it is a good stock market bet.

While the consumer obviously wanted a brave new market to develop, the shareholder looked to healthy returns from a monopolistic player.

Looking over the major utility privatisations it is not difficult to conclude that these tensions that existed have had a lasting impact on the structure of the private gas, electricity, telecommunications, water and rail industries that now exist or are emerging.

This paper will briefly describe the privatisation structures chosen and then, with the use of specific case studies, go on to examine the competitive and regulatory environment within each industry. Since this paper was written in 1996, the developments on these issues after that period can be found in Meek and Dee 1997; DOT & I 1998.

Utility industry overview

British Gas (BG):
Privatised 1986.

Regulator:
Office of Gas Supply – Ofgas.

Industry structure:
This state-owned monopoly was transferred virtually intact and unchanged into private hands although other companies were free to compete in the industrial market. For a variety of reasons British Gas has announced it will split vertically, separating its retail and trading arm from its international, distribution and exploration arm.

Development of competition:
Although competition was limited to very large users initially this threshold

has been gradually reduced. It was hoped that competition for domestic customers would be introduced in 1998 after it had been tested in two regional trials involving millions of homes. The first full-scale trial was held in the Southwest of England in April 1996.

British Telecom (BT):
Privatised 1984.

Regulator:
Office of Telecommunications – Oftel.

Industry structure:
Again, BT was privatised as an intact, vertically integrated monopoly. BT is currently the only company in the UK with a national integrated service.

Development of competition:
In 1982 Mercury Communications was also granted a licence and guaranteed seven years to operate without competitive restraint from any other market entrant. The duopoly review of 1991 brought this arrangement to an end and a number of other national and local companies have been given licences to compete with BT for fixed-line custom. Perhaps most importantly, the cable TV franchise companies represent the biggest challenge to BT. More than 50,000 of BT's customers are now switching to cable telephony every month. At present BT cannot provide entertainment services down its own lines. Despite the growth in competition, all companies depend on interconnection agreements with BT. The way these interconnection agreements operate is the subject of a current and wide-ranging Oftel consultation.

Water:
Privatised in England and Wales in 1989.

Regulator:
The Office of Water Services – Ofwat.

Industry structure:
The ten regional water companies of England and Wales sold as water and sewerage services and allocated specific areas of service. The Office of Water Services regulates these companies and a number of other private companies which are responsible for the supply of water only. Privatisation was prevented in Scotland due to fierce opposition.

Responsibility for pollution was removed from the ten privatised companies and assigned to a different regulatory body. All ten privatised water companies are effectively vertically integrated regional monopolies.

Development of competition:
No attempt has been made to introduce domestic competition in this industry although in theory the companies can compete for the custom of very large industrial users but only if the company boundary catchment areas meet.

Electricity:
Privatised in 1990 and 1991.

Regulator:
The Office of Electricity Regulation – Offer.

Industry structure:
In England and Wales the industry was split vertically and horizontally into three generating companies and twelve regional distribution and supply companies.

In Scotland the industry was sold as two vertically integrated companies. The national grid was also privatised as a national company. In Northern Ireland electricity is generated by four companies while one company provides the transmission, distribution and supply. Over the past year there have been a number of company mergers which has enabled the generators to acquire distribution and supply networks.

Development of competition:
While competition has so far been limited to large commercial users from 1998 it is hoped that the domestic market will be opened up to full competition. Nuclear generation has remained in public hands although the Conservative government was still committed to its privatisation in 1996.

Barriers to competition – the dominance of incumbent suppliers

The post-privatisation experience of BT is important for a number of reasons. First, this company was the first major utility to be privatised and obviously has the longest track record as a regulated private company which still has a monopoly for some services. Second, it is currently the only utility company to face competition in the domestic market. Lastly, this competition means that BT must allow its competitors to have access to its own nationally integrated network.

Given that the structure of vertical integration was chosen for gas and water and is growing dominant in the electricity sector as generation and supply companies merge, the experience of BT over the last twelve years offers valuable pointers for the future.

The majority of BT shares were sold privately in 1984. Twelve years on, BT is still massively dominant. It controls over 90 per cent of the revenue from calls from the residential market and 83 per cent of the entire market. More than 96 per cent of the revenue from exchange line rentals goes to BT. More than 95 per cent of households that have a phone are connected to BT.

This dominance of the market is underlined in other ways. There is no doubt that there has been a flurry of activity in the UK telecommunications industry over the last few years but this has meant little to the average UK residential user. In 1994, Oftel proudly announced that more than sixty licences had been issued for the supply of telephone services (Oftel 1994). Of those, forty-four were issued to companies that will have nothing to do with the residential fixed-line market and are concerned only with provision of international services or for fixed links for mobile networks. Fourteen others were issued to cable companies interconnecting with other cabled areas. Three others were issued to companies limited to small city areas. As far as CA is aware, only two of the licences were issued to companies with geographically ambitious plans and only one of those plans to compete with BT in the local call market within one region.

BT and others have frequently referred to the UK's four mobile operators as offering a genuine competitive alternative to the incumbent (Oftel 1995b). This is highly misleading. In a unique survey of more than 2,500 mobile users the CA unearthed a catalogue of dissatisfaction and problems relating to mobile use. In all, we found that just under 40 per cent wanted to abandon the contract they signed. In short, mobiles do not offer a realistic alternative to fixed-line networks. The technology is not designed to be used indoors and prices charged for calling mobiles are more akin to calling abroad (Meek 1996).

Cable television companies which also offer a fixed-line telephony service are a more serious competitive threat to BT. However, they have formidable barriers to climb. The problems in dealing with an incumbent operator are exposed with the way Oftel is grappling with the problem of how to allow cable companies and other competitors fair access to BT's network. BT owns and controls the only comprehensive network in the UK and as with other utility industries where economies of scale prevent the construction of a competing infrastructure, competitors must have access to the incumbent's network. Almost all calls made in the UK are routed at some point along a BT wire. Until now Oftel has retained a detailed control of interconnection arrangements in the UK. However, it now wishes to impose network charge caps on BT where genuine competition has yet to emerge.

Competitors to BT and CA have warned Oftel that such a scheme could give BT far too much power by allowing it to link its network charges to its own retail tariff giving competitors virtually no scope to develop imaginative new tariffs in order to compete with BT. In addition, the CA has concluded that such a system would be utterly dependent on watertight anti-competitive measures and rigidly enforced non-discrimination measures so that BT Retail was subject to exactly the same charges as competing companies (Consumers' Association 1996a).

By contrast, where cable companies have constructed their own local networks where they are not dependent on interconnection with BT they have shown an extraordinary ability to introduce imaginative and competitive tariff structures including free local call delivery.

Whatever the outcome of this debate it underlines yet again the very real practical difficulties the regulators have in dealing with vertically integrated incumbent operators.

BT and number portability

- Perhaps the clearest example of how a privatised company can abuse its incumbent advantage is how BT delayed the introduction of number portability for UK residential users.
- Both the government and Oftel correctly recognised that customers were being deterred from changing their telephone company supplier because they had to change their telephone number to do so. In 1991 a new condition was added to BT's licence giving Oftel the power to insist that BT provide a porting service. The licence condition also allowed BT to recoup 'reasonable' costs incurred in providing this service.
- The cable companies have argued forcibly that the absence of number portability has been the biggest single barrier to the introduction of effective competition in the UK (MMC 1995). In fact, a survey carried out by the CA among over 1,000 domestic consumers in March 1995 showed that 70 per cent of people would consider changing telephone operator if they could retain their existing telephone number. Further, the survey also showed that although there have to be significant cost savings on offer before most people would consider changing their telephone supplier those savings must be higher still if their existing phone numbers need to be changed (Consumers' Association 1995a).
- The CA has consistently argued that operators, particularly BT, should not be seen as 'owning' certain numbers. The mechanism by which numbers are allocated should be seen as an industry infrastructure which is commonly held. Ideally cost and quality of service should be the only criteria people use to choose between companies. The lack of number portability, or the prohibitive cost of such portability, acts as a barrier to effective competition.
- In the beginning of 1994 several of the cable companies wanted to introduce NP but throughout that year they were unable to agree commercial terms with BT. There are basically three costs involved in setting up number portability: the costs involved in setting up the capability; the costs incurred for every customer who ports a number; and the extra costs incurred in routing calls to a customer who has ported – the additional

conveyance costs. Fundamental disagreement emerged between BT, Oftel and the cable companies on the allocation of these costs.

- BT insisted that the company to which a customer was switching should be responsible for the additional conveyance costs and despite the fact that BT stated publicly that it supported the introduction of NP, this form of cost allocation effectively scuppered the whole plan. In addition, BT's solution would mean it would have absolutely no incentive to reduce its own costs involved in number portability as it could pass them on to its competitors.
- As Oftel and BT could not agree terms for cost allocation the whole issue was referred to the Monopolies and Mergers Commission. In oral and written evidence to the MMC investigation the CA argued that lack of NP has permitted BT to sustain an overwhelming market share while offering uncompetitive prices (see below). The CA also stated that it was sceptical of BT's claim to support NP as BT's interests in the foreseeable future appeared to lie in preventing its introduction (MMC 1993).
- It took the MMC around eight months to carry out its investigation and it concluded that additional conveyance costs should be split between BT and its competitors. It also ruled that as more efficient methods of porting numbers are established then BT will bear more of the costs. Although number portability can now go ahead BT has successfully delayed its introduction for around two years – two crucial years for the growth of the cable networks. It remains to be seen what other tactics BT can use to delay effective introduction for even longer.

There are other threats to wide cross-sections of captive BT customers. Currently when BT reduces the cost of service that cut is applied universally – this is called geographic averaging. Although it means that BT can focus its price cuts in ways which benefit business users more, it also means that BT cannot raise prices or maintain high prices in remote or rural areas where there is unlikely to be competition in the near future, in order to fund price cuts to undermine competitors elsewhere. This regulatory constraint is a logical consumer protection, it promotes efficiency and guards against monopoly abuse.

The fact that BT is vigorously campaigning to have this constraint removed is one of the clearest examples of the way incumbent operators attempt to rebalance their tariffs in ways which leave some consumer groups defenceless (British Telecom 1995).

But it is obviously not just BT which clearly exploits its position as the incumbent player in a market which it dominates. British Gas has been subject to two MMC referrals. The first, which was an investigation into the company's service to large customers, found that British Gas was abusing its dominant position and the Office of Fair Trading was given the responsibility of making sure that the company did not purchase more than 90 per cent of any new gas sources (CRI 1995b). The more serious second referral into the non-domestic arm of the company's business found that there was an 'inherent conflict of interests which makes it impossible to provide the necessary conditions for self-sustaining competition' (MMC 1993). The MMC recommended that British Gas be restructured to break up its vertical integration but the government rejected this suggestion.

The advantages of vertical integration have not been ignored by company directors in the electricity industry. During 1996 a series of proposed mergers and acquisitions provoked widespread debate about the threat to competition in this industry. Manweb lost a strongly contested takeover bid from Scottish Power. Given the vertical integration that already existed in Scotland, large sections of the entire industry now operate in this way.

Over the past few years it has become clear that the advantages that the incumbent companies have made it extremely difficult for market entrants and for competition to emerge on a sustainable basis in the domestic sector.

Incumbent advantages can also be used by companies in their efforts to diversify to compete in other industries. SWEB is using its existing data banks to access information on customer profiles to spearhead its launch into the gas business in the Southwest. SWEB customers are receiving SWEB Gas promotions in their electricity bills. Other market entrants clearly have no such advantage.

Barriers to competition – keeping consumers in the dark

For sustainable competition to emerge in privatised industries there needs to be a lot more than the correct industry structure and effective regulatory intervention.

The CA believes that a barrier to competition exists wherever consumers cannot make informed choices between companies. In the context of the utility industries, customers should ideally have access to accurate information about service and price.

Telephony company tariffs are the hardest to compare. All UK telephony companies have at least six different UK charges depending on distance and time of call. Most then have another twelve international charge bands. There is now a plethora of charges relating to premium and mobile numbers. The problems do not stop there. Some companies charge connection fees while others have minimum call charges, some do not charge for local calls on the same network. As everyone's call pattern is different it is virtually impossible to compare tariffs accurately.

Although models existed which roughly compared the various tariffs available there were no studies based on data from real telephone users. To plug this gap the CA carried out the first independent tariff analysis using real call pattern data. In all we made over half a million calculations on nearly 9,000 calls from real bills to compare the prices offered by individual companies. When the CA averaged out the bills and analysed them it has been found that BT is the most expensive. Virtually every company in every charge band works out to be cheaper according to the CA's analysis (Consumers' Association 1995b). We also used analysis to examine BT's much heralded price changes in June 1995. It has been shown, for example, that the BT's heavily promoted one penny per minute local weekend rate would make only a tiny impact on the vast majority of bills.

Not surprisingly BT have disputed the CA's findings but even though it is the only body that can access information based on the vast majority of call patterns it has been reluctant to hand over this data for independent analysis. With help from Oftel the CA has persuaded BT to part with some call pattern data which the CA are currently testing to find out if it can be used effectively.

Until the CA ran the tariff analysis consumers depended almost entirely on the claims made by the companies themselves. The same will be true in the gas industry in the Southwest. Full domestic competition was piloted in the Southwest in 1996 before a wider pilot was launched in 1997 ahead of full deregulation in 1998. Five companies with entirely different tariff packages have challenged British Gas in the domestic market in this first pilot area.

SWEB Gas is offering two tariffs which, it claims, undercut BG by at least 17 per cent. Total offer savings of 15 per cent and Calortex 20 per cent. The Gas Consumers Council has already accused SWEB Gas of attempting to mislead consumers on savings available and using high-pressure selling techniques which include duping customers into signing contracts (GCC 1996).

The regulators themselves have acknowledged that consumer information is crucial for sustainable competition. Oftel concluded that their own market research has highlighted several barriers to choice, including a lack of independent information, and it has underlined the need for price comparisons based on individual calling patterns.

The CA has also found that the provision of useful information will be a key issue in the deregulation of the electricity industry in 1998. The CA carried out a major survey of nearly 1,000 electricity customers in December 1995. When asked for reasons why they would not switch from their existing supplier, 33 per cent said price and service comparisons were too hard and a further 27 per cent said it would simply be too much hassle (Consumers' Association 1996b).

The National Consumer Council has also stressed that a clear and ongoing commitment to the provision of accurate information on suppliers will be crucial and that 'real choices can only be made by well-informed consumers' (NCC 1996).

Misleading the public

Perhaps the most damning evidence of how confusion about prices and cost comparisons acts as a barrier to effective competition is how passengers are being consistently misled in the new-look and semi-privatised British Rail. By far the most complicated of the government's privatisations, the UK's previously integrated national network is being split into seventy separate bodies. There will be twenty-five companies that actually operate train services – called train operating companies or TOCs – and these companies will lease track and rolling stock from other companies.

The government hopes that the gradual introduction of competition will lead to improved services and reduced prices. Eventually it is hoped that two or more TOCs will operate services on key lines in competition for the same passengers. Competition already exists on a number of key routes in the South of England and Wales.

Even though a competitive structure of twenty-five operating companies was chosen, in theory these companies must cooperate on the setting and retailing of fares and timetable and service information.

As most passengers have no choice in the ticket offices where they make purchases all TOCs are required to sell tickets not only for their own services but for services run by other TOCs even if they are in direct competition. The licences given to the TOCs state that they must retail tickets on an impartial basis – if a passenger asks for the cheapest fare for a journey they must be told about the cheapest service regardless of which TOC runs it.

The CA carried out an extensive investigation to test this theory (Consumers' Association 1996c). The CA painstakingly identified journeys where at least two companies were in direct competition for the same passengers. The CA made 250 separate enquiries and purchases at twenty-eight stations and telephone enquiry points. In the majority of these cases the questions were put to sales points run by the TOC which set the higher of the two competing fares for the journey. Despite the fact that the CA investigations asked for the cheapest fare available every time, in nine out of ten cases the answers were more expensive than necessary.

Overall, the total amount quoted and actually charged for these 250 tickets came to £13,013. If the TOCs had given neutral, unbiased sales advice, as their licences clearly state they must, that total should have been £7,591. In many cases individual fares were overpriced by more than £50. Our investigation also found that TOCs were also giving biased information about timetables and services.

Since this investigation and the flurry of publicity it provoked, the CA has called on the government to review ticket retailing and halt the sale of TOC franchises until a solution is found. In short, where passengers have a choice, they are not being told about their options. If one does not know that one has a choice there cannot be effective competition.

Regulation

As stated above, the government turned to regulatory intervention to act as a substitute for the discipline which competition imposes on markets. To carry out this task the UK's utilities regulators have five main functions: licensing; promotion of competition; the calculation and imposition of price controls; the extraction of information from companies and publication of industry information; and consulting with consumers.

The scope of these general functions coupled with the government's commitment to let the market dictate strategic policy means that the regulators have become pivotal players to all interested 'stakeholders', including consumers. Increasingly campaigning and lobbying efforts are focused in this direction.

Unless real competition exists it is important from the consumers' perspective to measure the performance of the regulators in five main ways. Success in:

1 imposing tough but realistic standards of service on the industry;
2 protecting domestic consumers from monopolistic price hikes while ensuring that they receive a fair share of price reductions as a result of price caps;
3 the promotion of sustainable competition;
4 defending marginalised or vulnerable consumers; and
5 ensuring continuity of supply.

It is often assumed that these bodies must bravely and objectively balance conflicting interests while carrying out their statutory functions. This is far from the case. According to statute the primary duty of the water, electricity and gas regulators is to protect the interests of shareholders. Defending consumers is a secondary objective and subject to the primary duty. In contrast to the UK approach, US regulators must attempt to balance interests between shareholders and consumers.

It is worth noting that while the UK government is still reluctant to follow the US statutory example it did not choose to substitute the priority given to shareholders with primacy given to the promotion of effective competition.

Given this unambiguous primary role of the regulator and the absence of effective competition in these industries, the CA has consistently argued that a strong counterbalance should be established alongside each of the regulators in the form of independent consumer bodies.

Only one of these bodies was established, however – the Gas Consumers Council. In the electricity, water and telecommunications industries consumer representation is organised in the form of committees established within the regulator with few resources and compromised independence. In

1996, the CA asked nearly 1,000 electricity users who they would turn to for help if they could not solve a problem with their supplier. Only 3 per cent named the correct body unprompted. The CA even found that an entirely fictitious body – the Electricity Consumer Council – had a better profile than the real thing. Incredibly, the electricity regulator has said that arrangements for complaint handling will remain largely unchanged when the domestic market is opened up to full-scale competition in 1998.

BT makes only two guarantees to its customers to keep appointments for installing and repairing lines. While the electricity regulator has imposed standards with compensation on the electricity companies they are far from onerous. For example, they have to give only two days' notice of planned interruptions to supply. When we examined the actual compensation levels paid out to consumers we found that in one year only one customer in 1,100 who had their supply cut actually received compensation.

Apart from some services run by BT these companies do not have to compete for domestic custom. It is critical therefore that the regulators make sure they do not abuse that power. Yet in 1994 the CA found that fewer than half of a sample of 1,200 people who had complained to a utility were satisfied with the outcome of that complaint. Amazingly, a third of those who complained to BT, their local electricity company or water company received no reply to their initial complaint. Compared to similar surveys the 1994 survey showed that complaint handling by these companies was actually getting worse.

In contrast the CA have in the past applauded the progress made in the gas industry. The fact that gas is the only utility industry to have a strong independent consumer voice and that British Gas has thirty-nine service standards to satisfy and its complaints-handling procedures appear to be by far the best is no coincidence. However, during the eighteen months before writing, the service offered by British Gas nose-dived with mushrooming numbers of complaints coinciding with dramatic staff cutbacks. This underlined the need for swift regulatory action when quality standards are not met.

BT

After more than ten years of privatisation, successive measures to introduce a more competitive environment, several price control reviews and the birth of a range of new telecommunications companies, Oftel has recently admitted that the prices paid by domestic consumers have dropped by just 1 per cent in the period 1990/1 to 1994/5. On the other hand, businesses have benefited from a 20 per cent drop in prices over the same period (Oftel 1995c).

To be fair to Oftel, residential users have started to benefit from real cuts in prices over the last few years but there is no doubt that BT's manipulation of its cuts in the 'basket' of services that count towards its price cap has meant it has focused price cuts where it faces most competition. The CA has consistently stated that price controls should be targeted. Until as recently as 1993, BT could satisfy the conditions of its price control yet make virtually no significant cuts in prices up to 1996 which would benefit domestic users.

Water

Water prices have provoked the most widespread controversy since privatisation in the UK. Apart from the debate which has erupted about the metering of domestic water use, analysis shows that domestic, unmetered water bills in England and Wales have risen by 39 per cent in the period from 1989/90 to 1995/6 (CRI 1996). This figure allows for inflation.

These dramatic price hikes have funded a massive overhaul of the industry infrastructure. In short, much of the cost of this investment has been passed on directly to consumers in the form of higher bills. Consumer groups have questioned why this has been necessary in the water industry and not in other industries where there has been a similar overhaul of the infrastructure, such as telecommunications.

A CA report in 1994 concluded that the rise in domestic consumers' bills has met an estimated 83 per cent of the cost of the companies' investment (Consumers' Association 1994). In the 1993/4 period the water companies paid out dividends totalling £583.8 million – an increase on the previous year of 9.4 per cent (CRI 1996).

Electricity

The electricity regulator has stated that electricity prices for the domestic consumer have dropped by around 7 per cent in real terms (Offer 1994). However, this analysis over five years obscures the fact that prices have actually risen on occasion as the electricity companies have the power to pass through increases in generation costs. For example, an independent analysis of domestic electricity prices put the drop at just 2.8 per cent in the period from 1990/1 to 1994/5, indicating that the significant drop in costs has been over the 1995 period (Electricity Industry 1995). Of course these cuts in electricity prices have not been translated into cuts in bills as VAT at 8 per cent was added to domestic fuel bills from April 1994.

The most controversial cost pass-through is the fact that the regional electricity companies are actually required to purchase a proportion of the electricity they sell from nuclear sources. The cost of this is recouped through the fossil-fuel levy which accounts for around 10 per cent of the domestic bill. This subsidy to the nuclear industry is one of the clearest examples of how government rhetoric about imposing market principles on the utilities has been shackled with uncompetitive constraints.

Gas

According to Ofgas, gas customers have fared better with a cut in fuel costs of some 20 per cent since the industry was privatised, although much of this boils down to a sharp drop in the cost of natural gas. Unlike the situation with BT the price-cap formula applied to British Gas means that price caps must be applied to domestic consumers. Despite this welcome rule business customers have seen the bulk of tariff reductions. In 1985 domestic customers paid 54 per cent more than industrial customers and 19 per cent more than commercial ones. By 1992 the equivalent figures were 122 per cent and 31 per cent, respectively.

The impact on the vulnerable consumer

While it is useful to note how price changes impact on the 'average' or 'typical' consumer, it is important to analyse how the marginal or vulnerable consumer is coping.

As utility services are essential and relatively price inelastic the regulators clearly have a social function to make sure demand is met. But as we have seen, under the present regulatory framework, whereby prices are subject to broad controls, the regulated companies attempt to satisfy the control mechanism by focusing their price cuts where they face the most competition. This focus on the most lucrative markets means that low-income consumers are increasingly marginalised in the tariff packages and pricing structures available. The introduction of discounts for direct debit payment plus extra charges imposed on those with pre-payment meters means a considerable gap has opened up between the tariffs available to domestic users with bank accounts and those imposed on others or those with payment difficulties.

The regulators have also overseen massive geographic variations in the price of utility services. The most expensive water rates in the UK are currently more than four times the cheapest, yet the UK national social security system is largely blind to regional variations. Electricity users in Northern Ireland now pay 20 per cent more than those in England.

The non-discrimination clause

- In addition to the universal service obligation imposed by the regulators on all the incumbent operators there are non-discriminatory measures written into statute. When fixing tariffs electricity suppliers 'must not show undue preference to any person or class of persons, and shall not exercise any undue discrimination against any person or class of persons' (Electricity Act 1989). The other regulators must impose similar clauses.
- However, Ofgas recently ruled that discounts offered to customers who can pay through their direct debits are not discriminatory despite the fact

that this new tariff undercuts the tariff imposed on those with pre-payment meters by around 12 per cent (GCC, 1995).

- There are now millions of electricity and gas customers on pre-payment schemes who pay more for their fuel than other users on standard tariffs.
- A similar debate on cross-subsidy has emerged in the water industry. As water charges currently reflect rateable property values any move towards the mandatory provision of water metering would mean those homes which had the lowest rateable value would be hardest hit. Although Ofwat has ruled out compulsory metering it is keen to promote its use so that costs reflect usage. As a consequence 7 per cent of all households in England and Wales now have a metered water supply and while unmetered bills have risen by 39 per cent since privatisation measured bills have fallen. The Centre for the Study of Regulated Industries has concluded that those with an unmeasured supply are effectively subsidising the high cost of meter provision to a minority.
- A consequence of gas and electricity pre-payment is that the companies which offer or impose this on consumers are able to bring down their disconnection rate. The number of households which have their supplies cut has fallen dramatically as a direct result of an increase in pre-payment meters. While this is to be welcomed, it is worrying to note that the regulators have done virtually no research to investigate whether a dramatic increase in self-disconnection has paralleled the increased use of pre-payment.
- The non-discriminatory measures imposed on these industries seem to be working against low-income groups in two ways. First, these clauses stop regulators acting on behalf of specific groups to the detriment of others. For example, the Low User Scheme imposed on BT which guarantees a discounted rental if the call costs fall below a specified amount has to be offered to everyone including those on high incomes who have small telephone bills. Second, where companies do discriminate against the interests of those on low incomes the regulators are failing to act.
- To help solve this contradiction the UK's National Consumer Council has argued that the regulators should be given a clear duty to consider the needs of low-income consumers.

But it is not only a regulatory loophole which acts against the interests of some consumers; the lack of genuine competition is also to blame.

Last year BT disconnected nearly 800,000 of its own customers. These staggering disconnection rates are an appalling reflection of how an incumbent operator can neglect its own customer base. Disconnecting this number of people would simply not be an option for a company which had to compete for most of its customers.

Although a significant proportion of the total remain disconnected, approximately 40,000 reconnect within a few hours of being cut off. The CA argues that clearly the company is doing something wrong if it cannot persuade so many people to pay before they are disconnected. This cavalier attitude with such a large number of customers is perhaps the clearest example that the company does not believe it faces a competitive threat.

Keys to the future

Despite the obvious advantages the incumbent operators have and the lack of effective competition across virtually every domestic market the regulators have won a number of important battles.

- The gas price formula is targeted to benefit domestic consumers and it links permitted increases with the achievement of specified levels of quality of service.
- A range of comparable performance indicators have been established by Oftel which it is hoped can be used by consumers to compare companies.
- Oftel have also launched a wide-ranging consultation about the scope and funding of the universal service obligation imposed on BT.
- And, despite the fact that a large number of service quality guarantees do not offer consumers adequate protection, they are now established and consumer groups can lobby to have them toughened.
- Increased choice and the range of services on offer have meant more households have chosen to have a phone. Connection rates are up from 78 per cent before privatisation to 92 per cent now.

While these and other successes are clearly welcome, CA has become increasingly concerned that the odds are stacked against the domestic consumer for the reasons outlined above. The outcome of two current regulatory initiatives will signal whether the domestic consumer is likely to see the benefits of competition in the future. First, Oftel's attempts to change the rules on anti-competitive behaviour and, second the success Ofgas and Offer have in implementing full-scale competition in 1998.

Oftel and anti-competitive behaviour

Potentially the most serious problem from the consumer's perspective that has emerged from the debate on the utilities is the inadequacy of current UK competition policy. The CA has consistently argued that anti-competitive restraints almost always act against the interests of the consumer but there seem to be no effective statutory mechanisms that work against these constraints.

Clear and effective competition policy is particularly important in order to deal with incumbent privatised companies as there are a host of regulatory problems associated with a dominant vertically integrated company:

- the difficulty in identifying predatory pricing;
- the difficulty in imposing accounting transparency;
- problems in accounting for and identifying cross-subsidy; and
- problems in ensuring network access for market entrants.

The Australian Hilmer Report on National Competition Policy concluded that: 'The disadvantages of the UK scheme have been seen as relatively weak deterrence flowing from the absence of a prohibition; the absence of third party rights, leaving affected parties without remedies such as damages or injunctions; and reliance on potentially slow government enquiries' (Hilmer 1993). The CA would endorse this view.

To plug this statutory hole Oftel have proposed that it should adopt sweeping new powers to deal with anti-competitive behaviour (Oftel 1995a). It would streamline investigations into unfair behaviour and give Oftel the right to publicise its findings. It would also prohibit the abuse of a dominant position and give the director-general of Oftel the power to define what he considers to be such an abuse. BT's competitors have rightly complained that BT can use predatory pricing to squeeze out competitors without breaking any statutory rule or licence condition. In 1993 Oftel received around 100 fair-trading complaints covering issues such as predatory pricing, unfair cross-subsidy and misuse of customer or competitor information.

The introduction of these measures would mark a pivotal shift in the ability of a regulator to grapple with a dominant vertically integrated monopoly and the CA fully supports the move. While new primary legislation to improve the UK's competition policy would obviously be preferable, this is a good second best.

BT's public relations retaliation has been formidable and the argument is growing increasingly bitter. Despite its overwhelming dominance of the UK residential market it is clearly in BT's interest to publicly exaggerate the competitive threat it faces. Not only does this encourage a myth that the company is a success in a genuinely competitive environment it helps give BT the public relations upper hand when it accuses Oftel of being heavy handed.

BT has won over significant support. In February 1996, an article in *The Times* headlined 'Don't let regulation stifle the voice of market forces' concluded that 'BT achieved its monopoly by state intervention, not competition. But after a dozen years of intense regulation in the private sector, aimed at creating a fully competitive market, it is fair to assume that BT's continuing dominance now owes something to its competitive performance' (*The Times* 1996). On the contrary, as has been demonstrated in this chapter, BT still has a huge incumbent advantage.

Competition in 1998

Plans to introduce unbridled competition in the domestic electricity and gas markets in 1998 will mark the biggest upheavals these industries will face since privatisation. From the consumers' perspective this should herald a new era of competitive pricing and a choice of tariff plans. Companies will have a genuine competitive incentive to make sure they have well-monitored quality of service guarantees.

The regulators must ensure that the companies involved do not squander this opportunity. Incumbent suppliers must be kept in check and fair and transparent interconnection arrangements must be found and enforced. Accounting transparency must also be imposed on vertically integrated, incumbent companies and those which have expanded through cross-utility mergers as an insurance against predatory pricing.

Consumers must not be exposed to misleading information and the regulators must accept that they have a responsibility to help consumers make meaningful comparisons between companies. Low-income and other vulnerable consumers must also be protected from discriminatory pricing.

Most importantly the right structures must be found to make sure competition has a chance. Offer has already been warned that the current plans for full competition in 1998 could lead to 'poll tax on wires' with the costs of implementing the planned competitive structure potentially outstripping the possible benefits that can be passed on to consumers (*Financial Times* 1996).

Despite the fact that full competition is being trialled in two regions in the gas industry Offer has so far ruled out a similar trial in electricity.

It would be the most spectacular blunder if the wrong framework for competition was chosen and consumers ended up paying more in a competitive structure that was not sustainable.

The UK's privatisation experience has not fostered a new era of competition in the utility industries. The objective of competition was not a central policy objective when the industries were sold and, so far, the only competition domestic consumers have seen is in the telephony market. Even there whole swathes of the market are still dominated by a monopoly provider.

Apart from isolated successes, the regulators, who are there to police the industry in the absence of competition, have failed to win a fair deal for domestic consumers. Worse still, the regulators are constrained by statute which stacks the odds against low-income groups in particular and the domestic user in general.

References

British Telecom (1995) 'A Framework for Effective Competition', BT's response to Oftel's Consultative Document of December 1994. March.

Consumers' Association (1994) 'Water, Are You Paying Too Much?', *Which?* July.
—— (1995a) 'A Framework for Effective Competition', UK Consumers' Association response. April.
—— (1995b) 'BT Beaten', *Which?*
—— (1996a) 'Pricing of Telecommunications Services from 1997', UK Consumers' Association response to the Oftel consultation document. February.
—— (1996b) 'The Competitive Electricity Market from 1998', Consumers' Association response to Oftel consultation document. February.
—— (1996c) *Which?*, January, p. 8.
CRI (1995a) 'Centre for Regulated Industries', *Financial Facts 1993/94*, p. 5.
—— (1995b) *The UK Regulated Industries Financial Facts 93/94*, CRI. June, p. 49.
—— (1996) *The UK Water Industry, 1995/96*, Centre for Study of the Regulated Industries. February.
DOT & I (1998) *A Fair Deal for Consumers*, Department of Trade and Industry, March.
Electricity Act 1989, Vol. 18, No. 4, p. 16.
Electricity Industry (1995) *The UK Electricity Industry 1995–96*. September, p. xiv.
Financial Times (1996) 'Financial Times Power UK' newsletter. Issue 23, p. 6.
GCC (1995) Referral by the GCC relating to discounts for customers paying by Direct Debit, May.
—— (1996) GCC News Release, 15 February.
Hilmer, F. (1993) *Independent Committee of Enquiry into National Competition Policy*, Canberra: Australian Government Publishing Services.
Meek, C. (1996) 'Myth and Reality', *Consumer Policy Review*, Vol. 6, No. 1.
Meek, C. and Dee, S. (1997) *Utilities in Transition*, Consumers' Association, London.
MMC (1993) 'Telephone Number Portability', Monopolies and Mergers Commission, p. 159.
—— (1995) 'Telephone Number Portability', Monopolies and Mergers Commission, November, p. 145.
NCC (1996) NCC Press Release, 1 March.
Offer (1994) *1994 Annual Report*, Offer.
Oftel (1994) 'A Framework for Effective Competition', Oftel.
—— (1995a) 'A Framework for Action', Ch. 6, Oftel.
—— (1995b) 'A Framework for Effective Competition and a Better Deal for Customers', Oftel.
—— (1995c) 'Pricing of Telecommunications Services from 1997', Annex B, Table 3, p. 8, Annex document, Oftel, December.
The Times (1996) 'Don't Let Regulation Stifle the Voice of Market Forces', 5 February.

6

PRESERVING CONSUMER PROTECTION AND EDUCATION IN A DEREGULATED ELECTRIC SERVICES WORLD

Challenges for the post-modern regulator

Michael Shames

Summary

In February 1993, the California Public Utilities Commission (CPUC) initiated a process intended to comprehensively transform the state's electric utility industry into competitive wholesale and retail markets. The Commission's stated goal was to lower the cost of electric service to all of the state's customers while preserving high quality service. After an exhaustive administrative review process, the Commission issued a decision in December 1995 indicating its intent to phase out the electric monopoly and to permit all customers to select their own electricity providers. The California legislature assessed and largely adopted the Commission decision during its 1996 legislative session. AB1890 modified some of the terms of the Commission's ruling, but essentially codified the deregulation of the electric services industry and ordered that retail electric competition begin on 1 January 1998.

The CPUC decision, as codified by the state legislature in October 1996, will have profound impacts upon residential and small business customers who, historically, had been aggregated by the investor-owned regulated monopoly. Choices about the quality, nature and options of service that have been made by regulators and the monopoly would, instead, be made by customers. The Commission's proposed restructuring eliminates the retail monopoly, leaving customers to aggregate themselves and make their own choices.

This change in the electric industry will usher in new ways that this new commodity is offered to electric customers. This chapter suggests heretofore untested ways that residential and small business consumers are informed about these new choices in electric (as well as telephony and other energy) services. It suggests that the post-regulation regulators will have to change the way in which they have provided market oversight and information to consumers. Some market information tasks will need to be removed from the regulatory sphere and transplanted into the market place, the social and academic sectors. This chapter will identify new institutions and new regulatory functions that will facilitate the dissemination of market information.

The role of the regulator is also changed. Instead of regulating monopolies, the post-regulatory or 'post-modern' regulator will need to regulate the market place. This paper suggests some new and very specific challenges that the post-modern regulator will need to meet in order to bring benefits of the competitive electric retail market to small business and residential customers (herein referred to as 'small customers'). It concludes that the regulator's new role will initially change but not diminish due to the need to guard against the inevitable breakdowns of the nascent unregulated market place. But by utilising private and social sector institutions, these challenges can be met without increasing regulatory staff demands.

Background

When the California legislature ushered in electric retail competition it did not expressly address the ramifications that this transition would have on consumer protection. In AB1890, the legislature briefly addressed consumer protection matters by stating that the Public Utilities Commission could not enforce complaints brought against electric providers and that customers had to rely upon civil court remedies for problems with competing providers.

The following year, legislators turned their attention to the undermining effect of AB1890 on regulatory oversight of customer service. It attempted to remedy the problems created by AB1890 with SB477. This follow-up Bill was passed by the legislature in August 1997 and signed by the Governor the following month. It amended Public Utilities Code Sections 366–96 to do the following:

> The PUC will facilitate direct transactions between electricity suppliers and end use customers. Customers shall be entitled to aggregate their electric loads on a voluntary basis, provided that each customer does so by a positive written declaration (Sec. 366a).
>
> Aggregation of customer electrical load shall be authorized by the PUC for all customer classes. Aggregation may be accomplished by private market aggregators, cities, counties, special districts or on any other basis made available by market opportunities and agree-

able by positive written declaration by individual consumers [Sec. 266(b)].

No change in the aggregator or supplier of electric power for any small commercial customer may be made until one of the confirmations have been made:

1. Independent third-party telephone verification.
2. Receipt of a written confirmation received in the mail.
3. Customer signs a document explaining the nature and effect of the change.
4. The customer's consent is obtained through electronic means.

Moreover, no change in the aggregator or provider of electric power for any residential customer may be made unless confirmed by an independent third-party verifier [Secs 366.5(a) and (b)].

The commission shall compile and regularly update information on registered providers. It shall issue also public alerts [to] fraudulent acts by companies. And the CPUC staff will collect and analyze information and prepare easily understandable informational guides or other tools to help residential and small commercial customers understand how to evaluate competing electric service options [Secs 392.1 (a–c)].

Electric service providers offering service to residential and small commercial customers must register with the commission [Sec. 394(a)].

The PUC must accept, compile, and attempt to informally resolve consumer complaints regarding registered entities. However, residential and small commercial customers shall have the option to proceed with a complaint against a registered entity either through civil court system or through a complaint filed with the commission [Sec. 394.2 (a–b)].

The commission may enforce the provisions against registered entities as if those entities were public utilities as defined in these code sections. Thus a registered entity may have its registration suspended or revoked, immediately or prospectively, in whole or in part, if it is found to have made material misrepresentations, engaged in dishonesty, fraud, or deceit or if the commission finds that entity is not financially or operationally sound [Sec. 394.25(a–b)].

The PUC will implement the minimum standards for registered entities offering electrical services to residential and small commercial customers. These minimum standards will include:

a. Confidentiality: Customer information shall be confidential unless the customer consents in writing. This shall encompass confidentiality of customer specific billing, credit, or usage information.

b. Only an electrical corporation, or a publicly owned electric utility, that provides physical delivery service to the affected customer shall have the authority to physically disconnect or reconnect a customer from the transmission or distribution grid.
c. Customers may change their energy supplier only with adequate notice supplied by a registered entity to the UDC providing physical delivery service.
d. Notices describing the terms and conditions of service agreements, notices of late payment, notices of discontinuance of service, and disconnection notices must be readily understandable.
e. All bills shall have a standard bill format, as determined by the PUC and shall contain sufficient detail for the customer to recalculate the bill for accuracy.
f. An electric customer shall have a reasonable opportunity to have their meter tested to ensure the reasonable accuracy of the meter.
g. Registered entities may require customer deposits before commencing service, but the deposit cannot exceed more than the estimated bill for a three-month period.
h. PUC may adopt additional residential and small commercial consumer protection standards which are in the public interest [Secs 394.4(a–h)]. Each entity offering electrical service to residential and small commercial customers shall, prior to the commencement of service, provide the potential customer with a written notice of the service describing the price, terms, and conditions of the service. The notices shall include a clear description of the price, terms, and conditions of service, including:

    a. The price of electricity in a format in which small customers can compare and select among similar products and services on a standard basis. PUC shall require disclosure of the total price of electricity on a cents-per-kilowatthour basis, including the costs of all electric services and charges and estimates of the total monthly bill at varying consumption level.
    b. Disclosure of all recurring and nonrecurring charges associated with the sale of electricity. The notices shall also provide:

        1. An itemization of the services and charge or charges associated with each,
        2. An explanation of the applicability and amount of the CTC charge,

3. The potential customer's right to rescind the contract without fee or penalty,
4. Detail the customer's financial obligations, as well as the procedures regarding past due payments, discontinuance of service, billing disputes, and service complaints,
5. The entity's registration number, if applicable,
6. The right to change service providers upon written notice, and
7. A description of the availability of low-income assistance programs for qualified customers and how customers can apply for these programs.

And, if a service provider declines to serve a consumer, it shall, upon request, disclose to that consumer the reason for the denial in writing within 30 days [Sec. 394.5 (a–c)].

The California commission is required to maintain a list of residential and small commercial customers who do not wish to be solicited by telephone, by providers. The list shall include sufficient information for companies to identify customers who do not wish to be solicited, including a customer's address and telephone number. A company who solicits any customer on the list more than once shall be liable to the customer for $25 per violation [Sec. 394.7 (a–c)].

Finally, a consumer damaged by a violation of this article by an entity offering electrical service is entitled to recover all of the following:

1. Actual damages.
2. The consumer's reasonable attorney's fees and court costs.
3. Exemplary damages for intentional or wilful violations.
4. Equitable relief as the court deems proper [Sec. 396(a)].

This legislation also restated the Legislature's directive in AB1890 that the state's electric utilities, with oversight by the state Commission, conduct an education campaign prior to the commencement of electric retail competition.

These changes by the California legislature in 1997 represented an important and unprecedented first step in ensuring that customers had some rights and expectations in a competitive market for electricity.

Foundational assumptions

The recommendations in this chapter are premised upon the five foundational assumptions. Because of the dearth of historical study of electric industry deregulation, there is little authority in support or in contravention of these five foundational premises. Thus they are, by definition, controversial.

In order to anticipate outcomes of the deregulated electric market, I look to the recently deregulated American telecommunications market place. After ten years of experience with competitive long-distance (or 'InterLATA') services, over two years of competitive local–long-distance (or 'IntraLATA') services and numerous unregulated billing and collateral telephony services, there are some lessons from the telephony experience to be learned and heeded by the electric regulator.

Retail 'competition' will materialise more quickly than many expect, albeit not quickly enough for the small consumer

There is one question that few can answer conclusively: will retail electric service providers flock to serve small customers? In a world of significant transaction costs and the high costs of failure, the answer is – no. That is, in the initial years of the transformation to a competitive market, few providers will pursue the small consumer market.

As was demonstrated by the telecommunications market, only the large commercial and industrial customers have captured the significant cost reductions and innovations attributable to deregulation of long-distance (InterLATA) and local–long distance (IntraLATA) services (Consumer Action 1996).

But a market for these small customers will come more quickly than occurred in telephony. That is because of the convergence of information systems. Information companies, such as phone companies, the cable companies and the wireless providers, i.e. network service providers, will find ways of incorporating energy services into the portfolio of services that will be offered to customers (Schuler 1996: 34).

Thus, any regulatory body that is considering electric deregulation has an obligation to deal with this reality directly. The policy maker's task is not to ensure choices for the electric residential or small business customer. Choices, alone, are not enough. They may be too few choices (i.e. oligopoly) or they may not be meaningful choices (services differentiated by marketing technique rather than quality or price). *The real challenge for electric deregulation is to ensure that the small customer has access to network-based electric service competitors.* Each electric customer should have access to at least three telecommunications networks and each of those networks should be able to offer energy services, such as metering, billing and energy management systems.

This conclusion is premised upon two underlying assumptions. (1) It is in the small consumers' interests to have electric, gas and telecommunications services provided by a multitude of service providers where municipalities do not aggregate. (2) Technological developments will lead to an integration of energy and telecommunications services in the near future.

The best means of offsetting these transaction costs and the high risks associated with them is to try to capture economies of scope. This can be accomplished by integrating communications services with energy services. The fit is a natural one; most of the energy services that will be provided to customers will be facilitated by some form of communication network. Currently, cable and telephone conduit reaches nearly every urban home in California. Wireless companies plan to create a network for most California homes, especially in rural areas. Further, state electric utilities are investigating the installation of wireless networks to replace meter reading functions currently performed by employees.

It is not clear how soon this convergence will develop. In California it is not likely to occur before 2001. Pacific Bell, which recently merged with Southwestern Bell, has retreated from its pledge to upgrade its wire-based network to facilitate broadband services. Its attentions appear to be focused upon preserving its local phone service market share. Similarly, large cable companies, such as TCI and Time-Warner, have announced the scaling back of their plans to enter two-way telephony service and, instead, have focused upon Internet service provision.

Wireless companies are best positioned to provide the service, but few have publicly expressed interest. Satellite services are not yet two-way capable and are too high-priced to provide competitive service. Until wire-based and wireless services are prepared to offer communications capability between the electric meter and the service provider, there is little hope that the effect of convergence will be felt by the small customer.

Small customers may lose; big customers will reap disproportionate benefits

California's residential and small business customers will likely see few benefits and perhaps some cost increases at the commencement of competition, now scheduled for January 1998. It appears that large industrial and commercial customers will reap disproportionate benefits during the four-year transition period at the expense of the small customer. Of the 115 electric service companies that registered to do business in the state of California as of 30 September 1997, only four of them have indicated an interest in marketing to residential customers (*California Energy Markets* 1997: 12).

A primary reason for this is the manner by which California regulators have apportioned 'stranded costs' among customer classes. Stranded costs, in California, are the costs of uneconomic generating plant and electric purchase contracts that were incurred by the investor-owned utilities in the previous decades. Even though the stranded assets are largely generation facilities, the allocation methodology for distributing these costs was based upon generation, transmission and distribution costs. The skewed result of this flawed methodology is that small residential and business-class customers in

California will pay 25 per cent more than they otherwise would have for the stranded asset costs.

Another contributing factor is the means by which regulators are implementing the 'rate freeze' established in the AB1890 legislation. Because rates for all customers will be frozen at 1997 rate levels, only those customers who utilise 'direct access' (i.e. direct purchases from generators, bypassing the Power Exchange) will be exempt from the rate freeze. Customers with real-time pricing meters will be in the best position to derive benefits from a real-time pricing market.

Small customers will have theoretical access through 'load profiling', but few marketers have seized upon this very complicated form of bill aggregation. Load profiling – a non-meter technique to provide clearer market signals – will prove to be an interim and very inaccurate step. But it will not permit small consumers to reap meaningful benefits from the hourly-priced electric market. And it causes sufficiently serious 'bill settlement' problems with the distribution companies to have discouraged most marketers from pursuing load profiling services.

At the current time, real-time pricing meters are not affordable for most small customers. It is likely to be beneficial only for those customers with a high usage of electricity. Customers with low usage, particularly low-income customers with few appliances, are not likely to benefit. Indeed, if the cost of metering equipment is paid by the customer and/or the customer's pattern of usage tends towards system peak periods, then the customer could be worse off.

Near-term access to real-time metering will only happen if distribution utilities universally deploy such meters. However, proposals by California utilities to do so are irreparably flawed because they are proprietary, one-way communication systems that may inhibit innovation rather than promote it. The risk of creating an information monopoly for the incumbent utilities may outweigh rapid deployment of such meters unless open protocols and standards can be established prior to deployment.

In September 1997, the CPUC rejected utility proposals to universally deploy real-time meters (D. 97-05-040). The Commission cited the potential for utility meters to cause a barrier to entry by competing marketers as a primary reason for this rejection.

Current analysis presented to the Commission by small consumer representatives shows that an extremely modest number of residential customers could theoretically benefit from competitive energy services markets when such meters become available in 1998 (Tellus Institute 1996). For individual customers, the key factors affecting the ability to benefit are load factor and size. Among residential customers who participate individually in restructuring, those with low or average annual load factors, as well as average usage, are likely to face increasing annual costs for electricity. This is true even if those customers obtain anticipated overall electricity cost reductions from competition in generation. Small customers will not reap any measurable benefits from retail competition unless these customers can use energy management systems via 'smart meters' or home computers.

The California experience with local telephony competition presents a vivid example of a nascent market's bias against the small customer. In a report issued in October 1997, a consumer group found that the vast majority of telephone customers in San Diego County, California (1 million phone customers) were not aware that competition exists for local telephone service. Throughout the state of California, fewer than 2 per cent (200,000 customers of the over 8 million California phone customers) had switched from the regional Bell Operating Company (Pacific Bell) to a competing local telephony service company. The few customers who had inquired into switching to competitive alternatives found themselves confused, stalled, misled and treated rudely when attempting to switch services. The even fewer customers who successfully switch are faced with complex and convoluted pricing structures that require an unusually sophisticated knowledge of telephony mathematics (Utility Consumers' Action Network 1997).

Low-income customers will be hurt by cost shifting and lack of market power

Low-income customers who, by definition, do not have the income to participate more than marginally (if at all) in competitive markets will be in the worst position to take advantage of new market conditions. Consumer education and regulatory action on termination protection, credit policies, collection practices, licensing and sales guidelines will be critical.

However, low-income customers are not the only ones subject to fewer benefits from competition. Experience in banking and telephony deregulation in the United States shows that identifiable customer groups, including low-income, seniors, minorities, rural, lower educated and other historically vulnerable small customer subgroups will not only reap fewer benefits but will be subjected to greater abuses of the unsupervised market. For example, telephone and natural gas deregulation in Canada and the US attracted 'fly-by-night' operators who would offer services, collect upfront payments from unsuspecting customers and then disappear into the night. Additionally, creative but legal questionable marketing practices, as seen in telephone services that prey on non-English-speaking or senior citizen customers, increase the risks to customers who are particularly prone to scams due to limited market sophistication. In California, regulators discovered that newly created long-distance companies were owned and operated by persons who had migrated from the shady boiler rooms of precious metal, penny stock and even drug dealing.

These unscrupulous marketers saw the lucrative opportunities of exploiting unsophisticated consumers who were eager to capture the deals promised by the highly touted deregulation of long-distance telephone service and the collateral telephony products such as calling cards. Society's more vulnerable small consumers, in particular, will need special consumer protections and information to prevent abuse in the competitive market.

True competition may not materialise for small consumers when the markets are opened unless consumers are adequately apprised of their options

In order to increase the attractiveness of markets to both small consumers and potential providers, this chapter suggests that regulators must:

1 ensure that small consumers have adequate access to understandable and credible information to make informed choices;
2 create adequate consumer protection measures, including an industry code of conduct;
3 promote and encourage voluntary aggregation of small consumers; and
4 promote entry of new energy providers into markets to overcome the incumbent advantage that monopoly regulation has given existing utilities.

Regulators are beginning to realise a dreadful oversight in telephony deregulation. They failed to ensure that adequate market information was available to customers so that they can make meaningful choices. In long-distance telephone services, few Americans can compare the prices and quality of competing providers. *Consumer Reports* (1996), the consumer magazine relied upon by savvy consumers, announced in its May edition that comparison of long-distance service providers was a virtual impossibility due to the lack of standard offerings and the complexity of the service itself.

Only now are regulators appreciating that their efforts to inject competition into the telephony market will be chronically blocked by information failure. If a market is not adequately informed, it cannot be robust. Thus, the need to educate small consumers about how to assess and to purchase their electric service is a task the importance of which cannot be overstated.

American consumers have decades, if not centuries, of experience in assessing and purchasing necessary goods such as food, housing, insurance and electronic goods. Not only have they developed the sophistication to compare these common goods, they also are aided by forced disclosure of product information about ingredients, weights, nutritional value and unit pricing. Disclosure laws are the bulwark of competitive markets for these necessary goods.

Telephony services were deregulated without regard to the need for adequate market information. Small consumers had little experience in assessing or purchasing telecommunications service and this relative unsophistication revealed itself in the magnitude of consumer-related problems and scams that ensued. Previously unimagined abuses, such as slamming (unauthorised switching of service providers, operator-assisted calls, 976 and 900 services), overpriced pay phones, privacy intrusions and extortionist rates by many small (and larger) long-distance companies developed.

Remarkably, a residential consumer in America can be currently charged from 35 cents per minute to 9.5 cents per minute for an interstate long-distance call at the same time, the same distance and the same quality of call. This dramatic price differential for the identical service is a telling indicator of market information failure (Utility Consumers' Action Network 1997).

For this reason, consumer education and regulatory action on termination protection, credit policies, collection practices, licensing and sales guidelines must be addressed in advance of electric deregulation. Policy makers should require specific minimum actions as a precondition to competition, such as price comparisons, adequate regulatory oversight staffing, plain-English contracts and minimum supply reliability requirements. And industry codes of conduct combined with regulatory proactive and enforcement actions are necessary to protect against the inevitable abuses that have accompanied deregulation in similar industry deregulation.

Low-income, non-English-speaking and senior citizen consumers, in particular, will need special consumer protections and information to ward off the predictable abuse that they will attract. Policy makers must be particularly sensitive to the needs of low-income customers who, by definition, do not have the income to participate more than marginally (if at all) in competitive markets. They have the least to gain, yet the most to lose, in the deregulated market.

Even if a robust competitive market develops for *all* customers, there are likely to be many small consumers who, for a variety of reasons, will not participate in such markets as individuals. These small customers who choose not to shop around on their own will be automatically aggregated by some entity to ensure that they have the opportunity to receive electric service.

A report released by California consumer groups in April 1996 indicated that these non-participants can benefit from deregulation if they are automatically aggregated (Tellus Institute 1996: 4-1 to 4-22). For this set of small consumers, it is necessary that the negotiating, bargaining and planning capability be used by the aggregating entity to capture potential benefits. Otherwise, these customers will be effectively denied such cost benefits. The analysis shows that, absent aggregation, most small customers will see increased costs if they have to use real-time pricing to exercise the opportunity for retail wheeling – even if retail wheeling is assumed to reduce overall electricity prices by 10 per cent.

Consumer education by the post-modern regulator

Mandatory part of deregulating a market

In passing AB1890, the California legislature mandated a consumer education programme to precede the commencement of a competitive market. The Legislature stated in its revision of Public Utilities Code Section 392:

> It is the intent of the Legislature that (1) electricity consumers be provided with sufficient and reliable information to be able to compare and select among products and services provided in the electricity market, and (2) consumers be provided with mechanisms to protect themselves from marketing practices that are unfair or abusive. . . . Prior to the implementation of the competition transition charge, electric corporations, in conjunction with the commission, shall devise and implement a customer education program informing customers of the changes to the electric industry. The program shall provide customers with information necessary to help them make appropriate choices as to their electric service. The education program shall be subject to approval by the commission.

This state-wide consumer education programme commenced on 15 October 1997. The $73 million dollar advertising campaign financed by California electric ratepayers included a mass-media saturation of the state's electronic media touting the advantages of 'choice' coming to most of the state's electric consumers on 1 January 1998. In authorising this expensive, ratepayer-paid advertising campaign, the Public Utilities Commission hoped to prime the pump for a competitive market in electricity.

The ambitious education programme came under significant attack as amounting to an 'awareness' campaign, and not an education campaign. Criticisms of the plan were broad in scope, but the recurring critical themes were five-fold:

1 Education monies should be used to give tools to customers to use in comparison shopping and evaluation of electric services, not in raising general awareness.
2 Small business was not adequately targeted.
3 Outreach to underserved communities requires the use of community-based organisation, not mass media.
4 Education efforts should be better coordinated and integrated.
5 Any education effort requires a recognition of the role of alternative power, energy efficiency and aggregation.

To its credit, the California regulators appointed a 'blue-ribbon' panel to advise the Commission of the best way to educate consumers about the rapid changes set to occur on 1 January 1998. In a first-of-its-kind report to regulators about such a process, the Commission's appointed 'Consumer Education Advisory Panel' unanimously condemned a preliminary plan developed by the utilities for being overly expensive, poorly timed, inadequately targeted and bereft of education (California Consumer Education Advisory Panel 1997).

This panel stated that 'The proposed Consumer Education Plan will not enable all or even most Californians to participate in or benefit from restructuring in a meaningful way, and *it threatens to exclude those consumers who most need the information in order to participate*' (p. 2).

It identified the elements that must be considered for a viable consumer education plan and made specific recommendations to the Commission, the most primary of which were:

1 The establishment of a multipurpose interactive call centre which would integrate complaint in-take, consumer education and community-based organisation outreach efforts.
2 Reducing mass-media advertisements and focusing monies on social sector administered, community-based organisation outreach, small business and municipality education.

Use of interactive integrated communications centre for effective education

On the first point, the panel recommended that a toll-free phone number and an Internet web site should be developed and integrated for two-way communications; that is, it should be available to receive feedback from consumers and accept complaints. In sum, an Interactive Education Centre would be created.

It argued that the interactive centre is a very important element in public education about the restructuring because it could be:

- expanded to include complaint identification and handling, as well as customer referral to aggregators;
- linked with the CPUC's market monitoring functions to be used by the CPUC and others as a means of collecting information about potential problems in the development of the market;
- staffed and designed for a minimum five-year life span;
- serve as an informational clearing-house and public education centre as well as a source for customers to learn about potential marketers who serve their community.

The panel also noted that research commissioned by the United States

Small Business Administration (SBA) found that small business owners and managers consider television and radio to be among the worst methods of obtaining information (Office of Advocacy 1994). The SBA research found that, to be effective, information should be relevant to small business owners and managers. It concluded that relevant information comes from trade associations and other sources whom the owners and managers know and trust.

Education of underserved communities requires the use of the social sector

The panel also argued that in order to educate vulnerable and hard-to-reach consumers, such as low-income minority communities, monolingual seniors and immigrant families, an education programme had to utilise community-based organisations (CBOs) and small community organisations to serve as 'focal points' for specific populations (California Consumer Education Advisory Panel 1997: 23).

Cited as precedent was the 1996 California CNEP (Caller Notification Education Plan). Recognising that the introduction of CallerID would present new and important impacts upon telephone customers, the Commission required that Pacific Bell and other phone providers commence a 'bottom-up' education plan as a precondition for the commencement of CallerID service. The efficacy of this approach in educating customers is discussed in depth in Dervin (1995). This report, commissioned by the Commission's staff and delivered on 21 November 1995, establishes a number of important principles for educating customers about changes in utility service.

Some of the relevant hallmarks of this education plan were:

- i *Independently crafted messages*. Professor Dervin stressed the need for involving community representatives in co-production of campaign messages. For CNEP, the Commission approved the hiring of a nationally recognised media consultant to develop themes and mass advertising and sought the input of interveners to refine the proposed themes.
- ii *Use of community-based organisations (CBOs) to educate customers*. The professor emphasised the use of high involvement or high interaction outlets and recommended that at least 50 per cent of the campaign needed to be implemented out in the communities. Recognising the educational advantages offered by the state's existing network of non-profits, the CPUC required that these CBOs be hired to effect customer education.
- iii *Concerted education plan commencing six months prior to the beginning of the new regulatory scheme and continued through the transition*. The campaign must be iterative and sustained, according to Dervin. Accordingly, the CNEP began educating customers almost six months prior to the introduction of CallerID service in California. The plan proved to be so successful that

Pacific Bell could not accommodate the crush of customers seeking blocking protections, and implementation was delayed until customer responses could be completed. The plan was to continue for one year after the introduction of the service.

iv *Make the campaign relevant to customers*. Electric restructuring is going to require a new awareness by customers of matters that had been heretofore largely handled by the monopoly utility. It will be essential that customers are educated, in simple terms, as to why they should care. The message must be interactive and accessible to all customer groups, including multilingual and multicultural communities. In order for any mass education programme to be successful, these elements would have to be incorporated into any regulator-approved education plan. And the creation of the interactive education centre using low-cost telephony and on-line media would seem to be essential tools.

The role of post-modern regulator will change

In this new subsea-level environment, replete with its new characteristics, the regulator's role changes. The 'post-modern regulator' no longer builds the dike, but manages it and, presumably, reinforces it. Thus, it must identify weaknesses and take appropriate action to deal with them. The modern regulators used command and control tools to regulate companies. The 'post-modern regulator' takes a decidedly different approach. This chapter addresses two areas in which the post-modern regulator's role changes in relation to customer education and protection, namely the areas of:

1 public consumer information; and
2 deregulated market activity.

What the small consumer wants

Residential and small business electric customers have little time and modest economic incentives to become skilled in the art of electric service analysis. Their primary interest is in receiving a reasonably priced, reliable and non-discriminatory electric service. However, competitive markets, by definition, are not just or reasonable, they are just markets and have little regard for customer expectations of social equity. These markets are characterised by their penchant for segmenting customer needs (translated: discriminating among customers) and thus violating customer expectations for non-discriminatory service. Also, many California customers would prefer not to be bothered with having to study electric rate options unless there is an opportunity for meaningful savings. Because the size of electric bills is dwarfed by monthly mortgage or rent, insurance and auto loan payments, these customers would prefer to assert a right not to choose. For these customers, the effort required to judge and compare rate options does not result in savings large enough to justify the effort. The requirement to choose will be greeted with dismay. As will the proposition that by not choosing they will be penalised with relatively higher rates than those that do choose.

These customers are presently guaranteed, by law, a regulatory system that is supposed to deliver just, reasonable and non-discriminatory rates thus freeing these customers from the uneconomic effort of having to spend time and resources on divining the optimal energy option for their individual needs. These very tangible rights not to choose and to a guaranteed non-discriminatory service are abandoned with the advent of a competitive market which forces choice and customer segmentation.

This competitive paradigm falls foul of almost all of the customers' current expectations, save for its potential to deliver lower energy costs. And the latter potential is in no way guaranteed for many customers, such as rural, low-income or relatively unsophisticated customers.

If choice is to be forced upon this unwilling majority of electric customers then it must be meaningful choice. 'Meaningful choice' means that choice must offer true savings to all customer classes and subclasses, must be readily understandable and not result in lower reliability of service. Initially, the cost of securing this information must be nominal, if not free, in order to be accessible to most small customers. Later, as the market matures, transaction costs are reduced and bundled into other services.

Second, customers will expect rate predictability. Energy rates, like other necessities, such as telephone and housing costs, must be predictable and budgetable. Almost by definition, a competitive market place is characterised by price and supply fluctuations. This characteristic will clash with customer expectations.

Proponents of value-added services will find a customer base that will be reticent to embrace the new services. Even if they are valid enhancements, the small consumers' relative lack of experience with these services will justify an exaggerated wariness especially where there are few consumer protections to guard against bad choices.

As will be explained below, innovation and growth in this market will require stringent consumer protections and clear, concise and reliable market information, thus giving the consumer adequate freedom to experiment and, perhaps, make a mistake.

Change and enhance the regulator's consumer information activities

With the new reliance upon the competitive market to provide basic electric and telephone services for small consumers, the post-modern regulator's challenges are, in the simplest of terms:

a to promote a competitive market place with multiple buyers and sellers, and
b to arm all consumers with the information necessary to make informed choices.

These two elements are essential components of a competitive market. If either of the two elements is missing, then a competitive market will not materialise. This assertion is a basic economic axiom that is not disputed by any reputable party.

This underlying premise compels the post-modern regulator to ensure a multiseller or multibuyer market place using supply-and-demand forces. Supply requires using market conduct and incentives to ensure multiple sellers are serving all customers. Demand requires adequately informing all consumers of choices and ensuring that customers have the necessary economic incentives to choose among competitors. To succeed, the post-modern regulator will need to implement a three-part strategy for the transition to a competitive market place which involves:

1 Developing and disseminating price and quality comparisons of electric (and telecommunications) services;
2 Monitoring customer education conducted by private participants and administering education trust funds for electric (and telecommunications) industries; and
3 Working to help aggregate customers, especially traditionally underserved communities.

Price and quality comparisons

If a consumer is unable to comparison shop for utility services, then a competitive market will fail. In order to shop, a customer must be able to determine value. In order to establish value, the consumer must be able to compare price and quality. The old regulator apparently did not appreciate this point, as its efforts to educate customers about long-distance and local–long-distance services on the telecommunications side and demand-side activities in the electric industry have been woefully inadequate.

The Californian Department of Insurance has endeavoured to provide automobile rate comparison with mixed success – the quality of the rate survey appears to reflect the degree of commitment to it by each insurance commissioner. Yet despite its failings, it is far superior to its sister agency, the California PUC, which has no programme to make assessments and comparisons of rates and customer service records for telecommunications or electric providers.

It is inevitable that small consumers will be offered a number of energy services by marketers so as to gain market entry, including 'energy audits'.

Initially, consumers will have no historical basis upon which to assess such services, just as they had little experience with which to assess the solar hot-water heater sales schemes that plagued California in the 1970s. The result was a proliferation of poor quality installations, fly-by-night companies and a market backlash against this very promising demand-side industry.

In the transition to long-distance and local–long-distance markets, consumers have been bombarded with misinformation or malinformation for almost a decade.

Only now are national providers beginning to offer simple rates, despite years of complaints by customers that rate shopping was impossible. Yet, as mentioned above, the residential consumer in America faces interstate call charges ranging from 35 cents per minute to 9.5 cents per minute for an interstate long-distance call. This price differential for an identical service is a telling indicator of market information failure. A failure of which the California regulator appears to remain oblivious (see Utility Consumers' Action Network 1997).

A robust competitive market will require high-quality information with which consumers can make meaningful choices. Active governmental involvement in encouraging the dissemination of this information and providing resources by which consumers can quickly gain the market knowledge will help promote this emerging market. This point was recognised by the California legislature when it required that the CPUC staff collect and analyse information and prepare easily understandable informational guides or other tools to help residential and small commercial customers understand how to evaluate competing electric service options [Public Utilities Code Secs 392.1(a–c), mod. by SB477 (1997)].

Customer education by private and non-profit organisations

Beyond simply promoting price comparison information and evaluative services, the post-modern regulator will be obligated to monitor private consumer education by market competitors and non-profit organisations to ensure consumer information is accurate. This is not tantamount to 'censorship' of marketing materials. But there are concrete steps that can be taken by the regulator to improve the quality of consumer information in the market. These steps include:

COORDINATING PRIVATE AND PUBLIC PROSECUTION OF MISLEADING INFORMATION

For example, when companies engage in inappropriate marketing transactions, the state attorney-general, local district attorneys and consumer class-action attorneys can utilise the California Business and Professions Code to discourage such behaviours and gain remedies for victimised consumers. The post-modern regulator should serve as a clearing-house for complaints and references to attorneys. The regulator's public intake functions are the essential and low-cost means of identifying such abuses. The private or prosecutorial attorneys offices can expeditiously act once the regulator alerts them to a pattern of deceit. The regulator should also refer individual consumers to private attorneys for fact-specific complaints; this can be done by establishing referral panels at little cost to the regulator.

CREATING OF EDUCATION TRUST FUNDS

California has recognised the need to educate more underserved and vulnerable customer classes in order to avoid the inequities and abuses that have visited consumers in telecommunications and banking deregulation. The California Telecommunications Education Trust Fund serves as a reasonable model, albeit underfunded, for this task. This entity enabled the regulator to sponsor consumer outreach and education through community service agencies and other private and non-profit entities during 1991–5 by using penalty monies imposed upon telephone monopolies.

SERVE AN ADVISORY FUNCTION FOR MARKET PARTICIPANTS

During the transition period, the post-modern regulator should provide a service whereby it will review marketing materials voluntarily submitted by service providers to the regulator. By undergoing an accuracy review by the regulator, the market providers are protected against possible private action for misleading or false advertising. And the regulator is able to proactively prevent potential customer confusion.

Help aggregate customers and use the public entities' purchasing power

The consensus among industry observers (and the California consumer report mentioned above) is that small customers will need to be aggregated in order to gain adequate market leverage. Absent aggregation, these customers would fare poorly. This conclusion is not surprising given the experience with insurance, banking and other complex services, in which aggregation of small customers minimised transaction costs and increased market leverage. In newly established markets, like electric and telecommunications services, it is essential that aggregation occur quickly so as to give small consumers some opportunity to secure improved service and lower costs.

During the transition period to a competitive market, the post-modern regulator should be active in helping promote aggregation. It can serve as a coordinator for private companies to find customers. For example, it can distribute information to the state's customers about available aggregators in rural, inner city and other underserved communities. It can establish a telephone hotline where interested consumers can learn about the potential aggregators. The California PUC, for example, has established a reseller programme for cellular phone services so that duopolist cellular providers can face some competition. Cellular resale is a good idea, yet most consumers are unable to track down the names and phone numbers for these resellers. Lack of information is undermining the California Commission's effort to create a competitive market for cellular customers. Similarly, post-modern regulator's efforts to promote a competitive electric market will be frustrated unless the regulator ensures that information is being disseminated.

Moreover, the state of California and most municipalities throughout the state use their purchasing power to secure very low-cost energy services for its offices. For example, many municipalities have used their large phone costs to negotiate long-distance services for under 7 cents per minute for an interstate call anywhere in the US at any time of the day. This rate is some 33 per cent lower than the *best rates* that could be found for residential customers.

Public entities could bestow a tremendous benefit for their citizens by negotiating discounts for all residents in their area who choose to sign-on with the public entities' carrier. For example, if a municipality were to incorporate into its bid for electric services an agreement that the winning bidder will provide local and long-distance energy services to any resident at an agreed-upon price, then those residents who choose to take advantage of the service would be provided a very competitive price leveraged by a multimillion dollar energy bill. Moreover, customer service satisfaction would be leveraged by the fact that the entity could choose to abrogate the agreement if residents complained about chronic customer service abuses or neglect. This leveraging of public entity purchase power is not unique. The state of California has done it for health insurance customers through HIPC, a state-wide purchasing group for small businesses with two to fifty employees. Numerous other states and state pensions have bestowed similar benefits upon its residents or pensioners using that same leverage.

The post-modern regulator can work with the private market to aggressively promote customer aggregation. It can assist municipalities and other public agencies who seek to create cooperatives or serve as purchasing agents for electric or phone services. It can distribute lists of qualified aggregators along with customer information about how to evaluate these services. And it can list the aggregators' names and product information on the state-sponsored world-wide web site and make the information available at state offices. In short, it can help reduce the significant transaction costs facing any service provider seeking to break into the mass market.

Regulators must recognise and utilise convergence

As described above, real-time pricing and more advanced energy management services increase the importance of two-way communications. In recognition of this fact, many electric utilities have entered into partnerships with telecommunications companies to begin integrating electric and communications services. In time, communications companies, including cable, telephone and wireless companies, would begin to compete and merge with electric and gas service providers to provide energy.

The already-blurred line between these services would fade and the network provider would materialise. Currently rules are being promulgated in the telecommunications industries about uniform consumer protection that will subsequently be redeveloped by a new set of stakeholders in gas and, even later, electric restructuring proceedings. Yet many of the providers of telecommunications services will also be future providers of energy services. This convergence must be recognised by the regulators and addressed proactively.

Policy makers should identify policy issues that overlap the three industries and address them comprehensively so as to provide uniform policy guidelines, as well as to provide the benefits of innovative thinking in a single forum.

Increase its market conduct activities in light of its deregulatory plans

Upon the commencement of a deregulated market, the demand upon regulatory resources will increase due to the increased number of consumer complaints and enquiries spawned by an uncertain and transitional environment. A virtual or real direct access world would spawn a number of aggregators, brokers, marketers and other third parties offering services to individual retail customers or cooperatives. These transactions will likely spawn a multitude of complaints, disputes and disharmonies that will need to be addressed in a uniform and knowledgeable fashion. Similarly, in the telecommunications market the amount of consumer choices and consumer confusion will increase.

During the transition years, demands made upon the time of the postmodern regulator's staff for complaint resolution and investigation will increase. Funding levels would have to increase in order for staff to be trained, armed and capable of fielding the slew of complaints. For example, the CPUC has seen its staff swamped with a tidal wave of telecommunications service abuses ranging from benign, but irritating slamming (unauthorised switching of long-distance service providers) to outright 'scam artist' activity.

The significant changes in the electric service markets will substantially increase the number and complexity of complaints submitted by consumers, as happened in telephony. But because of the complexity of energy services, new types of complaints are expected, including similar ones to those spawned by telecommunications competition. Contractual disputes will abound, as will new billing, service and jurisdictional disputes. Information-based infractions (misleading advertising, unrealised expectations and fraud) will also develop into huge growth industries in their own right. Current funding levels at most regulatory bodies are simply inadequate for dealing with current demands upon the regulator. Future demand will likely dwarf current demand, thus further necessitating a new approach to dispute resolution.

The focus of the post-modern regulator's challenge will be one of monitoring market conduct. Not only will it need to be vigilant in guarding against market dominance problems (a function that the regulator has recognised as important) but it must also be attentive to whether the competitors are treating customers responsibly, are providing adequate service, and are not engaging in unintentional redlining. The problems will develop at a fast and furious rate. Most regulators are woefully under-prepared to track, let alone respond to, these problems. The California regulators' response to long-distance service 'slamming' has been slow and only marginally effective. Future problems spawned by local telephone and electric competition could make it appear to be a minor infraction.

A new institution for consumer education

The emerging role of special interest groups on business practices

The term 'special interest group' carries connotations of a self-interested and greedy public manipulator which thrives in the dark dankness of the back-room deal. Many see self-interest groups as a problem. But they are not. In fact, they offer a solution. Peter Drucker, renowned management guru and respected professor at the Claremont School of Management, has concluded after a lifetime of observing the market place that we have become a factionalised society – a society of institutions. And that, he suggests, may be a good thing.

In his book, *Post-Capitalist Society* (Harper Business, 1993), Professor Drucker opines that the third set of institutions, which he calls the social sector, will serve as a counterbalance to the traditional public sector of government and the private sector of business. He states that:

> Very little has been achieved by government as the doer in the social sphere. But where we have had non-governmental action by autonomous community organizations, we have achieved a great deal. The

> post-capitalist society requires a new social sector – both to satisfy social needs and to restore a meaningful sense of citizenship and community.

His point: government – he calls it the 'Nanny State' – has made marginal achievements in the social sphere. But non-governmental, autonomous community organisations – such as consumer groups, community planning groups, social service organisations and specific stakeholder groups – have accomplished a great deal. The community, according to Drucker, has to play a predominant role in business and in governance.

A third-player in the institutional triumvirate is made up of disparate special interest groups representing the factions within society. They are the environmental, ethnic, poor, religious, neighbourhood preservationists, and the consumer activists. They are what I call 'superconsumers', as they not only consume but shape the opinions of other consumers. They are the collective conscience of a community. And they will have an increasing impact upon business decisions, including daily business decisions.

The following proposal taps into the social sector to complement the work that will be done by the post-modern regulator. Moreover, much of the education effort will have to be provided by non-governmental and social sector entities.

Creating an independent watchful eye on the competitive market – the competitive institute

In 1996, California deregulated local telephony services. At the beginning of 1998 retail electric services in the state will be deregulated. As discussed above, the emerging telecommunications market place has spawned consumer abuses, confusion and barriers to entry by new competitors. Information necessary to consumers to compare the competitors and find real value in the emerging energy services requires the creation of a mechanism that will assist in the dissemination of relevant information to the industry and consumers.

This help could come in the form of an independent entity designed to collect basic information and evaluate the developing competitive service markets. It would be an independent, non-aligned entity to provide low-cost market information for consumers, market competitors and policy makers.

An independent and autonomous observer of the state's emerging energy services can provide a perspective beyond state jurisdictional lines, and beyond industry lines. Such a perspective would substantially supplement and complement the regulators' ability to consider where economies may be achieved or where other advantages may accrue from the coordination (or inclusion) of cable or telecommunications or other future technologies. This can be provided by a 'competitive institute'.

Such an institute may also document the aggregate effect on consumers of industry mergers. One complicating factor in the newly deregulated world of telecommunications is the remaining divergent bargaining power between consumers and service providers. The average consumer is relatively unorganised, unable to bargain effectively and is locked into contractual obligations set by carriers.

The competitive institute would develop a base of information that could be used by aggregators, consumers, policy makers and other market participants to rescale the bargaining power between consumers and carriers. By monitoring the industry for any increasing market abuses and other consumer problems arising from utility sales practices and by publishing obtained information, the institute could counteract potential or unanticipated adverse consequences of a merger. The benefits of monitoring include early detection of abuses, the filtering out of misleading information, and the identification of problems.

The institute would not duplicate existing functions of the regulator, the attorney-general or private consumer groups. The attorney-general's office is largely reactive, does not routinely suppose market conduct and does not regularly publish its findings. The regulators' offices – having to make ultimate market-shaping decisions – will benefit from an independent and objective view of the market. The institute would have the advantage of separate funding, an assigned task and resources dedicated to monitoring and mitigation of abuses. It would act independently, which is to the advantage of the Commission. That independence assures the citizenry that consumer interests will be effectively articulated.

Other consumer groups, while able to assist the regulatory and competitive process, cannot provide the quality of research and information that would be expected from such an institute. It will contribute to the new market place by detecting problems early, providing market-enhancing services and information.

Independence of the institute

A major requirement of the proposal is that the entity be independent. If it is seen as being aligned with a competitive interest or tied to a government interest, the information and analysis provided by the institute will lose value. This is why an underfunded 'think tank' created out of Pacific Bell/Southwestern Bell merger-savings and approved by the California Public Utilities Commission (1997) is irreparably flawed. It is an entity controlled by the Regional Bell Operating Company and will never be seen as having an autonomous existence. Thus, it is paramount that the institute be funded and governed in such a manner so as to retain some degree of independence.

Regulators could adopt the pre-existing model successfully employed by the CPUC in the administration of its Telecommunications Trust, described above. It would be an appointed blue-ribbon board, entirely independent from the industry, to serve as a governing board for at least the first five years. The relevant legislation could then provide for five-year board appointments. Board memberships would be required to have no financial relationship with any other operator within the telecommunications or energy industries. Those appointed to the board should have substantial background as recognised, independent consumer advocates or educators.

The institutes should be prohibited from being engaged in political campaigns and legislative (or agency rule-making) advocacy involving a substantial part of its operations. It must serve a charitable, educational purpose.

The institute should be, but is not required to be, affiliated with a state university. University affiliation provides for a higher degree of analytical rigour. However, the affiliation also creates overhead costs and restrictions that may not be cost effective. This is a question that would be determined based upon regional considerations.

Funding of the institute

The institute could operate adequately on a realistic budget of $850,000 annually for five years in order to provide it optimal funds and time to become self-sustaining. The $850,000 sum should be increased by 3 per cent each year for five years to allow for inflation. At the commencement of the sixth year the funding should be reduced by $100,000 each year for the subsequent five years, and would cease contribution entirely on the eleventh year. The alternative funding amount would provide adequate seed money for a permanent establishment.

Further, the ten-year phased-out time line will provide incentive, and opportunity, to obtain independent funding on a more permanent basis for the created entity. It can be expected that, after ten years, the institute will have developed the required expertise and authority and so be able to either sell its information or secure private grants. Corporations and foundations may contribute grant monies. Consumer education products may produce additional revenue. The proposed time line allows a successful institute the opportunity to obtain long-term funding, with no further contribution required from ratepayers through utility assessment or otherwise. The monies for this entity can come from one (or all) of three sources:

1. monies paid by state utilities seeking permission to merge or sell assets;
2. registration fees paid by any energy or telecommunications company doing business in the state;
3. funds from penalties assessed by the regulators against telecommunications providers who have violated regulatory rules.

Complaint resolution by the social sector

This discussion is built upon the axiom that where a complaint by a consumer cannot be readily resolved by a service provider, the consumer must have access to alternative redress at little or no cost to the consumer. Electric service, like housing, is a necessary commodity that warrants greater consumer protection than most other commodities.

Access to no-cost regulatory relief means that the consumer should not be charged any filing fees or assessed any costs for pursuing regulatory relief. It does not mean that the time spent pursuing a case or travel and out-of-pocket costs will be necessarily recovered by the complainant regardless of the outcome. This no-cost redress is essential if the regulator is to encourage consumers to bring examples of market failure to their attention. It is also necessary to level the playing-field advantage enjoyed by better-resourced providers.

While the Commission is obligated by law to provide dispute resolution services, it can encourage the industry to create its own resolution process, thus reducing regulatory costs and interference. The following proposal should be considered as a model that may be imposed upon incumbent utilities but voluntary for all other providers during the transition period, after which it should be totally voluntary.

As has been demonstrated in other industries, companies can establish their own external policing or oversight procedures, thus reducing the need for the regulators to closely monitor complaint-handling. Industry in the United States has used self-policing models such as the Better Business Bureaus for more common transactions. In complex transactions, such as the purchase of automobiles and homes, industry has established independent mechanisms, such as arbitration boards, to resolve complaints. Other countries have created public–private dispute resolution mechanisms, as will be discussed in greater depth below. However, until such private oversight or enforcement is established, the Commission is obligated by law to provide for that oversight.

The following alternative dispute resolution model is a sustainable complaint resolution process, that reduces regulatory costs and interference. It is an independent complaint resolution body that serves as a screening entity as well as a monitoring entity for regulators. The Australian Insurance Enquiries and Complaints Corporation is such an entity. It addresses complaints or claims by insurance customers who feel they have not been dealt with fairly by their insurer. Over 100 individual insurers participate in the plan.

It is industry-funded and managed, but it is overseen by a non-industry governing board which sets budgets and overarching policy. The non-industry governing board of seven individuals is comprised of three non-industry persons selected by industry and four non-industry persons selected by government. They are charged with protecting the public interest.

The office has a two-step process in resolving complaints. A customer who calls must have first made an overture to the company against which the complaint exists. The calls are received by intervention officers who develop a record of the complaint and attempt to resolve it informally. For each complaint that is resolved in favour of the customer, the company is charged a fee of A$600. For each complaint resolved in favour of the company, the charge is a modest A$200 administrative fee. Where there is clearly no basis for a complaint, the intervention officer does not open a file.

If there is no informal resolution, then the complaint goes before special arbiters who work for the entity and are answerable to its governing board. These arbiters are independent judges who are assigned the task of resolving a complaint, first through mediation and, failing that, arbitration. The arbiter's decision is binding upon industry but is not binding upon a complainant. Moreover, a complainant is not obligated to use this mechanism, thus ensuring that the complainant does not become a captive of the industry. Consumers will use the mechanism only if it is more responsive, easier and quicker than courts or regulatory enforcement agencies.

This model is appealing because it is self-sustainable, independent and sufficiently expert to resolve complicated disputes. It is a model that is readily adaptable to resolving disputes with electric or telecommunications companies. Most importantly, it is accessible and imposes no monetary cost upon the complaining consumer.

It is superior to the internal Ombudsperson or Informal Appeals Group model which is often sponsored by American industry. Its superiority is based on six distinguishing elements:

1 *Neutrality*. Because it is not internal to the company nor governed by the company, it is perceived by the customer as being more neutral and objective. Moreover, because of its neutrality, it can be relied upon by regulators who would otherwise have to intervene in such complaints.
2 *Due process*. The process established is open, fair and designed to make information available to the arbitrator and the customer. This openness and accessibility to information gives the customer a more level bargaining position.
3 *Economic disincentives to litigate*. Because the company is charged more as it pursues higher levels of arbitration, the company is given the proper economic incentive to resolve disputes early in the process. Otherwise, a company has little economic incentive to expediently resolve disputes.
4 *Universality*. The external complaint resolution process is applicable to all industry service providers. Thus, this model can be used, on a voluntary basis, by all providers. Their participation offers economies of scale and efficiencies that benefit all providers.
5 *Information gathering*. The information gathered by this entity can be shared with regulators, policy makers and assorted information

disseminators. This information substantially helps the market place in identifying market failure or patterns of abuse. Statistics on the nature of complaints received, the kinds of resolutions provided and the frequency of the complaints offer invaluable guidance for consumers, market participants and policy makers. If market failure is occurring, this process serves as the early-detection 'canary'.

6 *Case screening*. Because this process is a threshold process – that is, complainants must pursue this process prior to filing formal civil or administrative complaints – it could help screen readily resolved matters. The result is reduced demand upon and improved focus for enforcement processes by the appropriate regulatory agencies.

For these reasons, the creation of an external, neutral and universal complaint resolution process as a means of mitigating potential quality of service deterioration is an essential step in deregulation policy. The Australian model suggests that a one-time start-up charge of $2 million would be sufficient to create an office that could serve California's energy customers. The operating expenses of the entity could be recouped through administrative fees charged to incumbent utilities and other participating energy providers.

Other forms of low-cost redress

Referral to public and private attorneys for action

As part of its ongoing market conduct oversight responsibilities and customer education duties, the post-modern regulator will have to compile data about the complaint records, financial viability, prices and service quality of all service providers licensed to do business. Much of this data should be made available to consumers who are shopping for energy services through mechanisms discussed above. However, all of this data should be made available to complainants who have filed formal complaints to regulatory bodies about an energy provider.

The post-modern regulator's market conduct duties will also lead it to identify patterns of abuse or misconduct by energy service providers. As discussed above, the post-modern regulator should share its market conduct findings with public and private consumer attorneys who may wish to initiate civil class actions against one or more providers on a co-counsel basis. As co-plaintiff in more egregious cases, the agency could protect against settlements that are not in the public interest. Because, in most jurisdictions, the civil courts share concurrent jurisdiction with the regulator, these kinds of actions can be funded by the awards of specific and general damages for tortious actions as well as general consumer-related statutory damages. As an example, when companies engage in inappropriate marketing transactions, the state attorney-general, local district attorneys and consumer class-action attorneys could utilise the state's Business and Professions Code to discourage such behaviour and gain remedies for affected consumers. The post-modern regulator should serve as a clearing-house for complaints and references to the attorneys. The regulator's public intake functions are an essential and low-cost means of identifying abuses. The private or prosecutorial attorneys offices can expeditiously act once the regulator alerts them to a pattern of deceit.

The post-modern regulator's resources are best utilised as a collector and distributor of information first, and a prosecutor second. However, where no private attorneys are willing or able to pursue a case, as is often the case against fly-by-night violators, the regulatory staff will be obligated to self-initiate regulatory action or to instruct its staff to pursue civil or criminal remedies, where warranted.

Help lower transaction costs for aggregation of customers

Small customers will need to be aggregated in order to gain adequate market leverage to benefit from electric competition. During the transition period, the post-modern regulator should be active in helping promote aggregation by properly educating customers.

While the regulator should not directly assist energy providers, it can serve as a coordinator for private companies to find customers. For example, at little extra cost, it can distribute information to the state's customers about available aggregators in rural, inner city and other underserved communities.

It can establish a hotline where interested consumers can learn of the potential aggregators. For example, the CPUC's cellular reseller programme cited above could have been more effective had Californians had a place to find these regulator-created resellers.

Finally, the post-modern regulator should require the distribution monopoly to utilise the monthly bills it sends to small customers for distribution service costs to include periodic inserts that list aggregators' names and information about them. Similarly, other state mailers, such as the California Department of Motor Vehicles and tax-related mailers can be used to disseminate basic information. It can distribute lists of qualified, certificated aggregators along with customer information about how to evaluate these services. In short, it can help reduce the significant transaction costs facing any service provider seeking to enter the mass market.

Every customer should have access to a personalised energy usage profile

In order to effectively comparison shop, customers will need to understand their energy consumption patterns and history of usage. It is unreasonable to expect that customers will have saved their bills over the previous three years in order to obtain this data. However, the regulated utility distribution company (or UDC) collects a certain amount of historical data about its customers, which can be used.

The UDCs should be ordered to provide, upon request, an energy usage profile for an individual customer. This profile would include a chart and breakdown of monthly data for energy consumption and price paid for energy over the previous 12–24 months, depending upon the information storage practices of each UDC (typically, utilities save 13–18 months of customer usage data). It should be adjusted for weather and price changes. It should also include a comparison to other representative customers' data so as to provide a benchmark against which a customer can compare their usage.

The first energy profile should be offered at no cost to customers. Modest charges may be applied to subsequent profile requests. This profile would provide the basis upon which customers could gauge their historical energy consumption patterns, better assess their energy needs and gain a sense of the cost of their electricity. This profile could be released by the customer to retail energy companies to better enable them to choose appropriate services for that customer.

Compulsory disclosure of relevant information

The post-modern regulator should consider requiring either the industry itself or an independent entity to establish an 'industry scorecard' or comparable mechanism that would present provider information and independent research in an understandable format. This format should be straightforward and simple, thus allowing consumers to easily compare the services, prices and service quality offered by each of the competing carriers. The scorecard would combine information disclosed by competing carriers and independent research on other entities, and present it in an understandable format that consumers could use to compare services.

The scorecard would consist of various minimum standards that each provider must meet to be included in the comparison. Carriers meeting the minimum standards would be rated according to the quality of service provided in various categories. Areas in which standards and ratings should be established would include at least the following:

- average customer service call holding times;
- total service complaints and complaint resolution percentages;
- ratios of service representatives to total service calls in customer service departments;
- time elapsed between orders taken and service installation or modification;
- availability of written offers, terms of service and price lists to prospective customers;

- billing clarity and simplification standards;
- privacy policies for collection and disclosure of personal information; and
- fair and standardized late fee, termination notice, and collections policies.

Preferably, the providers themselves should be required to create and publish the scorecard. However, given the problems with service quality currently found in the telecommunications market, energy providers are likely to be resistant to providing accurate and straightforward comparisons. Thus, it is likely that the appropriate government agency or independent policy institute may be required to develop the scorecard, at least in the short term.

Registration, licensure and bonding

Each energy provider should be registered with the state for identification purposes. However, the registration process needs to be stringent enough to protect customers, but not so onerous as to create a barrier to entry. The post-modern regulator can develop a registration process for service provider companies that is not overly burdensome. The process should include some method of bonding as a necessary precaution for electric service oversight. Bonding is needed because:

a Electric service is a necessity and generally is more expensive than a phone service. Thus greater protection is warranted.
b The upfront costs of entering the electric services market are fairly low. Aggregators need only a computer and customer leads. Thus the bonding requirement will not put an undue burden on any prospective new entrant as its start-up costs are relatively low.
c Without a bond it is likely that complainants will not be able to recover damages caused by failed service providers.
d The bonding process itself serves as a useful screen against companies or individuals with a questionable financial past who seek to enter the electricity market. Bonding services will either decline to bond or require higher deposits from entrants with questionable records.

The amount of the bond could be established based upon the prospective number of customers to be served. For example, a local community aggregator planning to serve fifty residents could post a very modest bond, whereas a large aggregator planning to serve customers throughout the state would require a more substantial bond. The challenge for the regulator will be to establish a reasonable level of forfeitable security while not making entry into the market prohibitively expensive for an energy provider. It is assumed that a municipal or state entity providing an electric service would be exempt from a bond requirement.

Compulsory codes of conduct

In the nascent energy service market, companies and customers will be unclear about their responsibilities and expectations. In order to facilitate smoother transition to a robust competitive market and to make clear what expectations exist about customer service behaviour, the post-modern regulator should develop a minimum code of conduct that will be provided to all registering energy service companies. This code would provide guidance for companies and their employees for all retail transactions. It would be distributed to all employees of these energy service companies and provided to customers upon request. As they are minimum codes, they represent the 'floor' of what would be expected, but can be surpassed by companies.

In this new market, it is not desirable for regulators and law-makers to devise rules and regulations for all possible consumer problems. But regulators can use the minimum code of conduct as a basis for determining the appropriateness of company conduct where a specific rule and regulation does not fit the conduct. This code could include clauses that address the following basic obligations:

1 Customers deserve accurate and understandable information. The consumer has a right to price and service information that is presented in a cogent and understandable manner and which can be compared to like service offered by other providers.
2 Electric service is a necessary service that all customers need. Thus the treatment of customers must reflect the importance of that service and the detrimental impact caused to customers when the service is not reliable, safe and affordable.
3 Customers have the right to advance notice (in writing, no less than thirty days in advance) of any change in rates or service that affects the customer.
4 When denied service, a customer should be notified of the reasons for a company deciding not to accept the customer. This information must be provided promptly and in writing upon request.
5 Customers can be charged reasonable service deposits and will be entitled to return deposits within a year after service is initiated. Criteria which established the need for a deposit must be applied equally to all customers.
6 Customers must get a timely and knowledgeable response from a company when a written complaint is filed with the company.
7 All customers must be given toll-free phone access for complaints or follow-up enquiries.
8 No customer must be held responsible for any service which is beyond the customer's control.
9 A customer threatened with disconnection has the right to at least four-

teen days' advance written notice of the proposed disconnection, except in cases of fraud.

10 Where fraud is alleged by the provider, the customer must be provided with specific notice of the allegations, and the provider bears the burden of proving the fraud.

11 Each customer should:

- explicitly approve use of personal consumption information by any provider other than their own;
- be informed in writing of the potential adverse privacy impacts of any new technologies deployed by providers, and shall be informed before signing up for a new service;
- have a right of access to their customer-specific information;
- have a reasonable means to obtain and review and, when necessary, correct and amend information about themselves which is held by a service provider; and
- be allowed to choose among various degrees of privacy protection, with respect to both the outflow of information about themselves and the receipt of incoming intrusions.

12 Systematic abuses of customers or questionable practices of other energy providers should be reported to the authorities.

Focus upon underserved communities

Even under the old regulatory paradigm, certain residential customer groups have been underserved relative to other customers. In telecommunications rural areas, low-income and minority groups, especially those with language diversity, were not as well served as other customer groups. In competitive markets, underserved communities will increase as private markets function to stratify social and economic classes. Residential consumers will be cherry-picked because the underlying objective of the competitive market is to discriminate. Unfortunately, the social objective of non-discriminatory electric services is undermined by this competitive reality (cf. Public Utilities Code 451 *et seq*., 453 *et seq*.).

The post-modern regulator must be acutely aware of the problems faced by traditionally underserved communities. There have been numerous good studies about these problems, notably by the National Consumer Law Center. Regulators should be fully aware of low-income, senior, rural, ethnic minority, inner city and other readily identifiable subgroups that have been disserved in telecommunications, banking and airline deregulation. Because of the equity factors, this task cannot be left, exclusively, to the private market because that market is, and will admit to being, ill-equipped to address this equitable objective. Markets pride themselves in achieving efficiency, not equity.

Thus, it is incumbent upon the Commission to focus its attention on potentially underserved communities. In a competitive electric market, these underserved communities may also be technologically dictated.

For example, areas with distribution constraints or unusual climatic zones may prove unattractive to aggregators. The Commission will need to pay special attention to the intentional or inadvertent discrimination that is engendered by the competitive market.

Privacy and information dilemmas for the post-modern regulator

The deregulation of electric services raises a number of new privacy issues that had not developed in the tightly controlled regulated industry. Existing Californian law strictly prohibits disclosure of utility customer information. However, the statutory controls are not applicable in a competitive market which relies on free-flowing market information to enhance competition.

In promoting dissemination of market information, the post-modern regulator must take care to ensure that customers are able to maintain control over their personal customer information. A dilemma will arise regarding the secondary usage of customer information. As will be explained below, the absence of controls over secondary usage will chill, rather than enhance, the growth of a competitive residential and small business market.

Privacy: as addressed in California

Currently access to personal utility customer information in California is limited by law. The right to privacy is an inalienable right under Article 1, Section 1, of the California Constitution. In addition, Public Utilities Code Section 588 expressly restricts the basis on which a utility may share personal customer information, including customer service usage information, with civil penalties attaching to violations. Other statutes also restrict access to residential and business information. For businesses and residential customers, control of information about their electric consumption is important. Large industrial customers have expressed concern that competitors can estimate production levels of goods they manufacture and may be able to determine production methods based on billing data. For these customers, billing data would or could be regarded as a trade secret. For residential customers, consumption usage is certainly personal. Protection for personal information accessed by utilities from residential customers has been given more explicit legislative attention, in part through an articulation of privacy concerns attendant to rights of protection against unreasonable search and seizure (see California Constitution, Article 1, Section 13). Different categories of information have been accorded higher levels of protection than others, but customer usage data has been amongst the most sensitive and, as a result, the most restricted. Credit information is also protected under special statute.

In the emerging competitive market place, marketers will have an insatiable thirst for as much information about prospective customers as possible. They will want information about energy consumption patterns, income distribution, the number of residents, the time spent at home, the appliances they use and other personal information. Unfortunately, this information is not only valuable to electric marketers – it is valuable to any marketer. For example, if a customer is approached by an energy marketer, it would be reasonable to share consumption patterns, income data and personal information about the residents, because they all relate to energy costs. However, that same customer would not necessarily share that same information with an insurance company or an employer. Yet, those latter entities could purchase this information from the energy provider. This is called 'secondary usage', and absent controls over such usage, it could discourage customers from sharing information with energy marketers.

Privacy concerns are not limited to disclosure of individual information. They also apply to how customers are contacted by potential service providers. Customers must have a meaningful method for providing or withholding consent to the disclosure of personal information to third parties. Customers must also have an effective means for withdrawing their consent or inviting access by competitors to their personal information. They must also have the capacity to choose which producers will be given the information and have the ability to limit the purposes for which it can be used (Givens 1997: 5–6).

The dynamic tension between the privacy interests of the individual and of business, and the competitive market place's thirst for customer information creates a problem that will not go away. For markets to function efficiently customers require information about the products and services available, and providers require information about the demands of potential customers. But release of customer information intended to reduce the barriers to entry and enhance competition will result in undesirable marketing practices and competitive harm to businesses.

The clearest solution for the post-modern regulator includes placing a strict prohibition upon the secondary use of personal customer information collected by an energy provider, unless that customer expressly consents to secondary usage. There obviously will be some costs associated with obtaining customer consent to release information and with preparing the data and delivering it to eligible providers. The implementation of information access must therefore assess the nature and magnitude of all relevant costs, and provide a means to recover those costs and compensate the appropriate parties.

A number of important privacy and information questions are raised by the utility's custody of the information. Should competitors and incumbent utilities have equal access to customer information, and if so, at what cost, if any? What, if any, should be the privacy standards governing retailers? Should customers have the right to expressly permit release of personal information or should that information be released by default if the customer fails to act affirmatively to preclude release.

In addressing this matter, the California legislature included strict prohibitions in AB1890 against uninformed switching of electric service so as to prevent the 'slamming' that occurred in telecommunications competition. Slamming (unauthorised transfer of service) protection provides a degree of overall consumer protection, but does not fully address the issue of protecting personal customer information or the obligations to be placed upon the utility for protecting customer information currently held.

Proposal for information clearing-house

The major problem facing policy makers grappling with customer information dissemination will be one of accountability. Information, once released, is difficult to control and leaks are difficult to trace. Prohibitions against secondary usage are simple to mandate and difficult to enforce. Moreover, information that is properly disseminated may be inaccurate, and thus create a whole new set of problems.

One solution has been informally raised by the California Energy Commission staff. This promising idea involves the creation of a retail information management (RIM) cooperative process. RIM involves the management of customer energy usage information, including meter data and related information. It encompasses diverse activities including metering, data communication, database management, hardware and software interface protocols and dissemination of and access to customer information. The creation of a cooperative RIM system would assist in dealing with:

- the huge volume of data involved;
- the diversity of users (including monopoly transmission and distribution companies, power exchange, independent scheduling coordinators, competitive retail providers and so on);
- the diversity of data providers serving the retail market;
- accuracy and security of customer consumption and financial information;
- the separation of information management from the distribution companies, while ensuring that the retail market is accountable; and
- encouraging the dissemination of consumer information so as to aid the development of the retail market.

To address these needs and objectives, an RIM system could be readily fashioned. It would be a centralised cooperative non-profit entity comprising industry members, in much the same way that Visa is comprised of banking institution members. Similarly, the semiconductor industry created Sematech to coordinate research activities by the industry. The entity would manage retail customer meter and billing data. The entity would be accountable to its stakeholders and would be obligated to faithfully abide by privacy rules established by the state's regulators.

Some of the activities of the RIM would include:

- obtaining meter data for all customers;
- maintaining a central database or coordinated networked database system, consisting of meter data and appropriate customer and retailer information;
- disseminating specified packages of information in a timely fashion; and
- maintaining security and accuracy of information flows.

The concept is a valuable one, as it helps avoid the creation of disjointed and proprietary information systems by utilities and others who have a vested interest in creating barriers to entry. Low-cost access to customer information is the only way in which one of the significant transaction costs of retail competition will be overcome. However, low-cost access will need to be balanced against the need to ensure accuracy and accountability of that customer information. The RIM could prove to be a low-cost and effective means of balancing those interests while helping build a competitive energy services market.

Conclusion

The above discussion focuses upon the role of the post-modern regulator in the evolving electric utility regulatory arena. Instead of regulating energy monopolies, the post-modern regulator will need to preserve and referee the competitive market place. This chapter suggests some new and very specific challenges that the post-modern regulator will need to meet in order to bring benefits of the competitive electric retail market to small business and residential customers. It concludes that the regulator's role will initially change but not diminish due to the need to guard against the inevitable breakdowns of the nascent unregulated market place. These information, privacy and competition problems can be offset by an informed regulator who uses non-intrusive strategies to prevent and quickly respond to the inevitable market breakdowns. Utilising private and social-sector institutions will give the post-modern regulator an enhanced ability to meet the challenges without having to increase demands upon regulatory staff.

References

California Constitution, Article 1, Section 13.

California Consumer Education Advisory Panel (1997) *Report to Commission on Consumer Education Plan*, July.

California Energy Markets (1997) September, p. 12.

California Public Utilities Commission Publication (1997) D97–04.

Consumer Action (1996) *Report on Long-Distance Rates (Telecommunications)*, May.

Consumer Reports (1996) May.

Dervin, B. (1995) *Evaluation of the October 11 Pacific Bell CNEP on Call Number Delivery*, Ohio: Ohio State University Press.

Drucker, P. (1993) *Post-Capitalist Society*, Harper Business.

Givens, B. (1997) *Privacy Rights Handbook*, California: Avon.

Office of Advocacy (1994) *How Small Business Learn: Final Report*, National Technical Information Service, Springfield, IL, p. 1.

Schuler, J. Jr (1996) 'Telecom Act Has Electrics At It Again', *Public Utilities Fortnightly*, December, p. 34.

State of California Public Utilities Legislation 1997, Public Utilities Code Sections 366–96.

Tellus Institute (1996) *Can We Get There From Here? The Challenge of Restructuring the Electricity Industry So That All Can Benefit*, Tellus Institute and Wisconsin Energy Conservation Corporation, April, pp. 2–4.

Utility Consumers' Action Network (1997) *Local Telephony Competition: Dysfunctional and Disconnected*, October.

7

BUSINESS-INDUCED BARRIERS IN EXPLAINING THE EFFECTS OF DEREGULATION

Two Swedish case studies

Maria Bengtsson, Agneta Marell and Andrew Baldwin

Introduction

A great deal of interest has been directed towards the degree of influence that public authorities should be allowed to exercise on industry. The role and influence of the state has changed in this respect over time, not least during this century. Carlsson (1990), for example, has identified three waves of regulation in the US: at the beginning of the century, in the 1930s, and in the 1960s. Similar waves of regulation can be identified in the Swedish economy, where deregulation and regulation as political tools have been used to increase the efficiency of the national economy (Eliasson 1993). Recently (i.e. during the 1980s and 1990s) deregulation rather than regulation has become the 'recipe' for a healthy economy.

According to microeconomic theory, healthy competition is brought about by perfect competition. Although microeconomic theory paints an ideal and normative picture, it has come to serve as a model for deregulation in order to obtain the advantages provided by perfect competition. Many empirical and theoretical studies of deregulation, however, show contradictory results (Shreiber 1977; Williams 1980; Coffman 1977; Teal and Berglund 1987; White 1988; Thomson 1992; Marell and Westin 1992), which is an argument against the belief that deregulation automatically brings about healthy competition.

We argue that focusing solely on the removal or replacement of a set of rules and regulations is not sufficient to be able to predict the outcome of a deregulation. Little consideration has been levelled at the effects of the pre-deregulation competitive situation on the outcome of a deregulation (Pagano and McKnight 1983). The existence of advantages due to scale and scope economies (Scherer 1980; Sölvell 1987), superior resources and capabilities

(Barney 1991; Hunt and Morgan 1996) etc., are argued here to be barriers to entry of significant importance for the result of a deregulation. This chapter is an attempt to emphasise the crucial role that business-induced barriers at the time of deregulation play in explaining the disparate effects of deregulation.

Healthy competition – the goal of deregulation

Healthy competition

Originating from theories of perfect competition, the goal of deregulation can be summarised as achieving intensive competition among many companies. The intensity in competition is low in regulated industries either because of the restrictions that hinder new entry and stimulate a development towards a concentration of the industry, or because of restrictions that prohibit interaction among competitors. If an industry (due to regulation) consists of few firms, companies will tend to adapt their actions to each other rather than to compete. Yo and Ito (1988) and Scherer (1980) state that competitors in oligopolistic industries tend to avoid intensive rivalry, and become defensive in their actions. Scherer's (1980) explanation of the coordination of action in oligopolistic industries is based on Chamberlin's (1933) theory that companies adapt to each other without explicit collusion arising between them. Companies are aware both of the prevailing interdependency and of the fact that conflicting action worsens the situation for all companies involved. Companies therefore become passive in their competition if the degree of concentration is high.

A deregulation is supposed to result in new entrants and thus a decrease in concentration and an increase in the intensity of competition. Scherer (1980) argues that oligopolistic coordination ceases when the number of actors increases. It is then probable that the competing companies may have different views on what constitutes the most advantageous action for all concerned, and therefore act in rivalry. This is seen as healthy competition which is the goal of deregulation.

Economic effects due to healthy competition

Three economic effects are mainly supposed to follow from healthy competition, and these effects explain why healthy competition is the goal of deregulation. First, competition is assumed to lead to an effective resource allocation. Adamson *et al.* (1991), Banister (1990) and Kay and Vickers (1988) argue that the purpose with privatisation and deregulation is that the suppliers should be more efficient. Differences in profit potential in terms of long-term return on investment provide firms with the incentive to operate in a way that offers the firm a higher profit or return, and to be more effective in their resource allocation (cf. Caves and Porter 1977 and Porter 1980, amongst others). Regulation can also be costly, both in terms of administration and maintenance by the state. It might be expensive for firms to keep up to date with existing rules, changing rules and new rules (Wiedenbaum 1981). Furthermore, different regulations can be contradictory and therefore inefficient, incurring greater costs, as does the persistence of obsolete regulations.[1]

Closely related to the argument about intense competition and an effective resource allocation is the second assumed effect of deregulation, that prices will fall due to a more efficient resource allocation (Backman 1981). Perfect competition is considered to be synonymous with price competition, and, over a period of time, the mechanisms of the perfect market lead to an effective allocation of resources. Cost-effective companies survive, and prices stabilise at a level where supply and demand match each other, which is held to be in the interest of customers. Through deregulation similar effects are assumed to arise. Houthakker (1981), however, holds that there is no evidence that competition will lead to increased productivity and he questions the theory of perfect competition, arguing that it is static and lacks the ability to incorporate market dynamics (an essential issue which has been widely overlooked in theory).

A third, rarely mentioned, argument for deregulation and intense competition is that rivalry stimulates innovative behaviour and development within industries. Adam Smith (1776, 1976) describes competition as the 'invisible hand' that forces action, Porter (1990) shows that rivalry is an important catalyst in industries, and Schumpeter (1942) argues that competition is a significant driving force behind technological development. Hunt and Morgan (1996) argue that even if the entrepreneurial capability to invent is lacking, the competitive process forces companies to invent, i.e. to produce reactive innovations. The core of this type of reasoning is that vigorous competition gives rise to a pressure to improve and innovate, i.e. to dynamics. Diversity in competition is seen to be central. Porter (1990) considers that, in the presence of many local competitors, the pressure to create improvements and innovations in operations relative to competitors becomes greater.

Deregulation – a sufficient recipe for intense competition and efficiency?

At first glance the assumption that deregulation will increase competition seems to be relevant. But if we consider the fact that companies' actions affect the competitive conditions in the industry, the assumption is not that obvious. Competitive conditions in a regulated industry are complex and include dimensions other than those related to the political restrictions that regulate the industry. The complexity of deregulation is addressed by, for example, Foerster and Gilbert (1979), who argue that price, entry and concentration pre-deregulation do have an impact on the outcome of a deregulation. The authors emphasise that deregulation has to be seen in its entire context, as any effects of deregulation are the result of interplay. In view of the above we argue that it is not given that the intensity in competition increases automatically with the removal or replacement of political regulations. We believe that the outcome of a deregulation also depends on other barriers to competition than politically induced barriers. Entry barriers arise as a result of both state regulations and actions taken by firms within the industry. It is therefore crucial that the effects of deregulation are not analysed in isolation.

Business-induced barriers and resource advantages

The reason why it is important to not just analyse a deregulation in terms of politically induced entry barriers is that markets are imperfect. Business-induced barriers also exist within an industry. Actual competition takes place on imperfect markets, which implies that business opportunities can be imperfectly exploited by the companies within the industry (Dickson 1992). Industrial organisation theory (IO theory) distinguishes between different types of imperfect markets by analysing the structure of an industry. Common structural dimensions considered in traditional theory, are cost structure, number and size distribution, the degree of vertical integration, the degree of differentiation, the degree of diversification and the degree of research and development (Schmalensee 1988; Scherer 1980; Knickerbocker 1973; Worcester 1957; Coase 1937; Williamson 1975, 1981). The structural variables give rise to what we call business-induced barriers or advantages that hinder exit and/or entry into an industry, and thereby give rise to dependency between the actors (Bain 1956; Yip 1982; Sölvell 1987).

Sölvell (1987) summarises the literature concerning entry barriers that can be linked to different structural conditions within an industry. Concentration constitutes an entry barrier due to the potential for collusion (cf. also Yo and Ito 1988). Concentration and the existence of a dominant firm can also imply a high degree of familiarity as a consequence of repeated exposure to the brand name or to the product. An increase in familiarity is commonly argued to correspond to an increase in liking or to a more positive judgement, which in turn affects behaviour. The correspondence between exposure, familiarity and attitudes is widely addressed in existing literature (cf., amongst others, Ajzen and Fishbein 1977; Zajonc 1980; Anand and Sternthal 1991).

Other barriers that can be traced to market structure can be mentioned. An effective cost structure constitutes barriers due to economies of scale and proprietary learning; product differentiation leads to brand loyalty and switching costs; a high degree of diversification implies barriers due to economies of scope, opportunities for cross-fertilisation and cost of capital advantages; and finally vertical integration leads to barriers due to economies of joint operations, cost of capital advantages and price discrimination (Sölvell 1987).

Business-induced entry barriers such as economies of scope, economies of scale and/or proprietary learning give the incumbents advantages in relation to potential entrants. Thus a business-induced barrier can be defined as a relative competitive advantage due to actions taken by firms. This definition of an entry barrier implies that other advantages not studied to the same extent within economic theory need to be included. Hunt and Morgan (1996) focus on the firm and argue that a firm's resource advantage is of crucial importance for competition, and from our point of view such advantages commonly held by the incumbents within an industry also must be described as business-induced barriers to entry. Resource advantages can be both tangible and intangible, and Barney (1991) argues that a resource has to be valuable, rare, imperfect, imitable and have a low degree of substitutability if it is to be seen as a resource advantage. Business-induced barriers can thus include intangible advantages such as a superior entrepreneurial skill (cf. Hunt and Morgan 1996).

Barriers to entry and intensity in competition pre- and post-deregulation

The business-induced barriers that together encompass an industry can be described through the metaphor of walls, where an industry is surrounded by a wall which 'protects' the firms. This wall is comprised of 'bricks' of entry barriers, both politically induced and business-induced, and can be of varying height, depending on how well developed the entry barriers have become. If a potential new entrant desires to become an incumbent it has to overcome the wall of barriers surrounding the industry. The new entrant has to invest in the existing entry barriers (such as developed economies of scale, a developed distribution system or brand loyalty) if he/she is to overcome the barriers that encompass the industry. The intangible advantages are difficult to leapfrog as tacit knowledge and capabilities are not possible to build in a planned and codified way (cf. Kogut and Zander 1996). In this sense, both tangible and intangible entry barriers can be considered to be the shared assets of the incumbents, because entry barriers hinder potential competitors from entering the industry (Porter 1979). Entry barriers incorporated in the incumbent firms simultaneously act as exit barriers. An incumbent's well-developed distribution net functioning as an entry barrier against new entrants also requires enormous investment in dismantling if the incumbent desires to leave the industry. If entry costs can be likened to the difference in 'height' of the barriers surrounding the industries, the same can be said of the relevant exit barriers.

The discussion carried in this chapter has led to the following assumption:

regulated industries differ from each other, depending on the 'height' of the politically induced entry barriers and on the 'height' of business-induced entry barriers. Politically induced barriers can include price control, entry restrictions and other regulation, and business-induced barriers include action taken by firms (and can be said to express the imperfection of the market). A deregulation does not mean that all the entry barriers encompassing an industry are removed or replaced. If the entry barriers constitute mainly politically induced barriers combined with few business-induced entry barriers, deregulation may ease entry and thereby increase the intensity of competition. If, on the other hand, the industry is encompassed by mainly business-induced entry barriers combined with few politically induced entry barriers, the outcome of deregulation has to be predicted from an analysis of the competitive situation with respect to business-induced barriers. The composition of the business-induced barriers will still affect the competitive situation within the industry post-deregulation.

In Figure 7.1, we illustrate four possible competitive situations that can be used to describe competition before and after a deregulation. The competitive situation characterised by low entry barriers and intense competition can be compared with the competitive situation that in traditional theory is assumed to be a result of a deregulation. This situation is represented by an *0* in the figure and is the desired post-deregulation situation. Owing to low intensity in competition, two possible 'before' deregulation situations can be identified and the 'before' situations are represented by X_1 and X_2 in the figure. In both situations the intensity in competition is low as a result of the politically induced barriers that exist, but the height of the business-induced barriers varies.

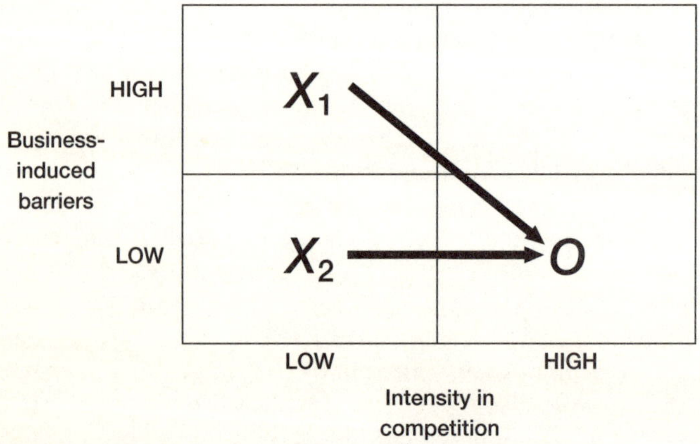

Figure 7.1 Competitive arenas before and after a deregulation

The study

Two industries have been studied: the postal industry and the taxi-cab industry. The postal service represents the pre-deregulated situation X_1 (the scale and scope advantages amongst others are high), and the taxi-cab industry represents the pre-deregulated situation X_2 (where mainly familiarity advantages exist). The study of the taxi-cab industry consists of secondary data collected by means of taxi-cab logs four months prior to deregulation, eight months after deregulation and four years after deregulation (see Gärling *et al.* 1995 and Laitila *et al.* 1995 for a detailed description). Personal interviews have also been conducted with representatives from the major taxi-cab dispatch services within Stockholm, Gothenburg, Malmö and Sundsvall, seven years after deregulation.

The study of the postal service industry is mainly a review of secondary data. The postal service industry has long been characterised by monopoly but competition was introduced in 1991 by a new entrant. The competition between the previous monopolist the Swedish Post Office and the new entrant City-mail has been the subject of legal discussions under Swedish competition law. Both competitors have presented many petitions to the government in order to ascertain whether the Post Office has been fair or unfair in competition, and official investigations have been conducted. These memorandums have been reviewed. Personal interviews with representatives from both companies have also been conducted.

Three main questions guided the data collection in both industries. First, what business-induced barriers to entry were present before deregulation? Second, what barriers to entry remained after deregulation? Third, how intense was the competition after deregulation? Entry barriers, for example scale advantages, brand loyalty, scope advantages and cost of capital advantages, are discussed qualitatively, and intensity in competition is measured as changes in price.

Deregulation of the taxi-cab industry

Removal of political rules

In this section of the chapter the development pre- and post-deregulation will be discussed. The deregulation of the Swedish taxi-cab industry in 1990 was fairly extensive in comparison to the deregulation of both the taxi-cab industry in a number of American cities, and of local and regional bus traffic in the UK. What distinguished the Swedish taxi-cab deregulation further was that the entire process was implemented simultaneously. The primary purpose of the taxi-cab deregulation was to guarantee free entry into the market. However, to ensure a certain standard among taxi-cab owners, e.g. economic capability and no criminal record, the test of the driver's knowledge and his/her suitability was sharpened, which meant that the suitability of taxi-cab owners was to be checked, and all taxi cabs were required to be equipped with receipt-writing meters.

The deregulation also involved the introduction of free price-setting and the abolition of the maximum rate. This meant that it became possible to adjust prices to different levels of demand and production costs, in that demand differences often depended on the time of day and geographic location. An additional requirement was that the applied rate was to be accessible to the passenger prior to the trip. A further effect of the deregulation involved abandoning the specification of geographic operating areas for taxi cabs. This made it possible, for example, for drivers in suburban municipalities to traffic inner city areas at peak hours. Removing these operating barriers allowed competition to arise between taxi cabs from different areas. Consequently, operating schedules were abolished. When taxi cabs were free to operate independent of location, it became no longer possible for the authorities to specify local or regional taxi-cab supply (in hours). Finally, the former requirement for all taxi cabs to belong to a radio-dispatch service (usually one per municipality) was also abandoned, making it possible to establish new dispatch services, and thereby increase competition. Apart from dissolving existing regulations, a few new restrictions were introduced. As mentioned above, the applied rate was to be accessible to the passenger and receipt-writing meters were required in all cars. All taxi cabs were also required to have a 'for hire' sign visible, a sign issued only to licensed taxi cabs. In return, taxi cabs with this sign were permitted to use traffic lanes reserved for public buses.

These deregulations were implemented in order to bring about a more efficient industry, new business concepts, an expanded market through new services, economies of scale and increased access; i.e. more taxi cabs, improved services and lower prices.

Number of dispatch services

One consequence of the pre-deregulation conditions within the taxi-cab industry was that all taxi cabs belonged to the only operating dispatch service within their geographical area. This dispatch service therefore had a monopoly over a restricted geographical site/area. This was the case throughout Sweden with the exception of Malmö. In 1987, the dispatch service in Malmö divided into two dispatch services in exception to the monopoly, and later further divisions were implemented. Consequently, Malmö had five competing dispatch services within the same geographical area at the time of deregulation in 1990. However, it should be noted that the number of licences were controlled in the same way as in the rest of Sweden. An analysis of demand was always made by both the County Administration

Board and the taxi-cab companies themselves to establish the need for more taxi cabs.

With the exception of Malmö, customers were generally aware of the existence of one dispatch service. In Stockholm and Gothenburg many customers were satisfied with the service provided in terms of access time, driver service travel time, the dispatch service and taxi-cab comfort (Gärling *et al.* 1995). Many customers also knew the dispatch service telephone number by heart, and a familiarity advantage existed within the industry that can be described as an entry barrier. The familiarity advantage was therefore stronger in Stockholm, Gothenburg and Sundsvall than in Malmö.

Post-deregulation development

After deregulation, new dispatch services were formed and established throughout Sweden. In many cities the previously monopolised dispatch services were divided into two or more dispatch services and many cities and municipalities experienced new entries into the market. In Gothenburg, for example, three new dispatch services were formed through the split-up of the previous dispatch service and through new taxi-cab entrants at the time of deregulation. In Stockholm, new competitors rapidly entered the market. New entrants and organisational changes in the former monopolist service resulted in four larger dispatch services. In both Stockholm and Gothenburg the former monopolist remained as the market leading dispatch service after deregulation and still today (1997) have a major influence. In Stockholm, 'Taxi-Stockholm' has 40 per cent of the market share. The closest competitors have a market share of around 20 per cent. The situation in Gothenburg is similar; the market leader has around 50 per cent of the market and the closest competitor has less than 20 per cent. No new dispatch services or traditional competitors emerged in Malmö, which meant that the incumbent full-service dispatch services remained the same. However, new dispatch services, such as mini single taxi cabs, have been established in Malmö.

Interviews with the market-leading dispatch services in Gothenburg revealed a tendency to reduce its relative power, in order to avoid unattractive attention due to a dominant position. 'Taxi Gothenburg's strategy is to systematically reduce their cruising fleet. As soon as someone retires or quits for any other reason, his or her place is not filled.

A new type of competitor, the 'single cruising taxi cab', entered the market in many cities. The 'single cruising cab' had no association with a dispatch service and operates entirely on its own. The relative number of single cruising taxi cabs in Malmö differs significantly from Stockholm and Gothenburg, in that approximately 40 per cent of the total cruising fleet does not belong to a dispatch service (compared to approximately 20 per cent in Stockholm and 10–20 per cent in Gothenburg). In Table 7.1 the number of taxi cabs per 1,000 inhabitants is shown. In Stockholm, Gothenburg,

Table 7.1 Taxi cabs per 1,000 inhabitants in different cities: 1990, 1994 and 1996

	1990	*1994*	*1996*
Stockholm	2.33	2.82	3.02
Gothenburg	1.21	1.54	1.76
Malmö	1.25	1.70	1.82
Sundsvall	1.01	1.37	1.31

Source: SCB T21 SM 9701, 9501, 9001.

Malmö and Sundsvall the numbers of taxi cabs have increased since the time of deregulation.

Intensity in competition – prices

In the autumn of 1990, immediately after deregulation, prices rose sharply within the taxi-cab industry (Gärling *et al.* 1995), and in January 1991, VAT was implemented for all transport services, which resulted in additional increases of rates. However, irrespective of VAT, rates increased more during the first eight months than the general price index accounted for (Laitila *et al.* 1995).

Prices began to fall after this initial period (Gärling *et al.* 1995). As illustrated in Table 7.2, prices for privately paid journeys were at a higher level in 1994 compared to 1990, although the increase is almost negligible if VAT is taken into account. Prices for public-subsidised trips, on the other hand, had decreased during the same period.

The studies by Gärling *et al.* (1995) and Laitila *et al.* (1995) had very few single cruising taxi cabs filling out the trip diary, as the 'single cruising taxi cabs' to a greater extent than others did not wish to participate. Since the interviews in this study reveal that the 'single cruising taxi cabs' often charge a higher price (particularly for unwitting customers at, for example, airports or bus stations), the picture of how rates have developed for private trips might be a little different. The tendency for an increase would perhaps be more unquestionable. It is also interesting to note that it is the single cruising cabs that have higher rates for private passengers (who constitute the sole customer segment). The larger dispatch services are unable to differentiate in the same manner in that loyalty and integrity towards the customer have to be maintained to a greater degree. Loyalty acts as protection for the customer, which means that loyalty as a business-induced barrier is an entry barrier to any new entrant desiring to set up a credible business.

The interviews also reveal that price differentiation or market segmentation within the industry in Stockholm and Gothenburg is acknowledged. The same service (i.e the same taxi cab, the same driver, with the same appearance) is offered to private customers, to customers that are publicly subsidised, and to customers employed by companies with agreements with a taxi-cab company, but different prices are charged. Publicly subsidised trips (i.e. the transport of disabled persons, patients and schoolchildren, and as a complement to public transport) are negotiated by county councils, local health authorities and those responsible for public transport. This means that the buyer has access to a great deal of information, and can therefore choose the best and cheapest alternative (i.e. the alternative that is most economically advantageous, not necessarily the cheapest alternative) that meets the agreed-upon criteria.

The price for transporting private customers from restaurants or to airports, for example, is charged at a higher level by the dispatch services, who also provide publicly subsidised trips. Customers using single cruising cabs are likely to pay an even higher price. This implies that prices decrease in some areas but remain constant or increase in other areas within Stockholm and Gothenburg, the two large municipalities in Table 7.2.

Most of the single cruising cabs charge a little extra premium, which is possible to do partly because of the customers' relatively low experience and consequential lack of information about the 'fairness in a price', and partly due to the customers' lack of information about when the next taxi cab will appear and what price will be charged then.

A different situation has evolved in Malmö (a large municipality, not included in the Laitila *et al.* study of 1995) than those in Gothenburg and Stockholm. Malmö had no monopolist at the time of deregulation and still lacks a market leader. The largest dispatch service has 15 per cent of the market share. The closest competitor is about the same size. The number of taxi cabs belonging to a dispatch service is lower than in Stockholm or Gothenburg. Prices in Malmö have been divided into three separate groups. First, the full service dispatch services generally charge a higher price than many of the 'mini taxi cabs' do. Second, mini taxi cabs have very low prices and are primarily marketed towards private customers. The interviews reveal a common assumption that the prices charged by mini taxi cabs do not 'make

Table 7.2 Prices for taxi-cab trips in SKr per kilometre, and SKr per hour (1990 prices, in SKr)

	Large municipalities		*Medium-sized municipalities*		*Small municipalities*	
	1990	*1994*	*1990*	*1994*	*1990*	*1994*
Price/trip kilometre						
privately paid	11.00	11.80	10.20	11.14	9.90	12.50
publicly subsidised	10.40	9.30	13.90	9.40	9.10	10.00
Price/trip hour						
privately paid	309	325	295	330	264	325
publicly subsidised	272	243	288	235	301	347

Source: Laitila *et al.* (1995).

ends meet' and that no serious company that pays all of its social insurance fees can charge such a low price. Furthermore, some time ago the dispatch services in Malmö started to notice a collaboration between some of the 'single cruising taxi cabs'. For instance, they started to buy automobiles in the same colour and by the same manufacturer. Third, some 'single cruising taxi cabs' charge a higher price, for similar reasons to those given in the discussion concerning Stockholm and Gothenburg.

The case of Sundsvall is similar to that of Stockholm and Gothenburg, with respect to prices and customer target groups. In Sundsvall, the dispatch service was divided into two separate dispatch services. They both provided service for the citizens of Sundsvall for about five years. After five years they merged, the reason being that cost efficiency would increase by the merger.

Deregulation of the postal industry

The Swedish Post Office has held a monopolistic position in the Swedish postal service for more than 300 years. The industry saw in 1991 the arrival of a competitor in one small niche of the postal service market, when City-Mail Sweden AB was established. This new entry into the postal service market was instrumental in leading to a deregulation of the postal service market in 1993. In this section the postal industry's development pre- and post-deregulation will be discussed.

Pre-deregulation period

The Swedish postal service market has effectively been a monopoly for centuries due to regulations that became more and more formalised. One of the underlying reasons for regulation was to guarantee delivery to the entire country. The postal service market has expanded both in size and scope during the twentieth century due to the efforts of the Swedish Post Office (cf. SOU 1962: 52). The expansion of the market can be exemplified by the introduction of different types of *korsband* (mass rates and group rates for different types of printed matter) that made possible the distribution of addressed and unaddressed printed matter and advertising parallel to the normal delivery of letter post. That in turn led both to increased contributions to margins to the rest of the Post Office's operations, and to an increased capacity utilisation of the distribution system. The expansion of the postal service played an important part in the build-up of the Post Office's nation-wide distribution system (Nyhetsposten Swedish Post Office 1996: 1).

Besides the increase in product segments the volume within each segment also increased during the twentieth century. Increased volume brought with it increased demands for measures aimed at further rationalisation and efficiency of the postal service. One such measure was the introduction of postal codes, which began in 1968. This numerical division of the country made it possible to increase the efficiency of the sorting and distribution of post, which resulted in discounts being offered for large distributions of post sorted according to the postal code (Jonason 1996). The Swedish Post Office also invested in a number of sorting terminals based on machine sorting of post. Another rationalisation that was introduced in 1981 was based on the differentiation of post according to handling time, handling routines and amount, i.e. first- and second-class mail (The Post Office financial report 1980/81). By differentiating between post that required immediate delivery and post that could be delivered after a few days, the logistics involved could be improved upon and made more efficient – allowing a 'smoothing out' of the flow of post and thereby decreasing the costs involved in the delivery of post.

The expansion of the market also meant that the traditional letter post decreased in relative importance for the total postal services market. Industrial post, i.e. large deliveries from firms to households, held an approximate 50 per cent share of the total market in 1996, while letters to private individuals took only 5 per cent. The remainder of the total market, i.e. 45 per cent, constituted stamped business post (Nerep 1997). The Swedish Post Office was and still is the only firm that can both deliver all types of post and deliver nation-wide.

The deregulation of the postal service market and new entry

CityMail Sweden AB entered the market in 1991, delivering industrial post to several postcode areas in Stockholm. The company's entry into the market gave rise to a debate about the necessity of retaining a postal monopoly in Sweden, resulting in the deregulation of the Post Office's lawful monopoly on 1 January 1993. One of the main objectives with this deregulation was to improve the efficiency of the postal service through the introduction of free competition. To ensure that the political goals concerning the postal services could be fulfilled, an agreement was reached between the state and the Swedish Post Office in 1994 which was to last until the end of 1996. The purpose of the agreement was to ensure that the political goals concerning the postal services would be fulfilled during the transitionary period that follows any deregulation. The Swedish Post Office undertook to deliver post 'overnight' and to maintain a nation-wide delivery service, which was considered a crucial goal for the Swedish postal services.

The deregulation made it possible for firms such as CityMail and Svensk Direktreklam AB to establish operations in the postal services. CityMail's business concept was to (1) establish operations within a delimited product and market area in order to build up a platform for further expansion in other geographical areas, and (2) to base operations on a different logic of distribution than that of the Swedish Post Office, thereby being able to offer its services at a lower level of price. CityMail's operations were geographically limited to Stockholm with a product range limited to large business deliveries, so-called industrial post. This meant that the firm established itself in a market segment that had previously constituted approximately 10 per cent of the Swedish Post Office's total market. CityMail's logic of production was based on distributing post that was pre-sorted, and by not having to sort post, they were also able to eliminate one stage of production, i.e. the sorting, and thereby eliminate the costs associated with this stage. According to the interview with the owner of CityMail the company gained competitive advantage relative to the Swedish Post Office through this, which in effect was a prerequisite to be able to establish operations in a previously monopolised market.

The intensity in competition after deregulation

The effects of deregulation can be described in terms of increased intensity in competition. It can be measured by the changes in price in different product and market segments. Other effects of deregulation can also be observed by investigating the two emerging patterns of competition between the two rival firms from their correspondence with official authorities about what was fair competition.

The deregulation of the postal services industry has led to markedly reduced prices within the area where competition occurs. After the deregulation, the Swedish Post Office introduced a new pricing system with different rates for volume deliveries and a rate for distribution in certain areas of the Stockholm region, which according to CityMail constituted 95 per cent of its distribution area. The Post Office claims that this area is a more lucrative market compared with certain rural areas, and that this reasoning lay behind the changes in pricing. The Post Office decreased its so-called "Stockholm prices" at the same time as the normal rates were increased in order to 'better meet the demands of our customers and to cover the costs of different types of distribution' (quotation from the Post Office's notice of the new price list for 1995 from 30 September 1994). The Post Office also offered discounts for volume deliveries addressed to the postal code areas exposed to competition. Several examples of the changes in price that were suggested can be found in Tables 7.3 and 7.4.

CityMail complained to the Swedish Competition Authority regarding the Post Office's notified changes in price. The assessment of the Swedish Competition Authority was that the Post Office's price differentiation was not contrary to competition law if the region in which the price differentiation is offered can be said to constitute a geographically relevant market. The Swedish Competition Authority also held that the Stockholm area could be considered a delimited relevant market because the competitive situation in this region differed in character from the competition in other regions.

Table 7.3 Changes in price for small post where the Swedish Post Office did not meet with any competition

Single letters and parcels and deliveries numbering less than 1,000		
Weight in grams	*Current price (in kronor)*	*New price (in kronor)*
20	2.86	2.95
100	5.72	5.89
250	11.07	11.16
500	17.86	17.86
1,000	24.11	24.11

Table 7.4 Drop in price for volume deliveries where the Swedish Post Office met with competition (all prices were dropped compared with previous levels, although the drop varies between the volume sizes)

Delivery volume	*New price for volume deliveries (in SEK)*	*Stockholm price when posted for delivery in Stockholm (in SEK)*	*Stockholm price from the rest of the country (in SEK)*
1,000–10,000 <20gm	2.85	2.25	2.45
1,000–10,000 >20gm	2.85	2.25	2.45
10,001–50,000 <20gm	2.75	2.15	2.35
10,001–50,000 >20gm	2.75	2.15	2.35
50,001– <20gm	2.65	2.05	2.25
50,001– >20gm	2.65	2.05	2.25

The Swedish Competition Authority therefore decided in November 1994 that there was no reason to intervene in the Swedish Post Office's use of Stockholm pricing.

The Swedish Post Office subsequently applied for approval of further more detailed action based on the 1995 price list (KKV dnr 682/95). From the Post Office's written comments on the Swedish Competition Authority's draft decision, it can be read that "the Swedish Competition Authority had opinion on the Post Office's volume discounts and could therefore not grant approval". As the Post Office acquired CityMail in April 1995, the case was formally dropped, but the Swedish Competition Authority decided to investigate the Stockholm price on its own initiative. After a while, the Post Office wanted to shut down CityMail, based on the argument that the company was not making a profit. However, during the acquisition, the Post Office had promised not to shut down the company if there were other parties interested in running the company. CityMail therefore re-emerged as a separate company, three-quarter-owned by foreign investors, one-quarter-owned by its previous owners.

The Swedish Post Office subsequently intensified its price competition relative to CityMail in its proposed price list for 1996, which included further reductions in price within the Stockholm region.

The Swedish Competition Authority shared the Post and Telecom Board's opinion, and therefore took an interim decision that the Swedish Post Office was forbidden to implement the new prices, punishable by heavy fines, until the case had been finally settled. Despite this, the Swedish Post Office continued its offensive pricing strategy by giving notice in May 1996 of its intentions to expand its Stockholm pricing, which included reducing the lower volume limit for delivery in Stockholm from 1,000 articles to 500. The Swedish Post Office also applied in autumn 1996 for permission to utilise Stockholm prices in Malmö, Gothenburg and a number of other cities in Sweden (KKV dnr 601/96; KKV dnr 1142/96). This application was made at the same time as CityMail announced its plans to expand operations to include Malmö and Gothenburg. The Swedish Competition Authority was hesitant over this proposed action in October 1996. Since then, the Swedish Post Office has given notice of its intentions to defy the decision of the Swedish Competition Authority, deciding to implement the new pricing system. According to the Swedish Post Office, this is due to the fact that if no price differentiation is implemented, prices must either be reduced over the entire country, or the higher price level must be maintained. Either strategy would make the Swedish Post Office profitable.

Besides the price competition described above, CityMail copnsultants, advocates and researchers have claimed that the Post Office has not been fair in its competition since the deregulation. The Post Office made use of exclusivity clauses, loyalty discounts, bonus systems and volume-based annual bonuses to retain the major customers (Nerep 1997). One case that drew much attention was the Post Office's contract clause in its agreements with business customers which meant that the Post Office was given the unilateral right to raise the price if a customer resorted to a competitor for partial distribution. By using CityMail for a certain amount of distribution, and thereby decreasing distribution costs for that area of distribution, a customer ran the risk of an increase in its total costs for distribution (KKV dnr 479/93). CityMail was unable to offer customers a total distribution solution because the company had neither nation-wide distribution nor a comprehensive product range.

CityMail claimed that, through its contract clause, the Swedish Post Office competed unfairly, and therefore complained to the Swedish Competition Authority, who instructed the Post Office in 1994 to cease its so-called *russinplockarklausul* (a 'skimming strategy clause', i.e. a clause that hinders customers from selecting only some services from competitors; this restricts new competitors' ability to only compete on the most profitable segements). The Swedish Post Office revised its *russinplockarklausul* to encompass only the product segment covering large deliveries from businesses, public authorities and other organisations (which entailed limiting the clause to CityMail's particular product niche), and to the Stockholm area (which was CityMail's geographical market). In 1995, based on previous decisions, the Swedish Competition Authority decided that the Stockholm area could be considered a delimited relevant market, which meant that there was no reason to take measures against the Swedish Post Office's use of the revised clause (KKV dnr 1417/94). This decision was recalled by the Swedish Competition Authority in 1996, due to changes in market conditions – new competitors had established themselves in the market, and CityMail had given notice of its intentions to expand its market geographically to include Malmö and Gothenburg.

Entry barriers and the outcome of the deregulations

The post- and pre-deregulation developments of the postal services industry, the taxi-cab industry in Gothenburg, Stockholm and Sundsvall, and the taxi-cab industry in Malmö differ from each other, with regard both to the business-induced barriers that prevailed in the industries before and after the deregulation and to the effects in terms of changes in price due to intensive competition.

Different barriers to entry before the deregulation

All the industries studied were characterised by a lack of competition and thus the intensity in competition was low before the deregulation. The business-induced barriers differed between the industries, however. On account of its former legal monopoly, the Post Office had been able to develop considerable, or 'high' entry barriers that encompassed the entire postal service market. These entry barriers included advantages of scope, where the Post Office had been able to develop and maintain a widespread range of products (which in effect defined the postal service), economies of scale in sorting the post, a widespread distribution system that covered the entire nation, combined with a capacity of overnight delivery even to rural areas (cf. Nerep 1997). The Post Office also has the advantage of loyalty due to the history and size of the company. These barriers can be said to be considerable business-induced entry barriers that, combined with the politically induced entry barriers, encompassed the postal services industry prior to deregulation.

The combined entry barriers in the taxi-cab industry consisted primarily of familiarity barriers. These were higher in Stockholm, Gothenburg and Sundsvall, due to the existence of a monopolist, than in Malmö, having five dispatch services at the time of the deregulation. The pre-deregulation situation for each industry is illustrated in Figure 7.2 with black dots in time 1 (T_1).

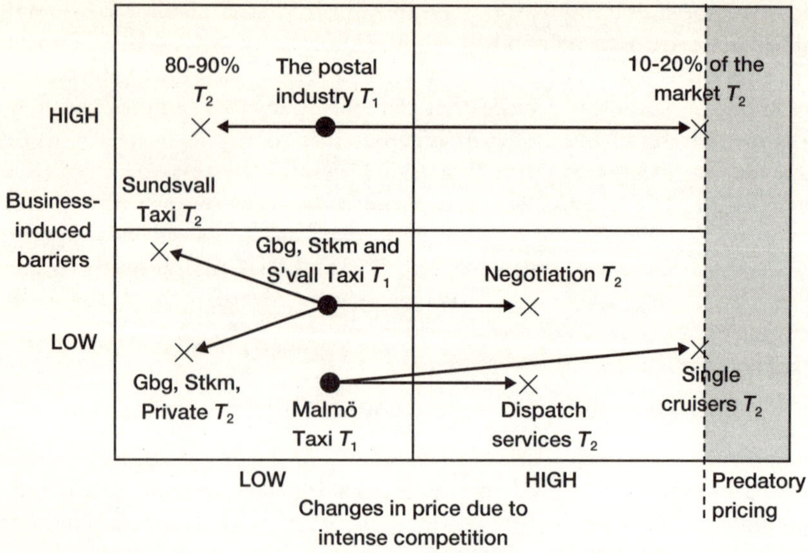

Figure 7.2 Business-induced barriers and intensity in competition before and after the deregulation of the studied industries

Changes due to the deregulation

The deregulation of the postal services industry gave rise to an intense competition in the product and market segments where CityMail and the Post Office competed (about 10–20 per cent of the market), whereas the intensity in other segments decreased in the sense that the price has increased but the entry or exit barriers remained at pre-deregulation level. The rates within the Stockholm region decreased step by step over the years, finally reaching a level that many claimed was predatory pricing (this, however, could not be proved). The decrease in price can be interpreted as a result of the deregulation and the competition that emerged between CityMail and the Post Office. It was possible, however, for the Post Office to use its monopoly power and replace the profit/loss within the Stockholm region by increasing its rates in other regions (although the Post Office argues that the increase and decrease in price was motivated by customer needs, and costs related to different products).

The increase and decrease in prices in different areas can also be explained from the exit barriers on the opposite side of the pre-reform advantages and entry barriers. The Post Office as an organisation has been built over a long period of time, whereas the current organisation is the result of a long series of reforms. Furthermore, the Post Office is a large organisation with in-built inertia tending towards centralised solutions and economies of scale. It is therefore fairly obvious that the Swedish Post Office would not be able to rapidly change its organisational structure or the logic of the postal services built up over time. Smaller, newly established firms often have a more flexible organisation, and can therefore develop new forms of organising operations in the industry. CityMail's rationalisation of the sorting process in distribution and the way in which the company cooperated with other actors in transportation instead of building up a distribution network as developed by the Post Office are examples of this kind of flexibility. One effect of deregulation is the opening-up of new ideas and solution of problems throughout the industry. In an industry such as the postal services industry, the in-built sunk costs involved obstruct such a development. Changes in price in order to defend the established business rather than as an effect of a reorganisation of the business are an observed consequence of deregulation.

In the taxi-cab industry, a number of common patterns emerged in Gothenburg, Stockholm and Sundsvall, where, for example, the price level decreased for subsidised trips negotiated by the public sector. For privately paid trips, prices increased or remained the same. A marginal increase only is noted for dispatch services, whereas it is argued that for single cruising cabs the average price level is above the dispatch price level. In Gothenburg and Stockholm, the number of dispatch services has not changed.

Malmö exhibits similar developments to those in Stockholm and Gothenburg, in that publicly subsidised trips experienced a drop in price. Fares for privately paid trips in Malmö provided by the dispatch services decreased, and the privately paid trips provided by some of the single cruising cabs are lower than the dispatch services' price. It is commonly argued that these prices are predatory, and therefore not consistent with the running of a serious business. Another interesting phenomenon can be observed in Malmö, where the single cruising cabs have recently begun collaborating (in terms of, for example, joint purchase of a car 'fleet'). Such a collaboration can be considered to be an increase in business-induced barriers, as existing collaboration in the industry constitutes a barrier for new entrants.

The price development in Sundsvall for public and private trips was similar to that observed in Stockholm and Gothenburg. However, Sundsvall's taxi-cab industry shows an interesting phenomenon, in that the two dispatch services (formed at the time of deregulation) have merged, with profitability given as the motive. As a result the business-induced barriers are now higher than they were before deregulation, as this cooperation has emerged within the industry rather than as an effect of political regulations. These arguments were illustrated in Figure 7.2.

From the discussion above we can conclude that the purpose of deregulation, to obtain a competitive situation with many competitors and intense competition, has not yet been fulfilled in the two industries studied, and that, as we have assumed earlier in this chapter, business-induced barriers influenced the outcome of a deregulation. It is only in the competition between the dispatch services in Malmö and in the competition in the negotiated taxi-cab market in Stockholm and Gothenburg that the 'ideal' corner is reached shown in Figure 7.2. Some parts of the taxi-cab industry and the postal service industry are unlikely to reach the ideal corner.

In conclusion the effects of the two presently deregulated industries studied here have not been those that were expected and we argue that this can be partly due to the business-induced barriers that existed in the industries before or at the time of deregulation. If an industry is encompassed by high business-induced entry barriers before deregulation, these barriers will remain after deregulation, and will most likely obstruct or hinder the development of the desired effects of deregulation. The dramatic changes in price in the postal service industry and the fact that these changes only occurred in smaller parts of the market can be explained, for example, by the heights of the remaining barriers to entry/exit.

It was necessary for the Swedish Post Office to use its power, due to the advantages built during the time as a monopolist, in its struggle to defend markets in the face of competition from CityMail in the post-deregulation period. The struggle included direct conflict with the Swedish Competition Authority on a number of occasions in order to apply for pre-emptive rulings on its pricing strategies. In the ongoing legal proceedings that have ensued since, both the Post Office and CityMail have presented a significant number of reports in defence of/against the Post Office's pricing behaviour. This indicates an unwillingness and/or impossibility on the side of the Swedish Post Office as the sole pre-deregulation incumbent to accept the effect of deregulation in terms of reduced market share, and the aggressiveness of its competitive counter-moves directed against CityMail must have at least caused potential new entrants to rethink.

Somewhat surprisingly, even in the taxi-cab industry with low entry barriers the removal of political regulations did not fulfil the desired outcome. It can, however, be assumed that other imperfections than those discussed above can obstruct the development towards healthy competition, as in the taxi-cab industry in Sundsvall and Malmö. In Sundsvall, the competitors started to cooperate with each other, thereby creating a competitive situation similar to the situation in pre-deregulation. The decision in Malmö to drive similar taxis is an example of the creation of familiarity advantages that gives higher business-induced entry barriers within the industry. The tendency to compensate for the loss of politically induced barriers by creating or strengthening business-induced barriers can be seen as a force that works against intense competition. The decrease in the intensity in the private market cannot, however, be explained by increased entry barriers in the same way, rather this is due to imperfection in information. For example, inexperienced customers do not know about existing rates, and therefore the price can exceed the price motivated by costs. Furthermore, inexperienced customers might choose a more expensive service since they do not know when a less expensive supplier will be available.

Conclusion

The main thrust of this chapter has been to emphasise the crucial importance of pre-deregulation business-induced entry barriers in understanding and predicting the outcome of deregulation. Our study has shown that business-induced entry barriers at the time of deregulation have affected the style of competition in the industries, producing outcomes that were neither expected nor desired. We have therefore found support for our argument that the removal or replacement of politically induced barriers does not automatically result in healthy competition since business-induced barriers remain and obstruct such a development. We have, however, observed that even if business-induced barriers are low the desired development might not be achieved. One reason is the imperfection of information and another is that firms seem to value cooperation more than competition.

The unwillingness to compete can be explained by the existing possibility to increase profitability by a cooperative solution, due to market imperfections as discussed within industrial organisation theory (cf. Tirole 1988), but also by the occurrence of mentally induced or cognitive entry barriers. Mental models of incumbent actors are slow to change, and a legally induced change in competitive condition does not necessarily mean that these mental models change overnight. The mental models of incumbents at the time of deregulation can therefore form mentally induced or cognitive entry barriers, which consequently affect the make-up of the competitive arena. Regardless of the height of the business-induced barriers within the industry, mental barriers that hinder firms from so-called 'healthy competition' can emerge. Firms that have co-existed with each other rather than competed with each other, due to politically induced barriers, may proceed with their co-activities even after the deregulation. Cognitive entry barriers, then, must also be added to the equation if an understanding is to be gained of how deregulation affects the emergence of healthy competition.

This explanation, both economic and cognitive, can be illustrated by the case of the taxi-cab industry in Sundsvall, where a merger has occurred between the two dispatch services formed at the time of deregulation. The goal of increased profitability has guided these two incumbents to 'regress' to a form of organisation strongly reminiscent of pre-deregulation market dominance, where efficiency is best gained through dominant position. It can also be argued, however, that the mental or cognitive attitudes of actors concerning the competitive situation can explain the merger, in that the cognitive frame of reference guiding the two firms remains similar to that which guided the industry in the pre-deregulation period (i.e. the industry is best served through a monopolist dispatch service).

The prevalence of mental barriers and the way these barriers guide actions taken by firms, and in our case obstruct a development towards healthy competition, can theoretically be explained using theories about mental models. Weick (1979) argues that preconceptions about the environment are generated through a process of learning that transforms data into information and action into experience which means that preconceptions and/or experiences of competition are manifested into action (see also Mintzberg 1989). Porac *et al.* (1989) came to a similar conclusion regarding action in strategic groups, stating that collective conceptions or mental models developed over time affect the strategic action of incumbent firms. Spender's (1989) 'industry recipes' and Bengtsson's (1994) climate of competition are another expression of how mental models in an industry steer action (see also Child 1988, 'cognitive fields'; Lija *et al.* 1992, 'business recipes'; Hellgren and Melin 1993, 'industrial wisdom'). Collective conceptions or mental models develop over time and are hard to change, which can explain, at least in part, why the style of action is stable over time. Inertia can therefore be said to exist in the mental models that govern the action of incumbents (Loasby 1991). Innate inertia therefore tends to exist in firms and in their logic of action, which means that they tend to 'continue as before' (Miller and Friesen 1980). This line of thought leads us to conclude that business-induced entry barriers (arisen through action) and politically induced entry barriers (arisen through formal rules) are intimately connected to mental models, and that the entry barriers that surround an industry must also include mentally induced or cognitive entry barriers.

This chapter indicates that deregulation may not be the only solution to problems in regulated markets. Business-induced and mentally induced barriers can thwart the aims of the removal or replacement of political regulation, thus creating new entry barriers that may obstruct or hinder new entry. However, our study is by no means exhaustive, and further research is therefore necessary to anchor these tentative findings. Studies of markets or industries that have already been deregulated can be used to determine the gap between expected and actual outcomes, seeking explanation in the form of changed entry barriers. Studies of markets intended for deregulation should concentrate on existing mental models and business-induced barriers of incumbent actors in order to heighten awareness of the importance of these in governing probable competitive behaviour in the post-deregulation period.

Note

1 Studies of regulations from the US support the statements above and show a connection between lower productivity and regulation (Backman 1981). Lindström (1991) among others, however, argues in the opposite direction that market-related regulations are motivated by the increase in efficiency, distribution and the protection of minority group interests (such as pensioners, the remote rural population, etc.).

References

Adamson, M., Jones, J. and Pratt, R. (1991) 'Competition Issues in Privatisation Lessons for the Railways', in D. Banister and K. Bulton (eds) *Transport in a Free Market Economy*, London: Macmillan.

Ajzen, I. and Fishbein, M. (1977) 'Attitude–Behaviour Relations: A Theoretical Analysis and Review of Empirical Research', *Psychological Bulletin* 84: 888–918.

Anand, P. and Sternthal, B. (1991) 'Perceptual Fluency and Affect without Recognition', *Memory and Cognition* 19: 293–300.

Backman, J. (1981) 'The Problem of Regulation', in J. Backman (ed.), *Regulation and Deregulation*, Indianapolis: Bobbs-Merrill.

Bain, J.S. (1956) *Industrial Organization,* New York: Wiley.

Banister, D. (1990) 'Privatization in Transport: From the Company State to the Contract State', in J. Simmie and R. King (eds), *The State in Action*, London: Pinter.

Barney, J. (1991) 'Firm Resources and Sustained Competitive Advantages', *Journal of Management* 17(1): 99–120.

Bengtsson, M. (1994) Konkurrensklimat och dynamik – en studie av interaktion mellan konkurrenter, Studier i företagsekonomi, Umeå Universitet.

Carlsson, B. (1990) *Den amerikanska avregleringsvågen* [The American Deregulation Wave], Stockholm: SNS Förlag.

Caves, R. and Porter, M.E. (1977) 'From Entry Barriers to Mobility Barriers: Conjectured Decisions and Contrived Deterrence to New Competition', *Quarterly Journal of Economics* 91: 241–67.

Chamberlin, E. (1933) *The Theory of Monopolistic Competition*, Cambridge, MA: Harvard University Press.

Child, J. (1988) 'In Organizations and their Sectors', *Organizational Studies* 9: 13–19.

Coase, R.H. (1937) 'The Nature of the Firm', *Economica* 4: 386–405.

Coffman, R. (1977) 'The Economic Reasons for Price and Entry Regulation of Taxicabs', *Journal of Transport Economics and Policy*, September: 288–97.

Dickson, P.R. (1992) 'Toward a General Theory of Competitive Rationality', *Journal of Marketing* 56 (January): 69–83.

—— (1996) 'The Static and Dynamic Mechanics of Competition: A Comment on Hunt and Morgan's Comparative Advantage Theory', *Journal of Marketing* 60(4): 102–6.

Eliasson, G. (1993) Preface in S. Fölster, *Frihet och ansvar istället för reglering*, Stockholm: SAF.

Foerster, F.J. and Gilbert, G. (1979) 'Taxicab Deregulation: Economic Consequences and Regulatory Choices', *Transportation Journal* 8: 371–87.

Gärling, T., Laitila, T., Marell, A. and Westin, K. (1995) 'A Note on the Short-term Effects of Deregulation of the Swedish Taxi-cab Industry', *Journal of Transport Economics and Policy* May: 209–14.

Hellgren, B. and Melin, L. (1993) 'Business Systems, Industrial Wisdom and Corporate Strategies', in R. Whitley (ed.), *The Social Foundations of Enterprise: Europe in Comparative Perspective*, London: Sage.

Hensher, D.A. (1988) 'Productivity in Privately Owned and Operated Bus Firms in Australia', in J.S. Dodgson and N. Topham (eds), *Bus Deregulation and Privatization*, Aldershot: Avebury.

Houthakker, H.S. (1981) 'Competition, Regulation, and Efficiency', in J. Backman (ed.), *Regulation and Deregulation*, Indianapolis: Bobbs-Merrill.

Hunt, S.D. and Morgan, R.M. (1996) 'The Resource-Advantage Theory of Competition: Dynamics, Path Dependencies, and Evolutionary Dimensions', *Journal of Marketing* 60(4): 107–14.

Jansson, K. and Wallin, B. (1991) 'Deregulation of Public Transport in Sweden', *Journal of Transport Economics and Policy* XXV(1): 97–107.

Jonason, L. (1996) Yttrande över postens överklagande av Konkurrensverkets delbeslut 1995-12-22 angående underprisättning av Posttidningar B.

Kay, J.A. and Vickers, J. (1988) 'The New Industrial Policy – Privatization and Competition', *Economic Policy*, October: 8–16.

KKV dnr 479/93, dnr 1417/94, dnr 682/95, dnr 601/96 and dnr 1142/96.

Knickerbocker, F.T. (1973) *Oligopolistic Reaction and Multinational Enterprise*, Boston.

Kogut, B. and Zander, U. (1996) 'What Firms Do? Coordination, Identity, and Learning', *Organization Science* 7(5): 502–18.

KTB (1984) *Behov av Taxitillstånd* [The Need for Taxi-cab Licences], KTB-rapport. 1984: 27, Stockholm.

Laitila, T., Marell, A. and Westin, K. (1995) Taxitrafikens egenskaper och taxikundernas uppfattning fyra år efter avregleringen, [Characteristics of the Taxi-cab Traffic and the Consumers' Attitude Four Years after Deregulation], KFB, 93-418-63.

Lilja, K., Räsänen, K. and Tainio, R. (1992) 'A Dominant Business Recipe: The Forest Sectors in Finland', in R. Whitley (ed.), *European Business Systems: Firms and Markets in their National Contexts*, London: Sage.

Lindström, B. (1991) *Den Reglerade Marknadsekonomin*, Stockholm: Industrins Utredningsinstitut.

Loasby, B.J. (1991) *Equilibrium and Evolution, An Exploration of Connecting Principles in Economics*, Manchester: Manchester University Press.

Marell, A. and Westin, K. (1992) 'Deregulation and Performance in the Swedish Taxicab Industry', paper presented at the sixth World Conference on Transport Research (WCTR), Lyon, France, 29 June.

Miller, D. and Friesen, P. (1980) 'Momentum and Revolution in Organizational Adaptation', *Academy of Management Journal*, 32(2): 333–52.

Mintzberg, H. (1989) *Mintzberg on Management, Inside Our Strange World of Organizations*, London: Free Press.

Nerep, E. (1997) 'Current Competition Law Issues in Regard to the De-(Re-)-Regulation of the Swedish Postal Services Market – Especially the Problems of Defining the Relevant Market, and Establishing Price Discrimination and Predatory Pricing', Stockholm School of Economics, Faculty of Law.

Nyhetsposten Swedish Post Office 1996:1.

Pagano, A. and McKnight, C. (1983) 'Economies of Scale in the Taxicab Industry; Some Empirical Evidence from the United States', *Journal of Transport Economics and Policy*, 17(3): 299–313.

Porac, J.F., Thomas, H. and Baden-Fuller, C. (1989) 'Competitive Groups as Cognitive Communities: The Case of Scottish Knitwear Manufacturers', *Journal of Management Studies* 26(4): 397–410.

Porter, M.E. (1979) 'The Structure within Industries and Companies Performance', *Review of Economics and Statistics*, May: 214–27.

—— (1980) *Competitive Strategy: Techniques for Analyzing Industries and Competitors*, New York: Free Press.

—— (1990) *The Competitive Advantages of Nations*, London: Macmillan.

SCB (1990) Statistical messages, T21 SM 9001.

—— (1995) Statistical messages, T21 SM 9501.

—— (1997) Statistical messages, T21 SM 9701.

Scherer, F.M. (1980) *Industrial Market, Structure and Economic Performance*, Chicago: Rand McNally.

Schmalensee, R. (1988) 'Industrial Economics: An Overview', *The Economic Journal*, September: 643–81.

Schumpeter, J.A. (1942) *Capitalism, Socialism and Democracy*, New York: Harper & Bros.

Shifrin, C.A. (1992) 'Swedish Deregulation Sparks New Service', *Aviation Week and Space Technology* 136(124): 50–1.

Shreiber, C. (1977) 'A Rejoinder', *Journal of Transport Economics and Policy* XI(3): 298–304.

Smith, A. (1776, 1976) *An Inquiry into the Nature and Causes of the Wealth of Nations*, R.H. Campbell and A.S. Skinner (eds), Oxford: Clarendon Press.

Sölvell, Ö. (1987) *Entry Barriers and Foreign Penetration – Emerging Patterns of International Competition in Two Electrical Engineering Industries*, Stockholm: Stockholm School of Economics.

SOU (1962) Postverkets organisation: betänkande avgivet av Postutredningen 1956, p. 52 (An official study of the post office organisation.)

—— (1988) *Trafikpolitiken inför 90-talet*, Regeringens Proposition 1987/88:50 [Transport Act 1987/88:50].

Spender, J.-C. (1989) *Industry Recipes – An Inquiry into the Nature and Sources of Managerial Judgement*, Oxford: Blackwell.

Teal, F.R. and Berglund, M. (1987) 'The Impact of Taxicab Deregulation in the USA', *Journal of Transport Economics and Policy* 1: 37–55.

The Post Office financial report 1980/81.

Thomson, I. (1992) 'Urban Bus Deregulation in Chile', *Journal of Transport Economics and Policy* 3: 319–27.

Tirole, J. (1988) *The Theory of Industrial Organization*, Cambridge, MA: MIT Press.

Weick, K.E. (1979) *The Social Psychology of Organizing*, Reading, MA: Addison-Wesley.

White, P. (1988) 'British Experience with Deregulation of Local Bus Services', in J.S. Dodgson and N. Topham (eds), *Bus Deregulation and Privatization*, Aldershot: Avebury.

Wiedenbaum, M.L. (1981) 'The Benefits of Regulatory Reform', in J. Backman (ed.), *Regulation and Deregulation*, Indianapolis: Bobbs-Merrill.

Williams, D. (1980) 'The Economic Reasons for Price and Entry Regulation of Taxicabs. A Comment', *Journal of Transport Economics and Policy*, January: 105–12.

Williamson, O.E. (1975) *Markets and Hierarchies: Analysis and Antitrust Implications*, New York: Free Press.

—— (1981) 'The Modern Corporation: Origins, Evolution, Attributes', *Journal of Economic Literature*, December: 1537–68.

Worcester, D.A. (1957) 'Why Dominant Firms Decline', *Journal of Political Economy* 65: 338–47.

Yo, C.-M.J. and Ito, K. (1988) 'Oligopolistic Reaction and Foreign Direct Investment: The Case of the US Tire and Textiles Industries', *Journal of International Business Studies*, Fall: 449–60.

Yip, G.S. (1982) *Barriers to Entry*, Lexington, MA: Lexington Books.

Zajonc, R.B. (1980) 'Feeling and Thinking, Preferences Need No Inferences', *American Psychologist* 35(2): 151–75.

8

PRIVATISATION IN MALAYSIA

A social and economic paradox

Winnie Goh and Jomo Sundram

Overview

Malaysia, in the early post-independence period (1957–69), essentially pursued a *laissez-faire* development strategy. Such a development strategy allowed the continued dominance of what were then the commanding heights of the Malaysian economy, namely plantation agriculture, mining, banking, and manufacturing by foreign (particularly British) capital and, to a lesser extent, local (essentially Chinese) capital during this period (Toh 1989). By the end of the 1960s, Malay participation, including that of state agencies, in the modern sector of the Malaysian economy was glaringly low. By 1969, such inequalities precipitated a major racial riot.

The Malay elite-dominated Malaysian Government's New Economic Policy (NEP) was designed to achieve ethnic redistribution goals. The NEP, introduced in 1971, was committed to reduce poverty and inter-ethnic economic disparities in order to achieve national unity. One of the objectives was to increase the corporate wealth ownership of the Bumiputera to 30 per cent by 1990. Thus, public enterprises – in the form of new statutory bodies, government corporations, government-owned or controlled publicly listed companies as well as government-owned or controlled private companies – became the means to achieve the government's objectives. Such government enterprises were involved in a wide range of economic activities: agriculture, manufacturing, transport, construction, finance and services. The heavy involvement of the state in the economy continued through the 1970s till the early 1980s.

By the early 1980s, the generally lacklustre performance of the Malaysian public sector, including public enterprises, required a policy response. Various reasons have been given to explain the generally poor performance of public enterprises. In many instances, state-owned enterprises have been hampered by unclear or contradictory objectives. Similarly, performance criteria have been ambiguous. In Malaysia, the so-called 'social' – usually ethnic redistributive, but sometimes also welfare – objectives were often invoked to circumvent profit, efficiency or other cost-effective criteria. Coordination problems have also been serious, especially with different levels of governments (federal, state, municipal, regional authorities etc.) as well as inter-ministry and other intra-governmental rivalries. With the proliferation of such enterprises in Malaysia in the 1970s and early 1980s, many were assigned or developed similar and often redundant functions. Monitoring and evaluation of public enterprise performance was virtually non-existent until the mid-1980s, and continues to remain weak and superficial.

The Malaysian privatisation

In 1983, Mahathir Mohamad, the Malaysian Prime Minister, announced the government's own commitment to privatisation. Two years after Mahathir's announcement in 1983, the Economic Planning Unit (EPU) of the Prime Minister's Department issued its 'Guidelines on Privatisation', which remained the main official document on privatisation until 1991. In February 1991, the government published the *Privatisation Masterplan* (*PMP*) document not long after the October 1990 general election, and just before announcing the rest of its post-New Economic Policy (NEP), or post-1990 economic policy.

Generally, privatisation has been defined in terms of the transfer of enterprise ownership from the public to the private sector. It can be strictly defined to include only cases of the sale of 100 per cent or at least a majority share of a public enterprise, or its assets, to private shareholders. Full or complete privatisation would mean the complete transfer of ownership and control of a government enterprise or asset to the private sector.

In Malaysia, therefore, the term 'privatisation' is often understood to include cases where less than half of the assets or shares of public enterprises are sold to private shareholders. In fact, privatisation is usually understood to include cases of partial divestiture where less than half of the assets or shares of public enterprises are sold to private shareholders, with the government retaining control through majority ownership. In fact, the definition of 'privatisation' in Malaysia is so broad that it includes cases where private enterprises are awarded licences to participate in activities previously the exclusive preserve of the public sector, as in the case of television broadcasting from 1984. Contracting out of services, especially at municipal authorities, e.g. involving garbage disposal and parking, and private ownership or even contracted leasing of public properties, e.g. enabling the imposition of tolls on roads previously built by the Public Works Ministry or the Malaysian Highway Authority (Lembaga Lebuhraya Malaysia, or LLM), are frequently equated with privatisation.

In Malaysia, when a public enterprise, legally formed as a government department or statutory authority, is privatised, it necessarily first entails corporatisation, or the formation of a limited company incorporated under the Companies Act 1965. On the other hand, the privatisation of a public enterprise which has been constituted as a limited company would merely entail a transfer in share ownership from the public to the private sector without any change in the legal form of the enterprise.

The official objectives in the Malaysian privatisation policy are:

1 To relieve the financial and administrative burden of the government.
2 To improve efficiency and productivity. Efficiency will be promoted through the introduction of competition, freeing governmental organisations from political supervision and rigidities, and the introduction of new employee incentives.
3 To facilitate economic growth. With privatisation, the economy is expected to be increasingly led by the private sector. With higher efficiency and profits, the government will be able to obtain additional revenue in the form of higher corporate taxes.
4 To reduce the role and size of the presence of the public sector in the economy.
5 To help in the achievement of national economic policy targets particularly with respect to restructuring the ownership pattern in the economy.

Arguments

Since 1983, a total of 165 projects have been privatised nation-wide. Of the total, 109 represented existing projects involving the taking over of the government's functions by the private sector, while 56 were new projects involving the construction of infrastructure and utility projects such as roads, power and water supply projects. Fifty per cent of the privatised projects involved the sale of government equity; 11.6 per cent of the privatised projects were undertaken through the build–operate–transfer (B–O–T) method; 11 per cent through sale of assets and 9.3 per cent through the build–operate–own (B–O–O) method (*New Straits Times*, 18 January 1996).

Advocates of privatisation in Malaysia, including the *PMP*, have claimed that there has been tremendous success in its privatisation policy. It has reduced the role of the public sector in the economy as well as the financial and administrative burden of the government. It has accelerated economic development and it will continue to open up new opportunities in the economic development of the country. The government was able to earn a one-off revenue of about RM2,063 million from divesting shares of enterprises to the public (see Table 8.1).

It has also boasted of total savings in capital expenditure from privatised projects since 1983 amounting to RM72.76 billion, and saving on annual operating expenditure, as of December 1995, was RM6.92 billion (*New Straits Times*, 18 January 1996).

Table 8.1 Proceeds from sale of equity

	RM million
Sports Toto Sdn. Bhd.	113
Malaysia Airlines Berhad (MAS)	469
Malaysian International Shipping Corporation (MISC)	90
Edaran Otomobil Nasional (EON)	29
Malaysian Shipyard and Engineering (MSE)	247
Perusahaan Padang Terap	51
Perusahaan Otomobil Nasional (PROTON)	177
Tenaga Nasional Berhad (TNB)	248
Telekom Malaysia Berhad (TMB)	639
Total	2,063

Source: Economic Report, 1993/1994, Ministry of Finance, Malaysia.

According to several – usually ideologically set – criteria, privatisation in Malaysia is making good progress, especially in terms of the government's own declared objectives. In terms of raising efficiency and productivity, it has been agreed that the establishment of STMB/TV3 introduced some competition into the television broadcasting industry previously dominated by the government's two channels. Also, since corporatisation in 1987, Telekom Malaysia has introduced several new services and improved existing services. As a result of privatisation, the Kelang Container Terminal's (KCT) average turnaround time improved from 13.4 hours in 1985 to 11.3 hours in 1987 and the average length of time that each container remained on the dock declined from 8 to 3.8 days. Also, throughput has risen from 244,120 TEUs (twenty-foot equivalent units) in 1985 to approximately 804,500 TEUs in 1994.

Since most privatisations have involved at least 30 per cent Bumiputera participation, the policy is said to have furthered the NEP's inter-ethnic wealth redistribution objectives.

The advocates of privatisation in Malaysia have not been honest in presenting a full and balanced record of what has happened with privatisation. Instead, a rosy picture has been advanced to mislead the public.

The sale of government-owned enterprises has indeed raised government revenue (see Table 8.1). Such one-off proceeds may relieve the government's financial burden in the short run, but it may result in forgone income in the long run. In the public flotation of the thirteen government-owned enterprises, the government has forgone considerable revenue amounting to approximately RM4.22 billion (Table 8.2). The forgone revenue has been seen as a result of substantial underpricing of shares in the initial public offerings. Table 8.2 reveals that high initial premia were obtained on the first day of secondary trading. Such underpricing of initial public offerings (IPOs) of the thirteen government-owned enterprises may have been deliberate in

Table 8.2 Estimated forgone revenue and initial premia on the first day of secondary trading

Company	*Volume of share (million)*	*Issue price (RM)*	*Volume traded on day 1 (million)*	*Turnover (%)*	*Price on day 1**	*Premium (%)*	*Revenue** forgone (RM million)*
Malaysian Airlines (MAS)	70	1.80	2.390	3.4	2.45	36.1	45.50
Malaysian International Shipping Corporation (MISC)	85	2.40	15.809	16.6	5.00	108.3	221.00
Sports Toto Malaysia	5.2	2.00	1.833	35.0	9.55	377.5	39.26
Tradewinds (M)	15	1.10	2.601	17.3	1.83	66.4	10.95
Cements Manufacturers Sarawak	5	1.30	0.828	16.3	2.17	66.9	4.35
Cements Industries of Malaysia	8.8	1.00	—	—	1.91	91.0	8.00
Kedah Cement Holdings	29.2	2.00	15.770	54.0	2.60	30.0	17.52
Perusahaan Otomobil Nasional	30	5.00	21.000	70.0	6.60	32.0	48.00
Edaran Otomobil Nasional (EON)	36	5.00	3.302	9.2	8.15	63.0	113.40
Syarikat Telekom Malaysia	470.5	5.00	29.895	6.4	6.10	22.0	517.55
Tenaga Nasional	625	4.50	51.932	8.7	8.75	94.4	2,656.25
Kelang Container Terminal	50	3.10	19.962	74.0	8.40	171.0	265.00
Petronas Dagangan	66.15	2.80	—	—	6.95	148.2	274.52
Hicom Holdings	82	2.10	—	—	—	—	—
Total							4,221.30

Source: KLSE Research Department.

* Closing prices.
** The difference between the issue price and the price on day 1 multiplied by the number of shares.

order to improve the likelihood of the share offer's success since failure could have adverse consequences.

In Malaysia, it is popularly believed that many cases of privatisation have strong influences from private interests who try to determine what is to be privatised, in what manner and to whom. Also, very often it has not even involved the formalities of an open tender system, as sanctioned by the official 'first come, first served' policy by which the government justified awarding privatisation opportunities to those who have supposedly first proposed the privatisation of a government property or activity.

For example, in 1986, it was announced that RM1.4 billion worth of water supply projects involving 174 schemes had been awarded to Antah Biwater without open tender. Antah Biwater is 51 per cent owned by the Negeri Sembilan royal family's Antah Sembilan Berhad and 49 per cent owned by the British water supply and treatment group, Biwater Ltd (Sundram 1995a).

Also in 1987, the government awarded the North–South Highway project on a B–O–T basis to United Engineers (Malaysia) Bhd (UEM). There was much controversy when the government awarded the project to UEM, then an ailing public listed company long suspended from trading on the stock exchange. The company had no previous experience in the construction of highways, yet it was awarded the project even though it has not submitted the best offer – in terms of cost, duration, consumer charges and subsidised financing requirements to the government – the apparent reason for the award was that UEM was controlled by an UMNO holding company, Hatibudi, in which UMNO president, deputy president, secretary-general and treasurer were trustees (*Asian Wall Street Journal*, 28 January 1988).

Another obvious example of favouritism is the privatisation of 144 local water authorities throughout Malaysia to manage, operate and maintain the urban sewerage systems for twenty-eight years (*Malaysian Business*, 16 December 1993). Indah Water Konsortium (IWK) Sendirian Berhad – a consortium of companies led by Vincent Tan's main listed vehicle, Berjaya Group Berhad, which has a controlling 20 per cent stake – was awarded the RM6.27 billion project without any tender process (*The Star*, 18 May 1993). Berjaya Group Berhad may have the experience in small road-building projects but it has never built anything the size of a national sewerage project (*Far Eastern Economic Review*, 1 April 1993).

Proponents of privatisation usually claim that enhanced efficiency will be achieved through the interaction of private ownership and competition. Thus, the market environment is an essential ingredient for the success of privatisation. It is widely recognised that public enterprises that routinely provide services such as supply of electricity, telecommunications, transportation, health and education, to name a few, are basically considered public monopolies, and suffer from a lack of product market competition. There is therefore a need to privatise such public entities in order to achieve both productive and allocative efficiency.

In Malaysia, privatisation of some public enterprises has not been accompanied by significantly increased competition and they have still remained virtual monopolies. In fact, in Malaysia there is the danger of such enterprises becoming private monopolies and very little chance of enhancing consumer welfare through privatisation. There is considerable evidence to show that, in Malaysia, increases in consumer charges for both utilities and services took place just before or after corporatisation and privatisation.

Review of various corporatised and privatised entities

Postal services

On 1 January 1992, the Postal Services Department (PSD) was corporatised, with the promise of providing better and faster services. Since then, there is evidence showing that Pos Malaysia (the name used since corporatisation) has been aggressively embarking on a massive corporate public relations exercise to enhance its image in providing fast mail delivery, polite services to the public and increasing efficiency and profitability.

In 1992, Pos Malaysia chalked up RM20 million in pre-tax profits, and by October 1993 it had chalked up further pre-tax profits of RM50 million (*Malaysian Business*, 1 April 1994). The question that needs to be asked is whether there was a need to corporatise and privatise the PSD to improve its efficiency and profitability.

The PSD had been financially stable with an impressive track record. It had been making profits yearly without any change in postal rates in almost ten years. In 1988, its revenue was RM186.3 million and profits were RM11.3 million. By 1990, revenue had increased to RM252 million, with profits more than doubling to RM44 million (*Business Times*, 31 December 1991).

The postal services in Malaysia were considered to be one of the best among developing countries as they were operating rather efficiently and providing relatively low postal rates. Table 8.3 provides a comparison of postage rates among various countries. Malaysia's domestic postage rate for a letter of up to 20gm was only 20 sen, the lowest in the region after India.

The Postal Services Department (PSD) has long been a monopoly and will probably stay a monopoly with privatisation. There are doubts with regards to improving efficiency since competition in this area is very limited. Fears among consumers regarding the adverse impact of rising prices and inferior services have increased after the proposed corporatisation. Fears about rising prices, which will disadvantage the consumers, have not been unfounded. The corporatisation of the PSD has already led to hefty increases in consumer charges.

Table 8.3 Comparison of Malaysia's domestic postage rates with those of Singapore, Indonesia, Thailand, India and Japan as at 1 May 1991 (RM)

Country/weight	*Malaysia*	*Singapore*	*Indonesia*	*Thailand*	*India*	*Japan*
Up to 20gm	0.20	0.30	0.31	0.22	0.14	1.24
21–50gm	0.30	0.45	0.61	na*	0.41	1.44
51–100gm	0.45	0.75	0.76	0.35**	0.47	3.50

Source: Rodhiah (1991).

* Not available as rate is based on a combined system, part of a marketing strategy.
** Surface service only, does not involve air service.

Table 8.4 Postage rates by destination for letters (RM)

Weight	*Within Malaysia*			*To Singapore and Brunei*			*To other countries*		
	Old rate	*New rate*	*% increase*	*Old rate*	*New rate*	*% increase*	*Old rate*	*New rate*	*% increase*
Up to 20gm	0.20	0.30	50	0.20	0.40	100	0.40	0.50	25
21–50gm	0.30	0.35	17	0.30	0.70	133	0.80	1.00	25
51–100gm	0.45	0.50	11	0.45	1.20	167	1.20	1.50	25
101–250gm	0.85	1.00	18	0.85	2.50	194	2.50	2.80	12
251–500gm	1.50	2.00	33	1.50	4.50	200	4.50	5.30	18
501–1,000gm	2.50	3.50	40	2.50	8.00	220	8.00	10.00	25
1,000–2,000gm	4.00	6.00	50	4.00	15.00	275	14.50	18.00	24

Source: Postal Services Department.

Table 8.4 compares postage rates before and after corporatisation, with postage rates rising tremendously in 1992 with corporatisation. For letters (weighing less than 20gm) posted to any destination within Malaysia, the postage rate has increased by 50 per cent; for letters with similar weight posted to Singapore and Brunei, the postage rate has increased by 100 per cent. For letters (weighing more than 1000gm) to Brunei and Singapore, the increase in postage rate has been tremendous, increasing by 275 per cent.

Table 8.5 compares postage rates for small parcels before and after corporatisation. The increase in postage rates for small parcels has been larger as compared to letters sent to similar destinations. For parcels of up to 100gm to destinations within Malaysia, the increase in the postage rate has been 100 per cent. For parcels of similar weight to Singapore and Brunei, the increase in postage rate has been rather alarming, increasing by 400 per cent.

A detailed study of Table 8.5 will show that postage rates for small parcels with weights exceeding 100gm have increased tremendously. For example, the postage rate for a parcel weighing between 251gm and 500gm to Singapore and Brunei, has increased by 609 per cent.

Table 8.5 Postage rates by destination for small parcels (RM)

Weight	*Within Malaysia*			*To Singapore and Brunei*			*To other countries*		
	Old rate	*New rate*	*% increase*	*Old rate*	*New rate*	*% increase*	*Old rate*	*New rate*	*% increase*
Up to 100gm	0.20	0.40	100	0.20	1.00	400	0.70	1.00	43
101–250gm	0.30	0.80	167	0.30	2.20	633	1.60	2.50	56
251–500gm	0.55	1.50	173	0.55	3.90	609	2.80	5.00	79
501–1,000gm	0.95	2.80	195	0.95	6.00	532	4.00	10.00	150

Source: Postal Services Department.

Since corporatisation of the PSD in January 1992, the promise of a more efficient postal service with faster delivery has been an elusive dream. S. Samy Vellu – the energy, telecommunications and posts minister – has commented that the PSD could handle 1 million letters a day, which increased to between 4 and 6 million during festive seasons (*Malay Mail*, 20 July 1994). Prior to corporatisation, it was found that Malaysia's postal delivery time averages less than two days for domestic mail. Also, with the introduction of air shuttle services between Malaysia and Singapore, 8 per cent of the mail could be sent on the same day, for example from Kuala Lumpur to Singapore (Rodhiah 1991)

After the comments made by the energy, telecommunications and posts minister, the *Malay Mail* carried out a survey in which it started mailing letters to its editorial staff at various destinations from post offices and letter boxes within the Klang Valley. It was found that, on average, it took six days for letters to be delivered within the Klang Valley. Table 8.6 shows 'Late delivery of mail in the Klang Valley'. A letter posted at a letter box in Jalan Raja Laut to Subang Jaya took eighteen days to arrive. In another case, letters posted on different days from 20 June to 5 July, to the same destination in Subang Jaya, arrived in a bundle on the same day (12 July 1994) (*Malay Mail*, 20 July 1994).

Toll-charges for highway use

Until the mid-1980s, the construction and maintenance of public roads in Malaysia were the sole responsibility of the public sector. But as domestic and external deficits widened and financing became more difficult, it was argued that the private sector should be involved in the construction and operation of roads. Thus the government allowed the private sector to undertake major ventures and to recover investments via user charges and tolls.

The 'build–operate–transfer' (or B–O–T method) has been used in the efforts to privatise the construction and operation of toll roads. Under this

Table 8.6 Late delivery of mail in the Klang Valley

Date sent (1994)	*Destination*	*Date received*	*Number of days required for letter to arrive*
30 May	Subang Jaya	17 June	18
3 June	Subang Jaya	7 June	4
28 June	Subang Jaya	12 July	14
29 June	Subang Jaya	12 July	13
1 July	Subang Jaya	12 July	12
4 July	Subang Jaya	12 July	8
5 July	Subang Jaya	12 July	7
6 July	Subang Jaya	12 July	6
31 May	Ampang	9 June	9
28 June	Ampang	7 July	9
29 June	Ampang	7 July	8
30 June	Ampang	7 July	7
30 May	Sentul	11 June	12
29 June	Petaling Jaya	5 July	6
30 June	Petaling Jaya	5 July	5
1 July	USJ	9 July	8
4 July	USJ	7 July	3
5 July	USJ	9 July	4

Source: *Malay Mail*, 20 July 1994.

method, the private sector constructs the facility using its own funds, operates it for a concessionary period, and finally transfers it to the government at the end of the stipulated period.

The North–South Highway or Expressway (NSE), privatised under the B–O–T method, in 1988, was granted a concession or licence for an agreed period (concession period), during which it earns revenue from operating the concession. The concessionaire has been granted a concession period of thirty years to collect toll charges from highway users. The toll charges are fixed subject to government approval.

The North–South Expressway's concessionaire, Projek Lebuhraya Utara-Selatan (or PLUS as it is more popularly known) is currently owned equally by United Engineers (M) Berhad (UEM) and Faber Group Berhad. There was much controversy with regards to the awarding of the North–South Highway/Expressway project to UEM, as it has no previous experience in construction of highways.

When toll charges were first introduced on the North–South Highway, they were set at 5 sen per kilometre. On 1 January 1993, the toll charges were increased by 50 per cent, from 5 sen to 7.5 sen per kilometre. After 1996, PLUS will be allowed to escalate its toll charges in accordance with the consumer price index (CPI), or by 6 per cent per annum, which ever is higher (Table 8.7).

Table 8.7 Johor Bahru to Bukit Kayu Hitam (800km) passenger car toll rates

Year	*Toll payable (RM)*	*Rate (sen/km)*
1994	60.0	7.5
1996	80.0	10.0
2000	101.0	12.6
2005	135.2	16.9
2010	180.0	22.6
2015	241.6	30.2

Source: Azizul (1994).

Based on the provisions of the concession agreement on the North–South Expressway, PLUS has recently requested a 33.3 per cent increase in toll charges from the present 7.5 sen to 10.0 sen per kilometre (*The Edge*, 25 December 1995). There was public outcry following the proposed toll hike by PLUS. PLUS has been able to collect approximately RM530 million in toll charges annually. It has been able to rake in 'superprofits' under a fixed quantum arrangement because of an 'explosion' in the traffic volume which was not foreseen earlier. The request to increase toll charges may not be rejected out of hand as this would make the government lose credibility in the eyes of the private sector, especially those involved in privatised projects. If the government rejects the requests, it may end up having to pay compensation of up to RM1 billion for the next three years (*The Edge*, 25 December 1995).

Passenger railway services

The corporatisation of Keretapi Tanah Melayu (KTM) on 1 August 1992 was a first step in the transition from an essentially public entity to a profit-oriented KTM Berhad, with an optimal balance between financial and public service objectives. Compared to the other corporatised or privatised entities, which are basically monopolies, KTM Berhad faces more competition as there exist alternative modes of transportation (road, sea and air).

It is felt that its outlook may not be as bright as Telekom Malaysia Berhad (TMB) or Tenaga Nasional Berhad (TNB). Yet, optimism runs high in terms of likelihood of listing in the stock exchange within five years. In order to do so, KTM Berhad has to quickly show a track record of profitability. In the years prior to 1988, KTM had operating losses of more than RM20 million. Thus one obvious option available to KTM Berhad to cut losses is to increase its fares (Philip 1992). On 1 January 1993, five months after corporatisation, KTM Berhad increased fares for the second time in three months (Table 8.8).

Table 8.8 Railways: passenger fare increases

	From 1.8.84 (sen/km)	*Effective 1.10.92 (sen/km)*	*Increase (%)*	*Effective 1.1.93 (sen/km)*	*Increase (%)*
First class	12.14	13.96	15	15.00	24
Second class	5.47	5.74	5	6.50	19
Third class	3.36	3.53	5	3.65	7
Supplementary charge for air-conditioned coach*	RM3.00	RM4.00	33	RM4.00	33
Berth charge for first-class coach*	RM15.00	RM25.00	67	RM25.00	67

Source: Passenger Division, KTM Berhad.

* This is a standard charge irrespective of distance.

Therefore, KTM Berhad was able to boast of good profits of RM5.7 million barely five months after corporatisation (*The Edge*, 20 November 1995).

The aim of privatisation of the railway service is ostensibly to provide faster and better service. Since corporatisation, railway services have been said to improve, but these marginal improvements may not justify the fare increases. Unfortunately for consumers, fares were increased twice within five months of corporatisation, thus implying a definite decline in consumer welfare.

The government medical store

The Government Hospitals and Health Clinics prescribed more than RM200 million worth of medicine in 1994. All government health institutions are required to order their medicines through the Government Medical Store (GMS). Bulk-buying through GMS has placed the government in a favourable position to negotiate generous price discounts from pharmaceutical companies, and newer drugs protected by patent legislation were available to the government hospitals at less than half their price in the private market. A large well-equipped and well-staffed pharmaceutical laboratory had been established with the GMS to ensure that the government got its money's-worth through the carrying out of random sampling of various items being purchased. Therefore, the GMS is a good model of how cost containment and drug quality assurance can be obtained (*Aliran Monthly* 1995).

The privatisation of the GMS in 1994 was a big surprise. GMS was taken over by Southern Task (S) Berhad as of June 1994, and hence given the monopoly to supply medicine to all government health institutions. Also, government health institutions have been constrained to buy medicine only from Southern Task, and prohibited to buy from other private pharmacies, even if the terms offered are actually better than those given by Southern Task.

Unfortunately, one of the first things that Southern Task did was to hike up the prices of the medicines it supplies (Table 8.9). Privatisation of health facilities may have some cost-savings for the government but it has resulted in disproportionate increases in expenditure for the public. Since GMS has been an excellent model of cost-containment and drug quality assurance, why was it privatised?

Table 8.9 Price increases announced by Southern Task in January 1995

Item	*Nature of drug*	*Price increases (%)*
Cimetidine	For treatment of peptic ulcers	15.0
Selegiline	To prevent the deterioration of Parkinson's disease	15.0
Human insulin	For diabetic patients	18.4
Codeine phosphate	For severe cough – often used in lung cancer cases	43.2
Imipenem	A powerful antibiotic	15.0
Ceftazidime	A powerful antibiotic	15.0
Cisplatinum	A cytotoxic agent for treatment of certain cancers	15.0
Simvastin	To bring down blood cholesterol levels	5.6
Mefenamic acid (Ponstan)	A painkiller	15.1

Source: Aliran Monthly (1995).

Telecommunications

The telecommunications industry in Malaysia has been undergoing a process of rapid modernisation and transformation since the late 1980s. Since the corporatisation of the Telecommunications Department (Jabatan Telekom Malaysia) in 1987, and its privatisation in 1990, better services – such as improved counter-services, the option of a detailed billing system reducing errors (for which one has to pay more), quicker responses to applications for telephone installations and complaints – have taken place. There is also an improvement in the penetration rate or lines per 100 population, with the annual rate increasing to 14 per cent from just under 10 per cent.

However, such improvements have not come without cost to consumers. Since its corporatisation in 1987, basic telephone charges have increased. A three-minute call unit used to cost 10 sen, but this was increased to 13 sen just before corporatisation in 1987, a 30 per cent increase.

In late 1995, there was a proposal to increase phone charges. The proposed increase is from 13 sen per unit (a three-minute call) to 45 sen per minute – an increase of 346 per cent. One of the reasons cited for the proposed hike is

Table 8.10 Annual profits of Telekom Malaysia

Year	*Profit (RM million)*
1987	4.9
1988	180.4
1989	365.5
1990	563.9
1991	1,080.0
1992	1,275.8
1993	1,527.2
1994	1,673.3

Source: Telekom Malaysia, *Annual Reports.*

modernisation and increased operating costs, but figures from the company's annual reports showed otherwise. Telekom Malaysia has been making 'superprofits' since 1991 (Table 8.10) (*The Leader*, 13 October 1995).

Conclusion

There is considerable scepticism about the benefits of privatisation of the various public enterprises reviewed earlier. In most cases, the transfer of ownership from public to private hands has not involved reduced user costs or significantly enhanced quality of services.

The manner in which the privatisation policy has been implemented needs to be questioned. There is a lack of public accountability and governmental transparency in the privatisation procedures. Therefore, privatisation in Malaysia has probably been most successful in contributing to the government's new economic policy (NEP) objective, particularly acquisition of wealth by Bumiputera. Thus, the Bumiputera redistribution goal has been clearly favoured at the expense of other stated objectives.

Privatisation is expected to be accompanied by the relaxation or abolition of monopolistic practices. There should be greater competition that would achieve greater efficiency and productivity when privatisation takes place.

In Malaysia, such desired improvements in the market place may not be achieved through privatisation, since there has been little evidence of increased competition associated with privatisation, and most privatised entities such as Telekom Malaysia, Tenaga Nasional Berhad (TNB) and Pos Malaysia have remained virtual monopolies.

Privatisation is certainly not the universal panacea to the large number of problems found in the public sector. In many instances, the problem of the public enterprises is not a problem of ownership *per se*, but rather due to the absence of explicit or achievable objectives. Privatisation may assist in the achievement of organisational goals with the changes it may bring, but this does not necessarily mean that privatisation is solely responsible for the improvements concerned. Hence, such improved performance of an enterprise may be wrongly attributed to changes in ownership *per se*. In the case of Kelang Container Terminal (KCT), the significant improvement in performance was not a result of a change in ownership (Goh and Sundram 1995). In fact, majority ownership did not go into private hands as the government still indirectly held on to over 88.7 per cent of the enterprise's stock. Studies of KCT's privatisation suggest that efficiency and productivity gains and improvement in performance have primarily been the result of managerial and organisational reforms by the new management rather than due to the ownership change *per se*. Also the increased profitability was a result of increased volume of imports and exports due to the economic recovery in the late 1980s in Malaysia (Table 8.11).

Privatisation, according to the *PMP*'s claim, is 'premised on the superiority of market over administrative directives in governing economic activity to achieve efficiency' and that 'government intervention in the economy will be minimal'.

But the pursuit of efficiency would only take place if all or at least the majority of the shares of a public enterprise or its assets are sold to the private shareholders. In Malaysia, complete transfer of ownership to the private sector is not a norm. The privatisation of telecommunications and electricity utilities (Telekom Malaysia Berhad and Tenaga Nasional Berhad, respectively) involved only partial divestiture. Table 8.12 shows that in the case of Telekom Malaysia, the government retained a holding of 75 per cent which was registered under the Ministry of Finance Incorporated, two and a half years after privatisation (Goh 1995).

In other cases, even when the government has relinquished all its shares, the mechanism of the 'golden share' has allowed the government to retain effective control and influence over firm behaviour, thus preventing efficiency-inducing changes (Naidu 1992).

It is important to have a comprehensive critical review of the myriad of problems faced by the public enterprises before implementing any relevant policy responses. It would be wrong to assume that, in all cases, privatisation may well be the superior option as such an option cannot be determined *a priori*.

Such a critical review with a view towards reform should consider the variety of modes of privatisation, marketisation and other reform measures as options in dealing with the public sector. In as far as the weakness of the public firms is concerned, possible reforms to restructure their management and institutional set-up, greater benefits through public accountability, coupled with a good reward system based on merit, may motivate workers to maintain and improve efficiency. Greater autonomy and greater exposure to competitive markets should create a strong sense of responsibility and greater commitment among public enterprises to cut waste and improve performance (Rugayah 1991).

Table 8.11 Relationship between growth of output to GNP, exports and imports before and after divestiture of Kelang Container Terminal

Year ended 31 Dec.	*Throughput (TEUs)*[a]	*Percentage increase*	*Turnover ('000)*	*Percentage increase*	*GNP*[b] *(RM mn)*	*Percentage increase*	*Exports of goods (RM mn)*	*Percentage increase*	*Imports of goods (RM mn)*	*Percentage increase*
1985	244,120	—	na	—	72,039	—	37,576	—	28,693	—
1986[c]	241,182	–1.2	na	—	65,851	–8.6	35,373	–5.9	26,592	–7.3
1987	273,335	13.3	75,185	—	74,679	13.4	44,597	26.1	30,041	13.0
1988	319,557	17.0	91,089	21.2	85,796	15.0	54,344	21.9	40,271	34.0
1989	393,954	23.3	107,756	22.2	96,447	12.4	67,824	24.8	60,858	51.0
1990	494,978	25.6	127,221	18.1	110,505	14.6	79,646	17.4	79,119	30.0
1991	603,257	22.0	151,370	19.0	123,530	11.8	92,220	15.8	90,771	14.7
1992	672,642	11.5	160,839	6.3	140,267	13.5	103,657	12.4	101,440	11.8
1993	759,251	13.0	171,640	6.7	157,900	12.6	121,214	16.9	117,423	15.8
1994	800,500	6.0	na	na	176,257	11.6	148,506	22.5	143,945	22.5

Sources: Jones and Fadil (1992); Negara Report; Department of Statistics, Malaysia.

a Twenty-foot equivalent units.
b GNP at current prices.
c Kelang Container Terminal was privatised in 1986.
na – not available.

Table 8.12 Substantial shareholders of privatised companies

Telekom Malaysia Berhad (privatised in November 1990)	
Share distribution as at 3 June 1993	*Percentage*
Malaysian – Bumiputera corporations	0.19
Bumiputera individuals	0.55
Government agencies (Minister of Finance Inc. holds 74.58%)	80.73
Nominee companies	2.19
Other local companies	0.13
Individuals	0.67
Foreign – Companies	1.70
Individuals	13.84
Total	100.00

Tenaga Nasional Berhad (privatised in May 1992)	
Share distribution as at 24 January 1994	*Percentage*
Malaysian – Bumiputera corporations	10.64
Bumiputera individuals	1.71
Minister of Finance Inc.	72.87
Other Malaysian individuals	2.84
Other companies	3.14
Foreign – Companies	8.71
Individuals	0.10
Total	100.00

Source: Annual Companies Handbook.

Therefore, a privatisation master plan should emerge from a critical review of the public sector. A variety of privatisation measures as well as other public sector reform measures should be considered as some among various options for improving the public sector as a whole in relation to growth, efficiency and equity development.

However, the *PMP* has failed to address a number of issues that resulted from the privatisation policy. It has inadequately monitored the post-privatisation conduct and performances of privatisation and privatised activities. It has been virtually silent on crucial questions of accountability and transparency. It has very little to say about market failure, even though the major candidates for privatisation are public monopolies. It has not addressed the issue of consumer protection and protecting the 'national interest', however defined, in an economy with much reduced public sector and considerably enhanced private sector. Unfortunately, it has been anxious in accelerating the pace of privatisation as an end in itself, instead of regarding privatisation as an option. To put it bluntly, the *PMP* is a disappointment on many scores.

Bibliography

Adam, C., Cavendish, W. and Mistry, P. (1991) *Adjusting Privatization: Case Studies from Developing Countries*, London: James Currey.

Aggrawal and Rivoli, P. (1990) 'Fads in Initial Public Offering Market?', *Financial Management* 19(1): 45–57.

Aliran Monthly (1995) 'Healthcare in Crisis', May.

Aminuddin, A. (1992) 'Tolls in Malaysia', in S. Azizul, 'Paying Too Much?', *Investors Digest*, April 1994.

Annual Companies Handbook (various issues).

Azizul, S. (1994) 'Paying Too Much?', *Investors Digest*, April.

Bank Negara Malaysia, *Annual Reports* (various issues), Kuala Lumpur: BNM.

Basheer, H. (1994) 'Privatization of Kelang Container Terminal: Labour Issues and Measures Adopted', paper presented at the Conference on 'Malaysia–Tanzania Roundtable Discussion on Privatization and Private Sector Development', organised by EDI and World Bank, Kuala Lumpur, 11–12 April.

Bhaskar, V. (1992) *Privatization and the Developing Countries: The Issues and the Evidence*, Discussion Papers No. 47, UNCTAD, Geneva.

Chee, S. (1990) 'The Political Economy of Privatization with Reference to Malaysia', in *Issues and Challenges for National Development*, Faculty of Economics and Administration, University of Malaya, Kuala Lumpur.

Cook, P. and Kirkpatrick, C. (1988) 'Privatization in Less Developed Countries: An Overview', in P. Cook and C. Kirkpatrick (eds), *Privatization in Less Developed Countries*, New York: Harvester Wheatsheaf.

Goh, W. (1995) 'Share Pricing, Performance and Consumer Welfare in Malaysian Privatization', M.Econ. dissertation, Faculty of Economics and Administration, University of Malaya, Kuala Lumpur.

Goh, W. and Sundram, J.K. (1995) 'Efficiency and Consumer Welfare', in J.K. Sundram (ed.), *Privatizing Malaysia: Rents, Rhetoric, Realities*, Colorado: Westview Press.

Jones, L. and Fadil, A.A. (1992) 'Kelang Container Terminal', in World Bank Conference on the 'Welfare Consequences of Selling Public Enterprises: Case Studies from Chile, Malaysia, Mexico and the UK', Washington, DC, 11–12 June.

Kartini, A.K. (1991) 'New Chapter in History of Postal Services', *Business Times*, 31 December.

Kelang Container Terminal, *Annual Reports*, 1993–4.

Kennedy, L.B. (1991) 'Privatization as a Method of Wealth Redistribution: The Case of Malaysian Telecoms', paper presented at the Seventh International Conference on Culture and Communication, Temple University, Philadelphia, 5 October.

Khor, E.L. (1992a) 'What Has Been Gained by Privatization', *Investors Digest*, July.

—— (1992b) 'Telekom's Take-off', *Investors Digest*, September.

Lloyd's List Maritime Asia (1993) 'Privatization in Port Klang', November.

Malaysia Economic Planning Unit (1985) *Guideline on Privatization*, Kuala Lumpur.

—— (1991a) *Privatization Masterplan*, Kuala Lumpur.

—— (1991b) *Sixth Malaysian Plan, 1991–1995*, Kuala Lumpur.

Malaysian Business (1989) 'KTM Privatization: Which Track?', May.

Martin, B. (1993) *In the Public Interest? Privatization and Public Sector Reform*, London: Zed Books.

Nadeswaran, R. (1995) 'Say No', *The Leader*, 13 October.

Naidu, G. (1992) *Private Provision of Physical Infrastructure: The Malaysian Experience*, EDI Working Paper, Economic Development Institute, Washington, DC: World Bank.

Patridge, B.E., Abd, S.Z. and Walton, J.R. (1995) 'Rhetoric Versus Reality: The Privatization of Telekom Malaysia', *Journal of Far Eastern Business* 1: 36–47.

Philip, K. (1992) 'On Privatisation Track', *Investors Digest*, October.

Rodhiah, I. (1991) 'Vibrant Postal in the Making', *Business Times*, 18 December.

Rugayah, M. (1991) 'Comparative Performance of Public and Private Enterprises in Malaysia', Ph.D. thesis, Development and Project Planning Centre, University of Bradford, England.

Soh, Eng Lim (1990a) 'Clue to Road Puzzles', *Investors Digest*, May.

—— (1990b) 'Tolling Side-Effects', *Investors Digest*, May.

—— (1990c) 'Not the BOT Way', *Investors Digest*, October.

—— (1990d) 'Open to Question', *Investors Digest*, October.

Sundram, J.K. (1993) 'Privatization in Malaysia: For What and For Whom?', in T. Clarke and C. Pitelis (eds), *The Political Economy of Privatization*, London: Routledge.

—— (1995a) 'Malaysia's Privatization Experience', in P. Cook and C. Kirkpatrick (eds), *Privatization Policy and Performance*, New York: Prentice-Hall/Harvester Wheatsheaf.

—— (ed.) (1995b) *Privatizing Malaysia: Rents, Rhetoric, Realities*, Oxford: Westview Press.

Telekom Malaysia, *Annual Reports*, 1991–4.

Tenaga Nasional, *Annual Reports*, 1993–4.

Toh, K.W. (1989) 'Privatization in Malaysia: Restructuring or Efficiency?', *ASEAN Economic Bulletin*, 5(5): 601–15.

Zainuddin Hj, A.R. (1994) 'Privatization: Malaysia's Experience', paper presented at the Conference on 'Malaysia–Tanzania Roundtable Discussion on Privatization and Private Sector Development', organised by EDI and World Bank, Kuala Lumpur, 11–12 April.

9

QUANTITATIVE ANALYSIS OF ECONOMIC REFORMS

Outcomes of the Indian manufacturing sector

Hiranya Mukhopadhyay

Introduction

The Indian economy plunged into a deep economic crisis during the Gulf War in the early 1990s. The rate of inflation was abnormally high by Indian standards, and the foreign exchange reserves had declined to three weeks of imports – about $1 billion. India entered into a standby arrangement – together with a supplementary loan – with the International Monetary Fund for a loan of over $1 billion. Furthermore, various reform measures were undertaken to increase the growth rate in a sustained way. However, five years after the reform, a shadow of recession is looming over the manufacturing sector and endangering the credibility of the reform of 1991.

This chapter provides an alternative explanation of the probable cause of the recession.

Economic reforms

India undertook a structural adjustment programme and various liberalisation measures in June 1991 after the Gulf crisis which intensified the strain on an already weak balance of payments situation. It was estimated that the direct adverse impact of the Gulf Crisis on India's balance of payments was $2.9 billion (Government of India 1991).

Major reforms were undertaken in broadly five main areas (see Government of India 1993). These were (i) industrial policy, (ii) trade and exchange rate reforms, (iii) tax reforms, (iv) foreign investment policy reforms, and (v) financial sector reforms.

Reforms in industrial policy:

a Industrial licensing was abolished for all except a select list of hazardous and environmentally sensitive industries.
b The separate permission needed by MRTP (the Monopolies and Restrictive Trade Practice) houses for investment and expansion was abolished.
c Access to foreign technology was made much freer.
d Private initiative encouraged in the development of infrastructure such as power, highways, telecommunications, shipping and ports, and airport and civil aviation.

Trade and exchange rate reforms:

a Import control through licensing has been virtually eliminated.
b Except consumer goods, almost all capital goods, raw materials, intermediates can be freely imported.
c Import duties have been cut sharply.
d The exchange rate determination was made market determined gradually.

Tax reforms:

a The maximum marginal rate of income tax was reduced to 40 per cent and corporate income tax was reduced from 65 per cent to 40 per cent by 1995–6. Again, while several exemptions were removed, the wealth tax on all productive assets was abolished.
b A process of simplification of excise duties began with the 1993–4 budget, with a moderation of the high rates of duties on some commodities, and removal of certain exemptions.
c The duty rates on imports have been sharply reduced, with the maximum rate falling from 330 per cent to 85 per cent in 1993–4 and to 50 per cent in 1995–6.

Foreign investment policy:

a Automatic approval of foreign investment up to 51 per cent was allowed and foreign technology agreements permitted for thirty-five priority industries which account for about 50 per cent of value added in the manufacturing sector.
b Foreign investment has also been liberalised in many other sectors.
c The Foreign Exchange Regulations Act (FERA) was amended to remove a number of constraints earlier applicable to firms with foreign equity operating in India and also to make it easier for Indian business to operate abroad.

Financial sector reforms:

- a New norms have been introduced related to income recognition, provisioning and capital adequacy.
- b A reduction in the statutory liquidity ratio (SLR), and this will most likely be reduced further in the future.
- c Banks are now allowed to approach the capital market to mobilise funds.
- d Private sector banks will be allowed to expand and new private sector banks will be allowed to be set up.
- e The interest rates have been gradually deregulated.

Overview of the achievements

The major goals of the reform process are to achieve a higher growth rate of gross domestic product (GDP) in a sustained way and to maintain a moderate inflation rate. While India has not been able to achieve a sustainable growth rate of 7 per cent even after five years of reform, the current rate of inflation is satisfactory when compared to its pre-reform level (Table 9.1).

The reform has failed to achieve positive results on the revenue front, when judged by the tax-to-GDP ratio. Between 1991–2 and 1996–7, the tax-to-GDP ratio declined from 10.9 per cent to 10.5 per cent, despite vari-

Table 9.1 Movements in key variables

Item	*1990–1*	*1991–2*	*1992–3*	*1994–5*	*1995–6*	*1996–7*
GDP at constant prices (% change)	5.4	0.8	5.3	7.2	7.1	6.8
Index of manufacturing production (% change)	9.0	−0.8	2.2	9.4	13.1	8.2
Agricultural production (% change)	3.7	−2.0	4.1	4.6	0.1	5.8
Exports (% change)	9.2	−1.5	3.8	17.9	21.4	4.0
Imports (% change)	13.5	−19.4	12.7	21.2	28.7	6.0
Foreign exchange reserves (US$ billion)	2.23	5.63	6.43	20.8	17.5	26.2
Inflation (WPI)	12.0	13.6	7.0	10.4	7.7	6.4
Total tax revenue (% of GDP)	10.8	10.9	10.6	9.8	10.2	10.5
Total expenditure (% of GDP)	19.7	18.1	17.4	17.0	16.3	15.9
Fiscal deficit (% of GDP)	8.3	5.9	5.7	6.1	5.5	5.0
Money supply (M3) (% change)	14.9	19.3	15.7	22.1	13.7	15.9

Source: Reserve Bank of India Monthly Bulletin (various issues); Economic Survey of India (1996–7), Government of India; Shome (1996).

ous reforms. There is no doubt that various reforms have eliminated distortions and diminished the cascading effect of taxes (Shome 1996), but they have failed to raise the tax-to-GDP ratio higher than its pre-reform level. Consequently, it has become very difficult to reduce the fiscal deficit-to-GDP ratio significantly and permanently, especially when the expenditure-to-GDP ratio has remained stable at around 17 per cent until 1994–5.

Exports and industrial growth have a mixed fortune. Growth in exports had been very promising during the last couple of years. However, it declined sharply from 21.4 per cent in 1995–6 to only 4.0 per cent during 1996–7. Many experts believe that infrastructural bottlenecks, especially congestion at various ports and slowdown in world demand, could be the plausible reasons.

The most alarming development during the current financial year (1996–7) is the shadow of recession over the industrial sector. The growth rate of the index of industrial production (IIP, manufacturing) had been rising steadily since 1991–2, when it registered a negative growth rate (Table 9.1). The growth rate of manufacturing was quite impressive during 1995–6 (13.1 per cent). However, the growth rate declined sharply to only 8.2 per cent during 1996–7. The performance of mining and electricity has been equally bad during the current fiscal year.

Another interesting feature is that the recession primarily is led by the consumer durables sector and partially by the basic goods sector (Table 9.2). Inventories have started piling up in many units of this sector and many companies are now offering attractive buy-back options. Furthermore, the situation may turn out to be worse as the large-scale inventory offloading to dealers would show up during the last quarter of 1996–7 in the company books.

Table 9.2 Index of industrial production: use-based

	Percentage change over previous year (April-October)	
	1995–6	*1996–7*
Basic goods	11.1	6.7
Capital goods	15.1	16.6
Intermediate goods	7.2	10.8
Consumer durables	30.2	9.7
Consumer non-durables	9.2	7.7
All goods	13.5	8.2

Source: Central Statistical Organisation (monthly bulletin), Government of India.

Note: For consumer durables, the turning point was April 1996. The growth rate declined from 40.8 per cent in March 1996 to 10.9 per cent in April 1996.

In many Latin American countries this type of business cycle – a boom followed by a recession – was noticed during the post-reform period (Kiguel and Liviatan 1992). Most of these countries adopted an exchange rate-based stabilisation programme, where exchange rate was used as a nominal anchor. The main reasons for the failure of the stabilisation programme in those countries have been the lack of supporting fiscal policy and the lack of credibility (Calvo and Vegh 1991).

Many experts believe that an infrastructural bottleneck and high borrowing cost are the main causes of recession in Indian industries during 1996–7. Both these factors are very important as far as industrial growth is concerned. But this offers only a partial explanation, because if this were true, then recession should have been across the board. How have capital-intensive sectors such as capital goods or intermediate goods maintained their growth rates? Why has recession been felt mostly in the consumer durables sector? The official explanation has failed to provide a satisfactory answer to these questions.

An alternative hypothesis

It is suggested that the growth rate in the consumer durables sector has fallen sharply during the first half of 1996–7 primarily owing to higher real interest rates (deposit rates). An increase in the real rate of return of saving has two offsetting effects. First, a higher interest rate decreases the present cost of future consumption, so that it is attractive to consume less now and more in the future and thus to save more today. Second, it is no longer necessary to save as much to achieve a level of future consumption, so that a higher real interest rate allows greater consumption today and tomorrow, and thus reduces the need to save today.

Therefore, the effect of real interest rates on current consumption becomes an empirical matter. Fry (1978, 1980) and Gupta (1987) found some support for a positive effect of real interest rates on saving. Schmidt-Hebel *et al.* (1992) did not find any such effect. Perhaps the substitution effect and income effect cancel each other out or liquidity constraints weaken the effects of intertemporal relative prices.

Deposit growth and inflation

The slowdown in the rate of growth of scheduled commercial banks' aggregate deposits witnessed in the second half of 1994–5 has continued until the first half of 1995–6. However, there has been a turnaround in the growth rate of aggregate deposits during the second half of 1995–6, to be more precise, during the month of January 1996 (Table 9.3). The growth rate of aggregate deposits further shot up to almost 16 per cent during April 1996. The upturn in the growth of deposits was responding to policy

Table 9.3 Total deposit of scheduled commercial banks

	Percentage change over previous year
27 October 1995	11.5
24 November 1995	11.4
29 December 1995	11.8
26 January 1996	12.9
23 February 1996	13.6
29 March 1996	11.8
26 April 1996	15.7
31 May 1996	16.3
21 June 1996	16.8
19 July 1996	16.9
30 August 1996	17.2
27 September 1996	17.0
25 October 1996	16.3
8 November 1996	17.0

Source: Centre for Monitoring Indian Economy (CMIE)'s monthly review of the Indian economy, December 1996.

measures; in particular, the increase in the ceiling interest rate for term deposits of up to two years' maturity and complete deregulation of interest rates on term deposits of over two years' maturity effective from 1 October 1995 (Reserve Bank of India Bulletin, 1996, p. 34). The deposit rate for over one year maturity was also deregulated in July 1996.

A careful examination of the growth rate of wholesale price index (WPI) or average consumer price index (CPI) reveals that there has also been a turnaround during December 1995. For example, the growth rate of CPI declined from 10.1 per cent in November 1995 to 8.5 per cent in December 1995 and further down to only 6.8 per cent in February 1996 (Table 9.4). A similar pattern was also revealed by the movements in the WPI.

Therefore, it would not be incorrect to conjecture that the upturn in the growth rate of aggregate deposits was responding to a higher real interest rate during January or February of 1996. In other words, there is preliminary evidence to suggest that the substitution effect of a higher real interest rate dominated the income effect. It may be noted that a representative consumer's decision is based on his/her *ex ante* inflation expectation; however, data on the rate of inflation in Table 9.4 are *ex post.* This distinction is trivial for deposits with short maturity periods (say, for example, 46 days' fixed deposit).

Table 9.4 Inflation rates

	Wholesale price index		*Consumer price index (average)*	
	1995–6	*1996–7*	*1995–6*	*1996–7*
April	10.0	5.0	11.3	8.5
May	9.9	4.5	11.3	9.1
June	9.2	4.5	11.7	8.8
July	8.4	6.0	12.9	7.7
August	8.8	6.2	13.0	7.5
September	8.9	6.6	12.0	8.1
October	8.5	6.7	11.1	8.5
November	8.4	6.7	10.1	
December	6.4		8.5	
January	5.0		8.1	
February	4.6		6.8	
March	5.1		7.6	

Source: CMIE's monthly review of the Indian economy, December 1996.

An econometric test of the alternative hypothesis

It is proposed to estimate a consumption function of the following type to assess the impact of higher real interest rate on private consumption, especially consumer durables.

$$C_i/Y_d = \alpha + \beta\, r_{int} + \gamma\, Y_{pd}/Y_d + \theta\, F_D/Y_d$$

where C_i = private consumption expenditure (i = aggregate, clothing and footwear, and furniture and furnishing appliances); r_{int} = real interest rate (deposit rate); Y_d = personal disposable income; Y_{pd} = permanent personal disposable income; F_D = fiscal deficit (centre plus states).

The direct effects of fiscal policies on consumption (or saving) operate through public deficit (or saving) and its composition (Marshall and Schmidt-Hebbel 1994). If the stringent conditions required for Ricardian equivalence are satisfied, a fall in public deficit – if it comes about through lower public spending – is exactly offset by an increase in private consumption. Because disposable income does not change, the reduction in private saving matches the rise in public saving. A fall in public deficit does not affect private consumption at all if it is achieved through higher taxes. But as disposable income is reduced by the size of the tax, the reduction in private saving matches the fall in public deficit (rise in public saving). However, it may be noted that the coefficient θ could be negative if the public sector has the preferential access to bank credit, forcing private consumption to adjust accordingly. This is an example of direct crowding-out. As has already been discussed, the alternative hypothesis is accepted, if β is negative. In other words, the substitution effect is stronger than the income effect. It may also be noted that a rise in the inflation rate may lead to higher saving and lower consumption owing to precautionary saving as a result of higher uncertainty despite a reduction in the real interest rate.

The equation was tested using annual data for the 1970–1 to 1994–5 period and the results are reported in Table 9.5. The equation was estimated by using the OLS technique, and every dependent or independent variable with a trend was divided by a common scale variable to get rid of spurious regression problems.

Furthermore, a lagged dependent variable has been added in each equation to check whether consumers adjust their consumption expenditure partially in each period or not. Finally, one dummy variable has been added in the equation for clothes and footwear to eliminate the outliers in 1976–7 and 1978–9.

It is interesting to note that aggregate consumption reacts to public deficit. Therefore, an increase in public sector saving does not lead to an equal increase in national saving, as it is partially offset by a decrease in private saving.

The short-run marginal propensity to consume out of permanent income is around 0.4 for aggregate consumption and less than 0.1 for other consumer durables.

The real interest rate has a significant and negative impact on private consumption expenditure, which clearly shows that a higher real interest rate reduces current consumption owing to the stronger substitution effect, and raises future consumption (saving). However, the coefficient of real interest

Table 9.5 Estimation results

	Aggregate consumption	*Textiles and footwear*	*Furniture and furnishing appliances*
Constant	0.11	−0.02	−0.02
	(0.45)	(0.52)	(−1.26)
r_{int}	−1.26	−0.31	−0.08
	(−2.31)	(−4.41)	(−2.51)
Y_{pd}/Y_d	0.39	0.09	0.03
	(1.79)	(2.19)	(1.92)
F_D/Y_d	−0.65	0.03	0.02
	(2.00)	(0.85)	(0.87)
Lagged dependent variable	0.60	0.04	0.79
	(3.88)	(4.82)	(6.37)
R^2	0.95	0.90	0.84
Adjusted R^2	0.93	0.89	0.82
h statistics	−0.48	−0.36	−0.08

Note: *t*-values are in parentheses.

rate is much higher for aggregate consumption than consumer durables. We do not make any attempt in this chapter to offer an explanation for this phenomenon.

Conclusion

An alternative hypothesis has been suggested and tested to explain industrial recession, especially in the consumer durables sector. Private consumers have postponed their consumption for the future owing to a higher real interest rate. Consequently, private saving, as proxied by the deposit growth rate, must have increased during the first half of 1996–7. The growth rates of bank deposits and IIP (consumer durables) started moving in opposite directions during April 1996. It may also be noted from Table 9.2 that the growth rate of capital goods, however, has not increased significantly, suggesting a decline in demand for funds (see also Bhaumik 1996, and Bhaumik and Mukhopadhyay 1997 on this point).

It is important to note that the total effect of a higher real interest rate may not result in a reduction in the consumption of durable goods. A higher real interest rate could generate higher income growth in a credit-constrained regime owing to higher saving and hence higher investment. Consequently, the total effect of a higher real interest rate on consumption may be positive.

However, as has already been argued, demand for funds had also declined during 1996–7 due to many reasons together with a decline in demand for consumer goods. Three important causes for this were: (i) very high lending rates, (ii) uncertainty that is also associated with political instability and (iii) infrastructural bottlenecks. It is now well established that producers do not invest in an uncertain environment owing to the presence of sunk-costs, rather they prefer a 'wait and watch' option. This has been a problem in Argentina, Kenya and Turkey during the mid-1980s when these countries' liberalisation programmes commenced. Mexico also had a pause in private investment, because private investors waited to see whether trade reforms would be reversed.

Therefore, a revival of demand for consumer durables does not necessarily imply a revival of demand for funds for investment, and it can also be conjectured that the total impact of a higher real interest rate on the consumer durables sector has therefore been negative during the first two quarters of 1996–7.

The policy implications of our results are very clear. First, the real interest rate (lending rates) should be reduced. A reduction in the nominal lending rates, however, may not be feasible at this juncture unless the deposit rates are also lowered. Second, various uncertainties that are associated with the non-transparent nature of economic policies should be minimised as early as possible. Finally, maximum priority should be given for removing infrastructural bottlenecks. Unless these steps are taken immediately, economic reforms will certainly fail to yield the desired results.

Appendix

Data sources and definitions

C_i: Private consumption expenditure data on various items have been obtained from National Accounts Statistics, Central Statistical Organisation, Government of India.

r_{int}: Deposit rate of one to three years minus the percentage change in the deflator of private consumption expenditure. This is the simple static expectation specification about the rate of inflation. We have also tried the partial perfect foresight assumption by taking the average inflation between today and yesterday and between today and tomorrow. The results donotchangemuchqualitativebothqualitativelyandquantitatively.Finally,we should have used the deposit rate for less than one year maturity, because then there is not much qualitative difference between the *ex ante* and *ex post* annual inflation. However, short-period fixed deposits with the commercial banks did not exist during the 1970s and 1980s. *Sources:* Reports on Currency and Finance (Reserve Bank of India) and National Accounts Statistics, Central Statistical Organisations.

Y_d: Personal disposable income. *Source:* National Accounts Statistics.

Y_{pd}: Permanent personal disposable income. First we have divided Y_d by aggregate consumption deflator to arrive at Y_d at constant prices. Then we have assumed expectations of the permanent values that are consistent with partial perfect foresight, defined as the simple average of the contemporaneous variable and one period into the future. Finally, the permanent disposable income at current prices is derived by multiplying the constant prices series with the consumption deflator (see Corbo and Schmidt-Hebbel 1991 for more on this point). Alternatively, we could have assumed static expectation specification for permanent disposable income.

F_D: The gap between total expenditure and total revenue (centre plus states). *Source:* Indian Economic Statistics: Public Finance, Ministry of Finance, Government of India.

References

Bhaumik, S. (1996) 'The Indian Financial Market: Issues, Problems and Policies', *National Institute of Public Finance and Policy*, New Delhi (mimeo).

—— and Mukhopadhyay, H. (1997) 'Liquidity, Crunch and Industrial Stagnation: A Fresh Look', *National Institute of Public Finance and Policy*, New Delhi (mimeo).

Calvo, A. and Vegh, Carlos A. (1991) 'Exchange Rate Based Stabilization Under Imperfect Credibility', *IMF Working Paper*, WP/91/77.

Corbo, V. and Schmidt-Hebbel, K. (1991) 'Public Policies and Saving in Developing Countries', *Journal of Development Economics* 36: 89–115.

Fry, M.J. (1978) 'Money and Capital or Financial Deepening in Economic Development', *Journal of Money, Credit and Banking* 10: 464–75.

—— (1980) 'Saving, Investment, Growth and the Cost of Financial Repression', *World Development* 8: 317–27.

Government of India (1991) 'Economic Survey: 1990–91', *Ministry of Finance*, New Delhi.

—— (1993) 'Economic Reforms: Two Years After and the Task Ahead', *Ministry of Finance*, New Delhi.

Gupta, K.L. (1987) 'Aggregate Saving, Financial Intermediation and Interest Rate', *Review of Economics and Statistics* 69: 303–11.

Kiguel, M.A. and Liviatan, N. (1992) 'Nominal Anchor, Stabilization and Growth: Some Thoughts on High Inflation Economies', in V. Corbo *et al.* (eds), *Adjustment Lending Revisited: Policies to Restore Growth*, Washington, DC: World Bank.

Marshall, J. and Schmidt-Hebbel, K. (1994) 'Chile: Fiscal Adjustment and Successful Performance', in W. Easterly *et al.* (eds), *Public Sector Deficit and Macroeconomic Performance*, Washington, DC: World Bank.

Schmidt-Hebbel, K., Webb, S. and Corsetti, G. (1992) 'Household Saving in Developing Countries: First Cross Country Evidences', *World Bank Economic Review* 6: 529–47.

Shome, P. (1996) 'Fiscal Policy in the 1990s – Needed Reforms and Ramifications for the Financial Sector', Sir Purshotam Das Thakur Das Memorial Lecture delivered at the Indian Institute of Bankers, Mumbai.

10

LIBERALISATION AND PRIVATISATION

India's telecommunications reforms

Moazzem Hossain

Implementation of the IMF and World Bank-led structural adjustment programme (SAP) in developing countries reached a peak with the support of Fund and Bank's adjustment-lending loans in the early 1980s. India, however, has been behind by almost five years in undertaking structural adjustment programmes to qualify for the loans. Nevertheless, the SAP has brought with it a strong wave of economic reform in India during 1991. Economic reform has been achieved using two major measures: trade liberalisation and privatisation of public enterprises. In this chapter, these measures are reviewed and their implications for the telecommunications sector of India are analysed.

Liberalisation

Liberalisation in developing countries has been extensively studied both within and outside the World Bank (Thomas and Associates 1991; Michaely *et al.* 1991). A large and growing amount of literature on trade policy reforms and their consequences has been surveyed in the last few years, particularly by Rodrick (1993). All these studies within and outside the Bank made at least one outcome of trade policy reform clear: that is, many developing countries have been pursuing the reform process unilaterally. India is not an exception (Srinivasan and Cañonero 1995). India pursued closed and inward-looking trade policies until the end of the 1980s, and then unilaterally embraced the outward-oriented policies by making substantial reductions in average tariff rates and removing many quantitative restrictions (QR) (Table 10.1).

There are numerous definitions of trade liberalisation, but the definition given by Krueger and Bhagwati seems universally accepted. Krueger (1986) defined liberalisation as 'any policy action that reduces the restrictiveness of

Table 10.1 Trade liberalisation in India, 1990–3 (percentage)

Average nominal tariff		*Tariff ratio*	*QR coverage*		*QR ratio*
Pre-reform	*Post-reform*		*Pre-reform*	*Post-reform*	
128	71	0.55	95	50	0.53

Source: Dean *et al.* (1994).

controls – reduces the scarcity premium attached to those controls'. Krueger defines liberalisation as a means of openness, that is the transformation of a closed economy into an open one where controls are minimised and/or removed altogether. Bhagwati (cited in Dean *et al.* 1994) emphasised neutrality of the trade regimes as the central aspect of liberalisation. Neutrality involves the removal of any bias from import-substituting regimes to favour domestic sale. There should not be any incentives against exports within a nation under a liberalised economy; rather exporters should be allowed incentives to increase exports by way of rebate or reducing duties on imported inputs.

The main trade liberalisation measures involve:

- lowering average nominal tariffs;
- narrowing the range of nominal and effective tariffs;
- shifting from quantitative restrictions (QRs) to tariffs (tariffication);
- a real devaluation of currency;
- the unification of multiple exchange rates;
- removing export taxes;
- removing export quantitative restrictions; and
- implementing export subsidies, rebates or compensation schemes.

With all these measures in hand a developing country must transform QRs into tariffs first, and then gradually lower these tariffs and make them uniform. Direct incentives to exports are not as important to export growth as real devaluation and import liberalisation. At the same time, exporters' access to imported inputs has been more important for export growth than internal export subsidies (Michaely *et al.* 1991; Thomas *et al.* 1991).

Privatisation

The industrial policy issues in developing countries were not only affected by the trade liberalisation strategy but also by the privatisation movement, which was initiated by the World Bank and the IMF through SAP. Like trade liberalisation, the privatisation agenda was endorsed for both more developed and developing countries alike. However, privatisation in developing countries has involved three main approaches: the 'big-bang' approach of Latin American and Caribbean countries, the 'go-slow and institutional' approach of the Asian and East Asian countries and the 'marketisation' political approach of the East European countries. These approaches have, of course, yielded different impacts in different countries. In India, the East Asian approach of 'go-slow and institutional' has been followed, so far.

In the Indian context, privatisation has mainly involved selling the state-owned enterprises (SOEs) and other government activities to the private sector (Edadan 1997). To enable the process to proceed with a reasonable pace India has an independent government agency in place. The subsequent review of the privatisation trends in India provides a clear picture about the shape and direction of privatisation in the country.

Privatisation trends

Privatisation of SOEs has been carried out by using a range of techniques. The most common techniques involve: direct sale of an SOE, public offer of an SOE, concession sale, joint venture, management buyouts, liquidation and lease. Table 10.2 provides figures for privatisation performance in India compared with the selected countries of South and Southeast Asia in 1994. In the South Asian region, Pakistan and Sri Lanka can be regarded as being relatively high privatisor countries, India as the medium privatisor and Bangladesh as the low privatisor. In contrast, in Southeast Asia, Malaysia is the high privatisor country, Indonesia is a medium privatisor and South Korea and Thailand are the low privatisors (South Korea is regarded as an East Asian nation).

Since 1991 the central government of India has introduced a programme of disinvestment of government shareholding across a wide range of public enterprises, bringing its share in a number of such enterprises to almost 60

Table 10.2 Privatisation performance, 1994

Country	*PR*	*GNP*	*PR/GNP*
Bangladesh	43	26,141	0.16
India	**4,395**	**289,374**	**1.52**
Pakistan	1,541	52,241	2.95
Sri Lanka	223	11,553	1.93
Indonesia	1,984	168,000	1.18
South Korea	3,274	355,672	0.92
Malaysia	6,638	67,163	9.88
Thailand	1,041	141,523	0.74

Source: Edadan (1997).

Notes: PR = privatisation revenue (US$ million); GNP = gross national product (US$ million).

per cent. The government of India has so far partially privatised the telecommunications and aviation industries. At the state level, Andhra Pradesh, Gujarat and Haryana have in fact permitted the privatisation of some poorly performing public enterprises (UNIDO 1995).

India's telecommunications industry

The development of an effective telecommunications sector is a key to the growing international competitiveness of India. The Indian authorities have at last realised its importance and launched several reform measures in telecommunications in the last seven years. Since 1991, the telecommunications sector has expanded exponentially as a result of the reform process. In 1972, the country had a million telephone lines and by 1994 it had 8 million telephone lines. It has been estimated that the rate of growth in the sector was more than 15 per cent per annum in recent years (World Bank 1995). The extent and implications of the telecommunications reform invite closer examination. The next section does this and considers the government's rate of success in implementing reform policies.

Telecommunication framework of India

Under the Indian constitution, only the central government can legislate on telecommunications. The central government has been the monopoly provider of telecommunication services through the Department of Telecommunications (DOT) which is under the jurisdiction of the central government's Ministry of Communications. Before 1989 a Telecom Board with a director-general at the helm steered the board on behalf of the central government. The DOT corporatised two of its operational wings in 1986. These are called Videsh Sanchar Nigam Limited (VSNL) responsible for international operations and Mohanagar Telephone Nigam Limited (MSNL) with operational responsibility for providing telephone services in metropolitan Delhi and Bombay, which comprise nearly a quarter of the total telecom network. The rest of the country remained under the jurisdiction of the DOT. In May 1989, the Telecom Board was replaced by a Telecommunications Commission with a much broader mandate than the board. Telecommunication operations were divided into five areas and headed by five full-time members of the Commission. These areas being: telecom policy, regulation, technical research and development, design and manufacture of equipment, and provision of telecommunication services. The secretary of the DOT also holds the position of Commission chairman.

India's present telephone density of one telephone per 100 persons is one of the world's lowest and is well below the world average of ten per 100 persons (Table 10.3). But with the planned establishment of over 20 million telephone lines by 2000 to meet the current demand for 40 million lines,

India is the world's second largest telecom market after China. The ambitious network expansion programme for the next five years will need around US$22.5 billion of investment.

Table 10.4 presents the information for the basic telecom structure presently existing in India. By the end of March 1995, the country had 9.38 million lines with installed capacity of a further 10 million lines. The demand for telephone sources over the last ten years has grown by almost 12.2 per cent with actual growth in installation of 11.8 per cent. The total workforce in Indian telecom services stands at 470,000 persons.

Table 10.3 Growth of access lines in the Asian region, 1993–2000

Country	*1993*	*2000 (estimated)*
India	0.9	2
Pakistan	1.0	2
Sri Lanka	0.9	4
Indonesia	0.9	5
Malaysia	13	25
China	1.5	5
South Korea	37	60
Thailand	2.7	9
Developed countries	48	63

Source: Jayasuriya and Knight-John (1996).

Table 10.4 Basic telecom information

Number of telephone lines as at 31 March 1995	9.38 million
Installed capacity of telephone lines	10 million
Demand for telephones (FY 1995)	12.5 million
Growth in telephone lines (FY 1985 to FY 1994)	11.8 per cent
Growth in telephone demand (FY 1985 to FY 1994)	12.2 per cent
Total workforce (telecom services)	470,000

Source: Hossain and Chatterjee (1996).

Recent reforms in telecommunications

A major programme is under way to expand and upgrade India's telecom network. Complete freedom of telecom equipment manufacturing, privatisation of services, liberal foreign investment and technology imports regulation are contributing to a quantum leap in growth. Concomitantly, the DOT will be restructured to remove its monopoly status as service provider. Most value-added services, including cellular phones and radio pagers, which were virtually non-existent, are poised for a massive increase in sales. The government is now set to open up a huge (Rs90 billion) basic services market which offers the largest business opportunities in telecommunications. In view of the above, the government issued a Telecom Policy Statement on 12 May 1994 which:

- allows new entrants to provide basic telephone services to supplement DOT;
- maintains DOT's status as sole provider of long-distance services and confirms that DOT will remain a government department;
- sets targets for providing all villages with access to a telephone by the end of 1997;
- endorses the existing policy whereby the private sector will be the main provider of value-added services;
- encourages pilot projects which envisage an inflow of new technology and management techniques, and generally involves foreign investment; and
- indicates that mechanisms will be set up to protect consumer interests and ensure fair competition.

Given the general nature of the new policy, the government issued implementing guidelines in September 1994. In summary these guidelines indicate that:

- a Telecom Regulatory Authority of India will be established as an autonomous body with a chairman and two members;
- new entry for basic telephone services will be permitted as duopolies (that is, DOT and one other operator) in the twenty 'Circles' into which the country has been divided;
- DOT will retain the long-distance monopoly for five years after which the decision would be reviewed; and
- foreign ownership of telecom operators will be welcome by up to 49 per cent of equity (from World Bank 1995: 104–5).

With all these changes in place, it is anticipated that the country will attract a massive amount of foreign investment from the world's major telecommunication companies. The next section will describe the proposed measures for implementation of the telecommunications policies.

Policy implementation

Implementation of new policies began in January 1995 with DOT calling for tenders from domestic and foreign participants for the operation of basic telephone services in twenty circles throughout India. One new entrant has been allowed per region on a non-exclusive basis as a local operator to bring in basic telephone services in competition with DOT. The bid process follows a two-step selection process.

The first step involves a technical and commercial evaluation of the bidders to conform with the technical specification and commercial eligibility conditions. A shortlist of compliant bidders is then prepared. The second step involves opening the financial offers of the shortlisted bidders in their presence which are then evaluated. The bidder with the best financial bid is selected.

- **Selection of private companies for basic services**: a total of sixteen companies participated in bids for providing basic telecom services in twenty 'circles' of which six companies were initially successful. The decision by DOT to restrict the operations of individual companies to three circles and to fix a reserve price for the bids resulted in retendering in thirteen telecom circles. Licences to initiate operations will be awarded after the entire selection process is completed allowing private services to be available by 1997.
- **Selection of private companies for value-added services:** the current status of major value-added services under the privatisation programme is stated value:

  (i) **Cellular:** eight companies have started cellular services in the four metros – Delhi, Bombay, Calcutta and Madras. Operations in twenty circles will be delayed.
  (ii) **Pager:** fifteen companies are initially granted licences to begin operations. However, issues like reserve price and bank guarantee led to the retendering of six circles.
  (iii) **E-mail:** companies licensed include ICNET, RPG-Sprint, Dataline and Research Technology, Wipro Infotech System & Services and Business Indian Information.
  (iv) **Video-conferencing:** this service is provided currently by the VSNL on a pilot basis. RPG Telecom and others will soon be entering this market.
  (v) **VSAT services:** licences for 64kbps satellite data communication services have been provided to Hughes Escorts Communication Ltd, Comsat Max Pvt. Ltd, Wipro Infotech, British Telecom and Amadcus (a joint venture between Telstra and IL&FS).

- **Selection of private companies for telecom equipment production**: in terms of production value, switching exchange is the most important segment followed by telecom cables and other transmission hardware. Production of terminal equipment and fax machines is also on the rise, with memory-aided operations and new facilities built into them. The largest and most diversified telecom equipment company was Indian Telephone Industries (ITI) which is currently under the pressure of private competition. The major private companies involved in telecom equipment production include: RPG Telecom, Tata Telecom, Bharati

Telecom, Shyam Telecom, Punjab Wireless and Punjab Communications. Table 10.5 lists major companies which are involved in producing telecom equipment by major items.

Recent developments

Indian telecommunications is one of a number of major industries which the government has been reforming by gradually introducing liberal trade policies since 1991. A few recent industry-wide developments have reinforced the policies. First, to meet the ever increasing demand for investment in the telecommunication sector, the union finance ministry plans to raise the ceiling on external commercial borrowings (ECB) from 35 per cent to 50 per cent of the total project cost. Second, to improve transparency in the tendering process for equipment purchases, the DOT is finalising its vendor rating system. The DOT spent more than US$2 billion each year in purchasing telecommunications equipment. The rating of vendors will now be based on the price quote (60 per cent weightage), on-time delivery (30 per cent weightage) and the rest on certification. Third, the VSNL and British Telecom (BT) proposed to form a US$500 million joint venture to make India a hub for international traffic. Under this venture, all international traffic to the UK from the Middle East, South Asia and Southeast Asian countries will be amalgamated in India, and then transmitted to and from the UK. This will lead to economies of scale and will allow BT to offer cheaper rates to the long-distance carriers of these countries. The bulk of the investment will go into an extensive undersea cable network to enable traffic

Table 10.5 List of private companies in the production line of telephone equipment

Item	*Name of company*
Small switch	ITI, Indchem, L&T, Meltron, Punjab Communications, Escorts, BPL and Northern Digital and Tata Telecom
Large switch	ITI, AT&T with French involvement (USA), Fujitsu (Japan), Siemens (Germany), Ericsson (Sweden) and GPT (UK)
Telephone instruments	Bharati Telecom, BPL System and Projects, Tata Keltron and Crompto and Greaves
Fibre-optic cables	Birala Ericsson Optical Ltd, Hindustan Cables Ltd, Optel Ltd, Sterlite Industries, Vikas Hybrids & Electronics Ltd
Jelly-filled telephone cables	Sterlite Industries, Finolex Cables, RPG Telecom, Hindustan Cables, Telephone Cables, Vindhya Telelinks, Upcon Cables, Usha Beltron, Nicco Corporations and Gujrat Telephone Cables

Source: Hossain and Chatterjee (1996).

from a number of countries in the region to enter the Indian hub. This venture will not change VSNL's existing relationship with other carriers such as Sprint, AT&T, Telstra, Deutsche Telekom, France Telecom, Hong Kong Telecom and others. Fourth, an additional public mobile radio trunking service (PMRTS) was launched recently in Bangalore by Anco Communications in collaboration with US-based Motorola. Motorola will supply the technology and the equipment and will offer the services under the name 'Team Phone'. The two-way radio is meant for use by a team of people and allows two-way interaction between team members.

The industry's growth in recent years has been mainly concentrated in the area of cellular phones. The number of cellular subscribers in the country exceeded 200,000 at the end of 1996. Table 10.6 presents an account of cellphone's growth from August to October 1996 in four metros in India. The table also presents the market share of each of the companies for this period. In Delhi circle, the growth of cellphone subscription month to month increased by 12 per cent and this is 13 per cent in Mumbai, 9 per cent in Chennai and 18 per cent in Calcutta.

Conclusion

The economic reform process in India commenced in 1991. After this period there was a huge demand created for both basic telecom services and value-added services through liberalisation, privatisation and foreign direct investment (FDI). To meet the large outstanding demand for basic telecom

Table 10.6 Market share of the cellphone brands/companies in four metros

City/brand	*August 1996*		*September 1996*		*October 1996*	
	Nos.	*Share*	*Nos.*	*Share*	*Nos.*	*Share*
Delhi	**69,740**		**76,519**	(10)	**85,653**	(12)
Airtel	42,339	61	45,163	59	49,153	57
Essar	27,401	39	31,355	41	36,500	43
Mumbai	**54,599**		**61,291**	(12)	**69,272**	(13)
BPL	25,687	47	28,685	–	31,690	–
Max	28,912	53	32,606	53	37,582	54
Chennai	**15,765**		**16,892**	(7)	**18,337**	(9)
RPG	7,265	46	7,892	47	8,725	48
Skycell	8,500	54	9,000	53	9,612	52
Calcutta	**15,356**		**17,136**	(12)	**20,190**	(18)
ModiTelstra	9,084	59	9,584	56	10,162	53
UshaMartin	6,272	41	7,552	44	9,578	47

Source: IRIS (1996).

Notes: Percentage changes in parentheses.

services, a target of 20 million lines and telephone density of two persons per 100 persons by 2000 was set by the DOT. However, a more recent estimate suggests that the demand for basic services by the end of the century will reach as high as 25 million lines, almost 25 per cent greater than planned by the DOT.

While price elasticity is critical for assessing future demand, wide discrepancy in elasticities across telecom circles can be found. The present telecom network is highly skewed and almost 25 per cent of telephone lines in India are confined to two cities – Delhi and Bombay. These two cities also have the highest telephone density – over nine times the national average. Future demand for telephones is expected to be driven primarily by the metro and large cities and by the rapidly growing states of Maharastra, Gujarat, Karnataka, Tamil Nadu, Andhra Pradesh and Uttar Pradesh. However, the last two years of political instability, particularly instability in the coalition government and the subsequent corruption charges against the former telecommunications minister, have contributed to a slowdown in the pace of economic reform. Consequently, the current agenda for the opening-up of the economy has been delayed. This had an adverse effect on the telecommunications industry's growth in recent months.

References

Dean, J.M., Desai, S. and Riedel, J. (1994) 'Trade Policy Reform in Developing Countries since 1985', *World Bank Discussion Paper No. 267*, Washington, DC: The World Bank.

Edadan, N. (1997) 'Privatisation Strategies in Developing Countries: External Debt and Domestic Economic Prospects', *Economic and Political Weekly* XXXII(27): 1608–19.

Hossain, M. and Chatterjee, S. (1996) 'India's Liberalisation in Communications: Some Preliminary Observations', paper presented to the Twentieth Anniversary Conference, Asian Studies Association of Australia, Inc., LaTrobe University, Melbourne.

IRIS (1996) Investment Research and Information Services In-house Publication, Private Consultants, New Delhi.

Jayasuriya, S. and Knight-John, M. (1996) 'Liberalization and Privatization: Telecommunications Reforms in Sri Lanka', paper presented to the Twentieth Anniversary Conference, Asian Studies Association of Australia, Inc., LaTrobe University, Melbourne.

Krueger, A. (1986) 'General Issues in Economic Liberalisation', in A. Choksi and D. Papageorgiou (eds), *Economic Liberalisation in Developing Countries*, Oxford: Blackwell.

Michaely, M., Papageorgiou, D. and Choksi, A. (1991) *Liberalizing Foreign Trade*, Vol. 7: *Lessons of Experience in the Developing World*, Washington, DC: The World Bank.

Rodrik, D. (1993) 'The Positive Economics of Policy Reform', *The American Economic Review*, Papers and Proceedings, 83(2): 357–61.

Srinivasan, T.N. and Cañonero, G. (1995) 'Preferential Trading Arrangements in

South Asia: Theory, Empires and Policy', IED seminar paper presented in May, Institute for Economic Development, Boston University.

Thomas, V., Nash, J. and Associates (1991) *Best Practices in Trade Policy Reform*, Oxford: Oxford University Press.

UNIDO (1995) 'Industrial Development: Global Report 1995', *United Nations Development Organization*, Oxford: Oxford University Press.

World Bank (1995) *Economic Developments in India: Achievements and Challenges*, A World Bank Country Study: Washington, DC: The World Bank.

11

THE OTHER SIDE OF THE NATIONAL COMPETITION POLICY DEBATE

Perspective on the public interest and community services

Eileen Webb[1]

Introduction

The engine that drives efficiency is free and open competition.
(Keating 1992: 1)

The 1990s have witnessed the seemingly wholehearted adoption of the view that competition is the cure for all economic ills. The mantra adopted by advocates of competition policy comes from the non-arguable premise that the Australian economy, and therefore the nation itself, can only prosper if it becomes more efficient and productive. As a result, Australian governments have been quick to adopt the recommendations of the Report of the Independent Committee of Inquiry into National Competition Policy (hereafter referred to as the Hilmer report) and embrace the objectives of National Competition Policy.

This process has seen significant changes to the fabric of the Australian economy. For example, we have witnessed a rapid move towards corporatisation and privatisation of government enterprises. Purported advantages which have been associated with government bodies in the past have been reduced and in many cases done away with in an attempt to make the government undertakings compete with private operations in an atmosphere of 'competitive neutrality' and through contracting-out of services traditionally the bastion of government agencies.

Whilst there can be little doubt that in general economic terms such views make perfect sense, the ensuing reforms have meant that some areas which traditionally have been immune from notions of the profit motive have now become exposed to a harsher, more competitive environment. It is arguable that certain areas, particularly aspects of education, health and community services, do not readily lend themselves to notions of competitive conduct.

One of the key selling points of Hilmer was the purported benefits to consumers which, it was confidently predicted, would follow from the implementation of the reforms. Nevertheless, as in the case of tax reform, promises of benefit to the community generally as a result of reforms invariably see some persons benefiting more than others. In the case of the Hilmer recommendations the driving force was notions of economic rationalism. Benefits are examined from the perspective of efficiency and cost saving. In such a case the importance of issues such as the environment, equity and consumer welfare which are not easily presented on a balance sheet may be underestimated. The quest for efficiency and competition may in fact have a downside amongst particular groups, invariably the more vulnerable in the community. An example of this is in the area of community services where the issues of equity and social justice have found themselves 'competing' with economic rationalism, which is overtaking all aspects of the economy.

The Hilmer reforms have seen notions of economic rationalism applied across the Australian economy including in the area of human services. This general application of the reforms is tempered by the recommendation in the Hilmer report and by section 1(3) of the Competition Principles Agreement which require that the application of the reforms to areas such as human services be made subject to considerations of the public benefit or interest when determining the costs and benefits of applying competitive practice in policy decisions or actions. Nevertheless it is arguable that, despite such default mechanisms, the protection of the human services sector will depend largely upon two factors. These are, first, the perspective taken by government of the public interest and, second, the level of commitment of those formulating policy to consider factors extraneous to, and more difficult to quantify, than numbers on a balance sheet. In the writer's view this will determine whether the safeguards will balance the possible pitfalls in the application of competition policy to human services. If public interest is regarded as referring to notions of efficiency rather than equity, the application of the reforms to community services may in fact undermine the objectives and philosophy of the sector.

This chapter will examine the climate which led to Hilmer and the legislative basis for the implementation of the recommendations. It will then examine notions of the public benefit or interest generally and discuss the possible interpretation of the term depending on whether there is an efficiency or equity focus. The chapter will then examine the effect of the reforms on the community services sector. It will be argued that in the absence of a competitive market place the efficiency and effectiveness which is supposed to flow from higher levels of competition will not materialise. Indeed in the writer's view unless governments, the community services sector and consumers are wary, notions of competition may in fact impede the effectiveness and smooth running of the community services sector.

Microeconomic reform and the ramifications of the Hilmer recommendations

> . . . an opportunity to facilitate reforms across all industries on a national basis by formulating common principles, policies and processes.
>
> (Taperell 1995: 1)

Background

Observers could be forgiven for concluding that discussion of competition policy reform began with Hilmer. In fact for almost twenty years Australian governments, like their counterparts in other Western economies, have adopted principles associated with the quest for globalisation. As a result the goal of economic growth through increased levels of efficiency and competitiveness became the prime focus for government policy makers. Over the years, and especially in the 1990s, such doctrines have permeated most if not all levels of the public and private sectors. These developments have also occurred against a global background where governments are distancing themselves from the concept of a 'welfare state'. We have witnessed a growing reluctance by government to become involved in areas where there has been a traditional expectation of government participation. In assessing the evolution of governments retreating from involvement in welfare issues the Australian Council of Social Service (ACOSS) has noted that 'a preoccupation with individualism and neo-classical economic theory has seen social goals increasingly couched in terms of individual choice and freedoms rather than citizens' rights and needs' (ACOSS 1996: 21).

The Hilmer recommendations

In the early 1990s the Labor government devised a strategy for the implementation of a National Competition Policy with a view to hastening microeconomic reform in Australia. Due to constitutional limitations on the power of the Commonwealth Parliament to legislate universally in relation to market conduct,[2] a cooperative process began in 1991 between the Commonwealth, States and Territories with a view to creating a national approach to competition policy. In October 1992, the Independent Committee of Inquiry into National Competition Policy was initiated. The committee, chaired by Professor Fred Hilmer, was the result of agreement by the

Commonwealth, State and Territory governments that there was a need for a standardisation of policy in this area.[3]

The committee saw its task as proposing the most effective form, content and implementation approach for a National Competition Policy that would support an open integrated domestic market for goods and services. The committee took a broad view which identified common themes and issues within the economy rather than the development of prescriptions for particular industries. The recommendations had a wide ambit and were of general application.

The committee reported on 25 August 1993. Agreement was reached on a number of reforms which can be summarised in six points:

1 *The Universal Application of the Trade Practices Act 1974 (Cth)*
The first major recommendation was that there should be general application of the provisions of the Trade Practices Act 1974 (Cth) to all government undertakings and unincorporated businesses. The Trade Practices Act 1974 is the pivotal piece of consumer protection legislation in Australian law. Owing to constitutional limitations, the Act generally applied only to foreign, trading or financial corporations.[4] Unincorporated associations were not subject to the operation of the Act.[5] In terms of its application to government, it only bound the Crown in right of the Commonwealth.[6] State and local government instrumentalities were therefore generally immune from the operation of the Act. This was particularly relevant to the provisions of Part IV of the Act which deal with anti-competitive conduct such as exclusive dealing and misuse of market power.

2 *Business conduct of the States and Territories*
There was a recommendation that the business conduct of the States and Territories be streamlined with attention to be paid to laws, regulations and controls imposed by governments. It was recommended that legislation should be examined and unless there were public interest grounds in not so doing, any potentially anti-competitive provisions were to be removed.

3 *Structural reform of public monopolies*
It was concluded that in order for there to be effective competition in certain industries, management and control of particular functions had to be kept separate. Three principles were stated:

a regulatory functions should not be performed by organisations operating in the market;
b the natural monopoly element of an industry should be separated from the contestable elements so as to remove incentives for cross-subsidisation and exclusionary conduct; and

c operations that are potentially competitive should be separated where efficiency gains are possible.

4 *Monopoly pricing*
The committee recommended the establishment in each State of a prices surveillance mechanism for public utilities and other corporations enjoying a high degree of monopoly power.

5 *Competitive neutrality*
The committee noted that competitive neutrality was desirable where the public and private sector were in competition in the same market. For example, facilities provided by government for government services were to be shared with private providers and, where applicable, rent paid by government enterprises.

6 *Access to essential facilities*
Essential facilities are those facilities necessary for effective competition and which cannot be duplicated economically; for example, electricity. The committee recommended a legal framework which would provide access to essential facilities by third parties.

Consideration of the public benefit

One point which has often been disregarded in discussions of the Hilmer report is that there was a recognition that certain public interest matters were important in any discussion of increased efficiency and competitiveness. There was recognition that if circumstances exist where efficiency is at the cost of other valued social objectives – for example, special benefits to particular sectors of society on equity grounds – it might lessen efficiency but nevertheless accord with community values (Hilmer 1993: 88; Johnston 1995: 4; 1996: 246). Therefore in the report itself there was a recognition that in particular areas, primarily human services, considerations of consumer welfare and social justice may need to prevail.

The legislative package

Movement towards the implementation of the policy framework was swift with the legislative package being introduced into the Federal Parliament on 29 March 1995. At the COAG (Council of Australian Governments) meeting in April 1995 all State and Territory governments agreed to the contents of the package. Four pieces of legislation were formulated.[7]

The Competition Policy Reform Bill 1995[8] introduced a wide number of reforms which saw all sectors of Australian business become subject to the provisions of Part IV of the Trade Practices Act.[9]

The legislative package also included three intergovernmental agreements, principally the Competition Principles Agreement which established agreed principles on matters such as:

- competitive neutrality between public and private sectors;
- prices oversight of utilities and other corporations with significant monopoly power;
- a regime to provide access to essential facilities;
- a programme to review legislation which restricts competition; and
- structural reform of public monopolies.

During the reform process there were submissions on behalf of various organisations such as Public Interest Advocacy Centre (PIAC), Australian Federation of Consumer Organisations (AFCO) and Greenpeace suggesting that the implementation of the National Competition Policy should be safeguarded by a national social justice package and protections for consumers, especially in the case of reform of utilities and uncompetitive sectors (Johnston 1996: 246). Upon its release, section 1(3) of the Competition Principles Agreement listed a series of public interest tests which were to be considered when determining the costs and benefits of applying competitive practice in particular policy decisions, the merits or appropriateness of a particular policy or assessing the most effective means of achieving a policy objective. The matters to be considered included:

- social welfare and equity considerations including community service obligations;
- government legislation and policy relating to ecologically sustainable development;
- economic and regional development, including employment or investment growth;
- government legislation and policies relating to matters such as occupational health and safety, industrial relations and access and equity;
- the interests of consumers generally, or a class of consumers, and the efficient allocation of resources.

Also again pursuant to the Competition Principles Agreement all Commonwealth, State and Territory legislation must be reviewed by the year 2000. If it is found the legislation impedes competition, it must be reviewed unless it can be established that the benefits of the restriction outweigh the costs and the objectives of the legislation. Similarly, it has been stated that competitive neutrality is to be implemented only to the extent that the benefits of its implementation outweigh the costs.

When determining whether a course of action is appropriate, policy makers are required to give consideration to the factors listed in section 1(3). This is particularly the case in circumstances where community services are involved. The question is whether the factors listed above can be quantified and given appropriate weight. This is particularly pertinent in an area such as community services where the impact of human contact and commitment is difficult to quantify, and may indeed be overlooked if our idea of public benefit is limited to more value for money.

What do we need to consider in determining the public interest?

> Just because the current Commonwealth Government is subject to political constraint in respect of these public policy agendas, we should not mistake their overall direction and their likely consequences. It is not surprising that the bureaucratic leaders of this reorientation of public policy have been central agencies of both levels of government. They are indeed the bureaucratic force behind the disestablishment of the welfare in favour of the compassion state.
> (Yeatman 1991: 45)

The reform process has caught consumers in its web due to the assumption that, as a result of increased competition, there will necessarily be a benefit to consumers. The problem which arises, however, is how do we measure the benefits to the public?[10] Similarly, when we consider the public interest when determining whether to adopt a particular policy, from what perspective will public interest be assessed? If the terms are examined from a value-for-money perspective the success or otherwise of the reforms may be measured by the gains made by consumers with improved choice, lower prices and a better quality of product. On the other hand, the term benefit may be examined from the perspective of the benefit to all consumers, not just those best able to avail themselves of cheaper prices and improved services. For example, although competition in relation to telecommunications has proved popular with consumers (Le Blanc 1995), consumer concerns may differ according to individual circumstances. Certain consumers may benefit from more services, more pleasant tones on inquiry lines and so on. Other consumers may be more concerned about paying the bill. The issue of balancing equity and efficiency is a vexed one.

Despite such statements governments are moving swiftly to embrace the reforms. Clearly governments have seen benefits financially. Nevertheless, the broader public interest, especially in the case of those who can least defend themselves, may be eroding.

So how are we to determine what is to be in the public interest? Craig Johnston (1996: 246) summarises the problem as follows:

> A concept like 'public benefit' or 'public interest' is a problematic one in a discussion of public policy. Fundamentally what is in the interest of the people is a matter for public debate and democratic decision making (i.e. by the people, not the limited number of players in the juridical system). In a legal sense:

- the content of public interest has no fixity and in legal deliberations, it refers a juridical body 'ultimately to its own idiosyncratic conceptions and modes of thought'; and
- a judgement of the comparative claims of competing public interests is essentially discretionary [footnotes omitted].

Public benefit or interest?

There is no precise definition of the terms public benefit or public interest. Nevertheless some guidance can be obtained from an examination of decided cases.

What is the public?

Certainly the term public does not need to be all-encompassing and does not include all the public at large. It has been recognised that it is sufficient if it includes a significant sector of the people.[11] The term may encompass more than simply consumers and could mean the benefit to shareholders through higher dividends, although the benefit is not spread widely throughout the community.[12] Consequently, depending on the interpretation of the term public, what may be in the interest of some members of the public may not necessarily be in the interest of others.

Public benefit under the Trade Practices Act

The term public benefit has been discussed widely in relation to applications for authorisation under the Trade Practices Act.[13] In order to obtain authorisation an applicant must establish that engaging in a restrictive trade practice, which would or could potentially be in breach of the Act, would result in a benefit to the public which could outweigh any detriment from a lessening of competition the conduct may cause.

Despite the pivotal nature of the term, the Act itself does not define public benefit. Public benefit has been given a wide ambit[14] and will include anything of value to the community generally, including the achievement of economic goals of efficiency and progress.[15] In *Re 7-Eleven Stores Pty Ltd* the court noted:

> . . . the assessment of efficiency and progress must be from the perspective of society as a whole: the best use of society's resources. We bear in mind that (in the language of economics today) efficiency is a concept that is usually taken to encompass 'progress': and that commonly efficiency is said to encompass allocative efficiency, production efficiency and dynamic efficiency.[16]

In *Re ACI Operations Pty Ltd*[17] the Trade Practices Commission (now the Australian Competition and Consumer Commission) listed a number of factors which in their view could constitute a public benefit, including economic development such as encouragement of research and capital investment, fostering business efficiency, particularly where this results in improved international competitiveness, employment growth and industrial harmony.

Although these considerations may attract criticism because of their centredness towards solely economic criteria there is also reference to improvement in the quality and safety of goods or services and the expansion of consumer choice, supply of better information to consumers and businesses to permit informed choices in their dealings, the promotion of equitable dealings in the market and steps to protect the environment. Also it has been noted that it is erroneous to equate anti-competitiveness with detriment. Anti-competitive behaviour may in certain circumstances be a benefit.[18]

Nevertheless there is a fear that too much examination of trade practices cases will result in the focus being too sharply on economic factors rather than taking a wider view.

Also, as we have discussed in the Competition Principles Agreement (CPA), certain matters are listed which are to be taken into account in determining the public interest. Section 1(4) of the CPA notes that these criteria are not to be taken into account when determining matters involving authorisation under the Trade Practices Act. Therefore the provisions of section 1(4) are not an extension of the criteria to be considered in relation to authorisation. Consequently, it may be inappropriate to take the criteria mentioned in decided cases under the Trade Practices Act into account when determining the public interest – clearly reference to the criteria listed rather than reference to any authorities on the Trade Practices Act is more desirable. Section 1(3) gives guidance with reference to such terms as social justice and equity. Nevertheless how much consideration will be given to such issues will depend on the viewpoint of those implementing government policy.

Public benefit from whose perspective?

Despite references in the CPA that in formulating policy decisions reference has to be had to social welfare and equity, Johnston (1996: 248, 257) utilises the examples of access to public utilities and a basic banking product to reveal a contradiction in the interpretation of the notions of public benefit or interest. Johnston states that welfare agencies dealing with low-income customers of utilities indicate that the affordability of the service – not in terms of value for money but in terms of whether low-income customers could purchase the essential service on an ongoing basis at all – is a key concern.

Value for money may not be an issue when finding the money is the problem. In the case of banking much attention has been given to the fact that there have been calls for a basic banking product which would be utilised primarily by lower-income earners. In examining the issue, the Prices Surveillance Authority noted that there were two issues to be considered: an efficiency argument and an equity argument (Prices Surveillance Authority 1995: 2; Johnston 1996: 251). The efficiency argument was based on the premise that universal banking should be encouraged and made feasible, even for marginalised members of society, for the benefit of society as a whole, and the equity argument that basic banking should be provided as a concession to assist marginalised members of society (Prices Surveillance Authority 1995: 2; Johnston 1996: 251).

In a nutshell, the low-income customer wanting such a product was, in the eyes of the bank, expendable. From the perspective of efficiency it may be better for a bank to shed such customers and therefore be able to provide more benefits to those customers who assist the bank in generating income. What is efficient and what may be a public benefit if a person is in the latter group may be overshadowed by equity issues and matters of the availability of services.

The dilemma faced in determining the whole idea of public benefit is the subjective determination of what is the public benefit – the greatest good for the greatest number or the equitable treatment of all persons within the 'public'.

Johnston refers to this conflict as a contest between equity in processes and equity in outcomes. The former refers to getting value for money with the main consumer issue being consumer protection. The concept is similar to the concept of benefit equity which calls for those who benefit from the supply of goods and services to bear an appropriate share of the costs. In comparison equity in outcomes refers to the equitable distribution of income wealth and public goods and the primary consumer issue is social welfare. This resonates with access equity which calls for those with an inability to pay for goods or services to nevertheless have access to some minimum level (Johnston 1996: 252).

How will public benefit be quantified?

The Competition Principles Agreement states that recourse is to be had to social justice, equitable and environmental factors. However, how are these matters going to be factored into the equation where the world is being seen through a balance sheet? For example, in the context of community services Hodge[19] suggests that when determining the desirability of increasing levels of contracting-out of government services there is a necessity to weigh up economic gains and the potential social and democratic impacts.

References to social justice and equity suggest that when weighing up the costs and benefits of applying competitive practice in policy decisions, due regard will be paid to these factors. The difficulty, however, is how public benefit is to be quantified to ensure the appropriate attention to issues such as social justice and equity.

The Commonwealth's Public Accounts Committee has noticed a considerable variation in the complexity involved in attaching values to social responsibilities and states that in some cases it may be impossible to quantify (Joint Committee of Public Accounts 1992: 66; Johnston 1996: 257). In addition, the committee has noted there needs to be evidence of the cost effectiveness of valuing social responsibilities before any such exercise is taken (Joint Committee of Public Accounts 1992: 66). Importantly, however, there was a recognition that determining the benefits of the services provided might involve relying on qualitative and less easily quantified data which should be seen as carrying equal weight to financial information (Joint Committee of Public Accounts 1992: 79; Johnston 1996: 257).

There is some cause for optimism, however, with a recognition that techniques such as environmental and social impact statements and multi-criteria analysis can be used to complement cost–benefit analysis (Private Infrastructure Task Force 1995: 96; Johnston 1996: 258).

If social justice and equity are to be factored into government decision making we must not lose sight of the fact that the role of government is to ensure adequate standards of living for all its citizens. There must be a recognition that notions of efficiency are only one factor amongst a myriad of considerations when formulating policy. Such policies cannot be formulated in a vacuum, and without proper consideration of the impact the decisions will have on the welfare of all citizens.

How can the public interest be assessed in relation to community services?

When formulating policies which will impact on community services an initial step will be how 'the public' is to be defined. It is suggested a similar approach could be taken to that adopted by the courts when determining whether there has been misleading or deceptive conduct pursuant to section 52 of the Trade Practices Act.[20] In the process of determining whether conduct has been misleading or deceptive the court first identifies the class of persons to which the representation was made. This can range from the public at large to a particular group of persons to a single individual. Once the class is identified the question is posed as to whether persons within that class would in fact be misled by the statement.[21] Despite the difference in subject matter a similar process could be adopted by policy makers. The first step will be to identify the class of persons involved. Although it is arguable the class could be the public at large, in the case of community services the persons involved, both providers and clients, have different concerns in relation to policy changes in this area to other members of the public. Although all members of the public have an interest in ensuring that all members of our society have access to certain minimal living standards it is submitted that in the initial stages of examining the impact of policy considerations 'the public' should be limited to those persons within the sector, or who operate within a particular part of the sector. Then once that class is identified there can be a consideration of the members of that class and consideration given to whether the changes are in the interest of 'the public' given the appropriate references to social justice, equity and so on. It is submitted that by limiting the class in this way it is less unwieldy and enables a more ordered approach to be taken to public interest considerations and the special concerns of that particular group.

When examining the effects on matters involving community services it is essential that an equity rather than efficiency viewpoint be taken. The very nature of the industry makes this the more logical approach. This need not be at the expense of efficiency. It is in the interests of the government and the community services sector to take efficiency into account. However, this must be balanced against the public interest questions. The nature of the industry, the providers and the clients make it imperative that the quest for efficiency does not override other relevant considerations.

An example of how this process may work comes from the adoption by some State governments of competitive tendering and contracting (CTC) guidelines. Such guidelines support utilising CTC in circumstances where it would be in the public interest, and establish a framework for assessing the case for CTC in the particular circumstances (ACOSS 1997: 38). Factors examined are an individual assessment of activities and services, identifying constraints, reviewing functions and assessing risk (ACOSS 1997: 39). Similarly in its report, *Competitive Tendering and Contracting by Public Sector Agencies*,[22] the Industry Commission has suggested that CTC be examined on a case-by-case basis with consideration of a number of listed factors.

Community services

> The relationship between government and community organisations has been one of co-responsibility even though the relationship has never been equal because of the power of the government as sole purchaser. The role of the community sector expanded because government recognised its strengths in service delivery advocacy and community development. Ironically the expansion of their role as providers of government contracted services may transform the community sector in a way which undermines the very strengths government and the wider community value in community organisations; their flexibility, responsiveness, diversity and autonomy.
>
> (AOSS 1997: 16)

Community services in Australia

Tang[23] defines community services as those services required by people who need support to function independently within the community. ACOSS classifies community services as including services involving child care, child protection and substitute care, accommodation, community care and support for independent living, individual and family counselling and support and financial counselling and emergency relief (ACOSS 1997: 14).

Community services in a variety of forms have existed in Australia since the early nineteenth century. Its humble beginnings were through the work of church or philanthropic organisations with little government involvement or assistance. This situation continued until the election of the Whitlam Labor government in 1972 which, through a combination of factors including the commitment of the government to social reform, altered community perceptions about the role of government in welfare and social policy. The changing cultural and societal mores of the period saw the commencement of two decades of expanding government involvement and assistance in relation to welfare and community services.

The relationship grew to involve a high degree of mutual cooperation. Indeed, ACOSS has noted:

> The boundaries of roles and responsibilities were often unclear but there remained an acceptance of non-government organisations as independent of government even where those organisations were solely reliant on government funding. At the same time the role of community services was expanding and state and federal governments took steps to enhance formal channels of advice to government to facilitate community sector and consumer participation in policy. This involved a range of processes including formal advisory councils, providing more support to peak representative bodies and funding development workers and forums at regional levels.

Community services in Australia have a variety of players that include primarily government and for-profit and not-for-profit organisations. Government involvement can be direct or indirect. It can be direct in its role as a provider of services, such as education and health. The contribution can be indirect either through financial assistance to fund community projects or organisations or through the mapping out of a legislative, policy or regulatory environment in which the organisations may operate. It is estimated that 35 per cent of all community services are provided by government bodies (Lyons 1993; ACOSS 1997: 15).

Organisations operating for profit provide 10 per cent of all community services and tend to deliver services which have a commercial reward, primarily child care and aged care (Lyons 1993; ACOSS 1997: 15). The largest and most varied contribution to the community services sector (55 per cent of all community services) comes from the not-for-profit organisations. These are funded to varying degrees by government, small business ventures and public donations. The services provided by the organisations may overlap with those mentioned above, or predominantly serve other equally deserving but less commercially viable pursuits.

With the advent of the Hilmer reforms and the move to economic rationalism community services found they were not immune from the cold winds of competition. Despite the comments discussed above about considerations of public benefit and the fact that the reforms may not be applicable to human services, the terminology and philosophy has permeated government policy and is reflected in the adoption of practices such as contracting-out in relation to the community services sector.

How have the reforms affected community services?

The reforms have had a varied impact given the variation of funding models used by governments to fund community services. As a general observation, however, the reforms have led to a tightening of procedures in relation to the granting of funds to community service organisations. Services traditionally dealt with by government departments have been put to tender on a wider scale, although this development has been primarily limited to expansion and establishment of new services (ACOSS 1997: 21). Also the system of funding in community services has changed in that the government will 'buy' products or services and look for the most economic and effective delivery of services (Struthers 1995: 4). Grants are being tied to agreed outputs (Struthers 1995: 4). Contracting has now become the norm, although it takes a variety of forms depending on the nature of the programme or the government department or jurisdiction involved (ACOSS 1997: 24). Innovations include the introduction by the Federal Government of a quasi-voucher system which purports to assist even-handed treatment by a recognised service provider. This is so whether it is a profit or not-for-profit organisation and subsidises the user of a service (for example, child care) rather than the provider of the service.

Reforms in the public sector consist of separation of purchasers and providers, the development of contracts and quasi-contracts and the operation of the trading systems based upon prices and user choice (Searles and Moon 1996: 1). The relationship between citizens and government is increasingly becoming a contractual one rather than the traditional one of the government as public provider (Struthers 1995: 4).

Indeed it has been stated:

> To respond to these challenges the social and community services industry will in turn need to become more professional in its

> management, particularly in its financial control systems. There is something deeply uncomfortable about the notion of selling the sorts of services you all work with and yet in principle that is the expectation under the National Competition Policy. . . . If the government decides that some communities require youth sport centres then it will specify what it wishes to purchase, open up a tendering process and then closely evaluate the outputs and outcomes received for the money invested.[24]

The bottom line is, however, that economic rationalist theories are fundamentally different from the values and motivation of the sectors discussed in this chapter. There are other factors to be considered which fall outside the economist's gaze including cooperation, networking and most importantly motivations underpinned by compassion rather than profit. Also, although there are some benefits in the adoption of the new policies there are significant pitfalls which should be considered in the application of the reforms to community service organisations.

Problems in applying competition policy to community services

> . . . the market itself only survives if parties to contracts are prepared to trust each other – to accept some basic non-market rules of human intercourse.
>
> (Hutton 1996: 11)

Some misconceptions

One point should be made at the outset. It is a common misconception that the Hilmer reforms will make community organisations more efficient thus inferring that they were inefficient and wasteful in the past. The reality could not be further from the truth. Australia has a highly targeted and efficient welfare system and compared with other OECD countries has one of the lowest levels of social spending and of taxation as proportions of GDP (OECD 1994, 1996; ACOSS 1997: 15).

Behind the rhetoric surrounding the implementation of competition policy there is the potential for benefits to the community services sector. ACOSS identifies a number of potential advantages for community organisations which include clearer service definition and performance expectations, greater certainty through longer-term contracts, the capacity for better forward planning and strategic management and improvements in service costing and data collection. Nevertheless there are a number of potential pitfalls where the creed of economic rationalism has and may continue to undermine the motivations of the community services sector. Indeed, the fact that these problems exist demonstrates that proper attention is not being paid by policy makers to issues such as social justice and equity. This chapter addresses a number of areas of potential and actual concern.

The creation of a general creed of economic rationalism

Economic rationalism is market driven and is based upon very different considerations and motivations from those espoused by, for example, the community services sector. How is one to quantify characteristics such as cooperation, willingness to volunteer and compassion. Where there is cause to examine the public interest issues in section 1(3) we have already discussed the difficulty in quantifying such considerations. In light of such difficulties, and given the fact that competition policy has overtaken the running of many government departments, real questions have to be asked as to how much attention, in reality, will be paid to such considerations.

Is there the opportunity for any competition at all?

In some areas of community services the whole question of competition and the selection of a provider from ranks of willing organisations is purely academic. Despite the overlap between profit and non-profit providers, in many instances it may quite simply be impossible to encourage competitive conduct. For example, there are situations where there are no alternative providers at all. This is the case particularly in rural or remote areas or where the project is not commercially viable enough to encourage the entry of a for-profit provider into the particular market.

The relationship between government and community organisations

Lack of negotiation and consultation

One of the criticisms of the implementation of the policy has been that the governments have been so keen to introduce reforms that there have been problems involving a lack of information, consultation and opportunities to discuss or negotiate programmes. Community organisations are being expected to make submissions, write tenders and so on with insufficient information and little assistance from the government departments involved. Also the reforms have been in many cases imposed on community organisations without consultation or with minimal negotiation. The problem with a lack of available information is a serious one. This lack of information means that it is difficult for community organisations to properly cost proposals. This difficulty is compounded by the short time frame made available for the preparation of applications for tenders and grants. A major concern is that responsibilities will be underestimated and therefore underfunded.

The expectation of more for less

Clearly there is a perception that government is trying to get blood out of a stone. Governments are reluctant to provide funding for support services such as research, accreditation and benchmarking. This has the potential to impede the ability of community services to evaluate the impact of the reforms and properly streamline their services (ACOSS 1997: 34). Similarly, it means that governments are generally uninformed about the effectiveness of the reforms. Also the emphasis of the cost factor on the contracting and tendering process may have two undesirable results. First, a contract may be awarded to a provider with more interest in profit and keeping margins down. In such circumstances it is unlikely that requisite attention is paid to more 'human' factors. Second, there is the risk that there will be advantage taken of the professionalism of persons involved in community services who will continue to provide a service, and just be funded for the bare service provided, and continue to do 'more for less'.

More accountability

With the reforms comes a need to be more 'accountable'. As a consequence we have seen community workers diverted from their duties to take up administrative functions to ensure all expenditure is accounted for. It is feared that such accountability requirements will impact on service delivery as more time is spent on administration.

The ironical thing is community service organisations are for the most part experts in providing services on a tight budget. Nevertheless, with the emphasis on accountability such organisations will be called on to verify at all times what they have been doing efficiently in the past. Valuable resources will, however, be burnt up recording what is already occurring.

Reduced independence

Despite the mantra that there will be less government intervention in the process, the reality is that although the government may become more distant in its knowledge and understanding of particular cases it will in other ways be applying more rigid controls to the community services sector. ACOSS notes that there are dangers to the core philosophy and purpose of community organisations because:

- contracting based on government priorities and specifications will lead to reduced independence and autonomy; and
- tight service specification will result in distortion of agency purpose leading community organisations to become little more than agents of government.

Government

Government efforts to distance themselves from involvement with welfare may cause them to lose sight of their public responsibilities and to be less able to meaningfully and efficiently contribute to the community services sector. Efforts to take the government largely out of the provider/client equation may see governments lose touch with the community services sector thus causing governments to make less informed choices and become unable to appropriately specify the requirements of the sector.

The relationship between community organisations themselves and their clients

Reduced funding and consequently services

The stretching of already scarce resources by the community services sector will increase. Less funding will cause greater prioritisation and some projects, although no doubt deserving, will suffer. This could also have the potential to affect the standard of services.

There is some apprehension that in tendering or in making applications there will be a tendency to undercut on price by accident (through calculations based on inaccurate or insufficient data) or by design (simply to be awarded a project). Increasing government expectations and a 'more for your money' attitude will have a detrimental effect on the quality of the product and the benefit to consumers.

Another concern is that in cutting funding more reliance is being placed on the commitment of individual sacrifice by community services sector workers. Put simply, reliance is placed on those working within this sector having a level of commitment which will see them put in extra hours and in many cases utilise or contribute their own resources to 'get the job done'. This could increase the level of 'burn-out' within the sector. Individual workers will attempt to do the same job with less resources and support. The levels of individual commitment are such that the process is unlikely, however, to slow down or decrease. The writer predicts that we will see individuals (even more so than now) doing the same job but working longer hours in order to provide services. The result will be increased levels of stress within the sector.

Collaboration

Competitiveness within the community services sector may work against the collaboration and cooperation of individuals or the development and provision of services generally (Tang 1997: 339). There is some difficulty in reconciling the nurturing of alliances between purchasers and providers and open competition (Mellors 1996: 3). Implicit in the non-contractual aspects of these alliances is openness and trust in an exchange of information between purchaser and provider (Mellors 1996: 3). The need for access to information is, paradoxically, considered a necessary precondition for both the operation of a competitive market and the capacity of purchasers to maintain expertise in community services sufficient to determine service standards and the degree to which they are fulfilled.

Related to this is the impact of competition upon the sharing or provision of information. Aronson notes:

> Economically rational people, the economists tell us, need lots of information. However, it is remarkable how wedded to confidentiality free marketeers can be when they come to assess the information needs of government and the public as regards outsourcing. In the area of outsourcing, basic contractual details such as performance standards and price are frequently kept secret for fear of prejudicing the contractor's competitive position.
>
> (Aronson 1997: 20)

In relation to these considerations ACOSS (1997: 31) has stated that in the context of tendering it would be ironic to exacerbate these problems through unnecessary use of tendering when so much of the reform agenda at state and national level is directed towards achieving better coordination and integration between services.

A reluctance to release information may also tell against the consumers of community services. Consumer influence is in proportion to their access to information. Consumer influence is exercised through choice of product, a theory which assumes that consumers have the capacity to exercise choice or viable options from which to choose. Many customers of community services are in a difficult position in relation to the provision of such information and the decrease in access to information as a result of a more competitive environment will further erode this situation.

Difficulties for consumers with high or complex needs

Another risk is the tendency for contracted services to select consumers for whom it is easier to provide and therefore produce outcomes at lower cost. This obviously disadvantages consumers with very high or more complex needs (Tang 1997: 341).

ACOSS recognises that there is a potential risk that services will be skewed in favour of clients with better prospects for successful outcomes and less attention will be given to people with complex and long-term problems. This is especially the case where incentives, for example through the linking of government payments directly to the achievement of certain outcomes, are offered (ACOSS 1997: 26).

A decline in community participation

The transformation of community organisations and the addition of often onerous responsibilities for those in management roles may see a reduction of persons wishing to volunteer to assist in certain ventures. This is to be lamented because when the 'human face' of an organisation is diminished the community services sector will suffer as a whole. For example, the employment of a large catering firm to replace a 'meals on wheels' operation may make economic sense. Through the resources of a larger, more specialised organisation the meals and the packaging may be completed more efficiently and for a cheaper price. Meals could be delivered in a short time. On its face everything appears fine. However, the element of community participation simply has not been considered. The philosophy of a project such as meals on wheels is not just to provide food but to provide companionship and support to its clients. This simply cannot be done when profit is the overriding motive. Meals would be prepared in a central location, more often than not in the local area and deposited on a doorstep to save time. In many cases the visit from a representative of meals on wheels is one of the few contacts with the outside world enjoyed by the elderly or sick. The companionship and contact provided by volunteers cannot be duplicated by private providers of similar services. It appears that price has been a major determinant in awarding contracts, but price alone cannot consider all benefits.

Consumer capacity to exercise choice

Community services consumers rarely exercise choice either because there is no choice to be made (in the case of involuntary use of community services), services are so scarce that the consumer must 'take what you get' or because community services consumers are unable or unwilling to exercise that choice (Tang 1997: 341). Where there is a profit motive there is a significant risk that the drive to produce a profit will work against the interests of consumers.

Uncertainty and disruption

Although competitive tendering may be beneficial on the face of it, chopping and changing providers is not good for community organisations or their clients. The nature of the services offered by the community services sector is such that it is desirable for there to be continuity over time. Relationships are fostered between the providers and their clients and trust and friendship are often developed. Such relationships should not be severed because another body has tendered at a lower price. Changes as a result of the tendering process are difficult at any level; however, it is submitted this is particularly the case in relation to the nature of the community services sector.

Conclusions

The scope of this chapter does not permit a discussion of detailed solutions for the myriad contingencies which government policy makers will have to consider when weighing up factors associated with the public interest. Similarly all the actual and potential shortcomings mooted above cannot be individually addressed. Nevertheless, some general recommendations can be formulated.

1 First, it is essential that governments retain a pivotal role in decision making in relation to community services. Although it would be difficult to retreat too far from an economic rationalist approach, governments need to accept that in certain circumstances it is impossible to apply competition principles. Where it is possible through the existence of a number of potential providers competition between providers through contracts and competitive tendering has the potential to improve services through opening the market to new players and also ensure that the industry is not afflicted by inefficiencies and complacency.

2 Although the impact of competition policy on community services may have some potential benefits government must remain mindful of its obligations to keep existing and potential providers fully informed in relation to projects to ensure accurate dialogue between all parties. The failure to consult and inform will not only place community services in a vulnerable and disadvantageous position when dealing with government departments but will also erode the goodwill between government and community service organisations. This can only result in a lesser standard of service for clients, a result neither governments nor community service organisations would desire.

3 The formulation of policy in this area must divert from notions of the profit motive and make recourse to 'human factors' the starting point. The difficulty in quantifying such matters has been addressed. Clearly emphasis has been on efficiency rather than social justice. One only has to

examine what has been happening – contracts, more government control, more for less interest in support. Nevertheless there is an obligation, moral as well as in the Competition Principles Agreement, to do so. The governments must ensure that consideration is being given to appropriate issues. In comparison look at it from a social justice and equity perspective. In fact, much-needed services may go out of business, attention to tenders and the lowest price simply cannot consider the existing relationships.

4 Although the benefits of tendering, especially in keeping organisations 'on their toes', have been acknowledged, there should be the opportunity to use discretion in determining whether or not an existing provider is made to endure a tender process. Where objectives are being met and the provider is performing well the disruption and uncertainty of the tender process may be counterproductive. The whole process puts members of the organisation under both a strain and a cloud of uncertainty. This cannot help but have some effect on performance. The tender process is especially dangerous and disruptive when it is perceived that the sole determinant is price. If the tender is awarded to another provider there is a significant settling-in period for even the most efficient operator. In relation to community services, however, this is made more difficult by having to formulate new relationships with clients. It is difficult for the provider and especially difficult for clients.

5 More attention should be paid to fostering the relationship between government and community services. The government should be encouraging dialogue with members and keep in mind that in so doing they are tapping into an industry populated largely by persons with a genuine commitment and enthusiasm for their sector. Instead of making themselves more remote from such persons, government should be actively seeking advice and encouraging input from members of the community services sector.

Until attention is paid to these factors the problem remains that the reforms will continue to be thrust onto sectors Hilmer himself felt were not applicable to the general thrust of competition policy. Social, welfare and environmental considerations are and always will be absent from the creed of economic rationalism.

Notes

1 B.A., LL.B.(Hons), LL.M., Dip. Ed. Lecturer in Law, Griffith University. The writer would like to thank Justin Malbon of the Faculty of Law, Griffith University, for his comments on an earlier draft of this chapter and Nigel Ridgeway, student at law, Griffith University, for his valuable assistance in researching this chapter.

2 The major constitutional basis for the Trade Practices Act is the Corporations Power (s.51[XX]).
3 CCH Australia Ltd, Australian Trade Practices Reporter, (1997) CCH Australia Pty Ltd Australia, p. 600.
4 In certain circumstances there was extended application through the trade or commerce or post and telecommunications power. Since the Hilmer reforms mirror legislation has been introduced by the state governments which extend the application of the Act to 'persons'.
5 Although some unincorporated associations were found liable indirectly in a number of cases; for example, see *Hughes v. Western Australian Cricket Association (Inc.)* (1986) 69 ALR 660 in relation to the cricket clubs.
6 Section 2A Trade Practices Act 1974 (Cth); see too A. Tonking, *Gentlemen and Players: Application of the Trade Practices Act to Government Bodies, Including those Corporatised or Privatised* (1992) QUTLJ 75.
7 The package was made up of: The Competition Policy Reform Bill 1995; The Intergovernmental Code of Agreement; The Intergovernmental Competition Principles Agreement; The Intergovernmental Agreement to Implement the National Competition Policy and Related Reforms.
8 The Competition Policy Reform Bill was passed by the Federal Parliament on 30 June 1995 and assented to on 20 July 1995.
9 To facilitate this there has been the insertion of the competition code under Part XIA and the Schedule version of Part IV.
10 On this subject see generally M. Hogan and G. Rogers (1997).
11 Johnston (1996: 246) citing Jacobs J in *Sinclair v. Maryborough Mining Warden* (1975) CLR 473: 487.
12 *Re Howard Smith Industries Pty Ltd* (1977) 28 FLR 385.
13 See ss. 88–90.
14 *Re Queensland Co-operative Consolidated Milling Association Ltd* (1976) 25 FLR 169, *Re 7-Eleven Stores Pty Ltd* (1994) ATPR 41–357.
15 *Re Queensland Co-operative Consolidated Milling Association Ltd* (1976) 25 FLR 169, *Re Travel Industries Automated Systems Ltd* (1993) ATPR(Com) 50–131.
16 *Re 7-Eleven Stores Pty Ltd* (1994) ATPR 41–357.
17 (1991) ATPR(Comm) 50–108.
18 *Re 7-Eleven Stores Pty Ltd* (1994) ATPR 41–357.
19 Hodge, G. *Contracting Out Government Services – A Review of International Evidence*, (1996) Montech Pty Ltd, Melbourne, as discussed in ACOSS (1997) op. cit. at p. 39.
20 Section 52 states, 'A corporation shall not in trade or commerce engage in conduct that is misleading or deceptive or likely to mislead or deceive'.
21 *Taco Co. of Australia Inc v. Taco Bell Pty Ltd* (1982) 42 ALR 177, ATPR 40–303.
22 Report No. 48, AGPS, Melbourne.
23 Anita Tang, 'Contracting Out in Community Services', *Administrative Law: Setting the Pace or Being Left Behind?*, L. Pearson (ed.), Australian Institute of Administrative Law, Sydney.
24 Glyn Davis, Director-General – Office of Cabinet, QCOSS 1995, extracted from Karen Struthers, op. cit. at p. 4.

Bibliography

Aronson, M. (1997) 'A Public Lawyer's Responses to Privatisation and Outsourcing', unpublished monograph.

Australian Catholic Social Welfare Commission (1996) *Competitive Care: Understanding the Implications of National Competition Policy on the COAG Agenda for the Community Services Sector*, Discussion Paper No. 11, Canberra: ACSW.

Australian Council of Social Service (1994) *Beyond Charity – The Community Services Sector in Australia*, Sydney: ACOSS.

—— (1995) *Volunteering in Australia*, Paper No. 74 Sydney: ACOSS.

—— (1996) *Reforming Australia's Community Services*, Paper No. 13, Sydney: ACOSS.

—— (1997) *Keeping Sight of the Goal – The Limits of Contracts and Competition in Community Services*, Paper No. 92, Sydney: ACOSS.

Australian Institute of Health and Welfare (1995) *Australia's Welfare Services and Assistance*, Canberra: Australian Government Publishing Service.

Hodge, G. (1996) *Contracting Out Government Services – A Review of International Evidence*, Melbourne: Montech Pty Ltd.

Hogan, M. and Rogers, G. (1997) 'Contracting of Community Services: Can It Be Done in the Public Interest?', in L. Pearson (ed.), *Administrative Law: Setting the Pace or Being Left Behind?*, Sydney: Australian Institute of Administrative Law.

Hutton, W. (1996) 'Friendship – The Commodity Money Cannot Buy', *Sydney Morning Herald*, 4 December, p. 11.

Independent Committee of Inquiry into National Competition Policy (1993) *Report of the Independent Committee of Inquiry into Competition Policy*, Canberra: Australian Government Publishing Service (referred to throughout the chapter as 'Hilmer').

Industry Commission (1995) *Charitable Organisations in Australia*, Report No. 45, Melbourne: Australian Government Publishing Service.

—— (1995) *Competitive Tendering and Contracting by Public Sector Agencies*, Report No. 48, Melbourne: Australian Government Publishing Service.

Inglis, J. and Rogan, L. (eds) (1993) *Beyond Swings and Roundabouts – Shaping the Future of Community Services in Australia*, Sydney: Australian Council of Social Services.

Johnston, C. (1995) *A Public Interest Perspective on Competition Policy*, Sydney: Public Interest Advocacy Centre.

—— (1996) 'Consumer Welfare and Competition Policy', 3 *Competition and Consumer Law Journal* 245.

Joint Committee of Public Accounts (1992) *Social Responsibilities of Commonwealth Statutory Authorities and Government Business Enterprises*, Canberra: Australian Government Publishing Service.

Keating, P. (1992) 'One Nation', Prime Minister's Speech, February, Australian Government Publishing Service, Canberra, p. 1.

Le Blanc, M. (1995) *Consumer Experiences of Telecommunications Competition, Consumers Telecommunications Network. For Whom the Phone Rings – Residential Consumers and Telecommunications Competition*, Sydney, NSW: CTN.

Lyons, M. (1993) *Australia's Non-profit Sector*, Working Paper No. 13, Sydney: CACOM.

Mellors, J. (1996) *Competitive Tendering and Contracting*, Canberra: Bulletin of Public Administration.

OECD (1994) *New Orientations for Social Policy*, Paris: OECD.

—— (1996) *Economic Outlook*, Paris: OECD.

Pearson, L. (ed.) (1997) *Administrative Law: Setting the Pace or Being Left Behind?*, Sydney: Australian Institute of Administrative Law.

Prices Surveillance Authority (1995) *The Social Responsibility of Banks*, Melbourne: Prices Surveillance Authority.

Private Infrastructure Task Force (1995) *Report – Economic Planning Advisory Commission*, Canberra: Australian Government Publishing Service.

Queensland Council of Social Services (1995) *Managing the Reform Process – Towards an Effective and Efficient Community Services System in Queensland*, Community Services Issues Paper No. 1, Brisbane: QCOSS.

—— (1996) *The Other Side of National Competition Policy*, Community Services Issues Paper No. 2, Brisbane: QCOSS.

Searles, W. and Moon, J. (1996) 'Preparing the Market: The Role of the State in Contracting for Community Services in Western Australia', paper presented at Annual Conference of Australian Political Studies Association, University of Western Australia, Perth.

Struthers, K. (1995) *Competition Policy – How is it Likely to Impact on the Community Services Sector*?, Brisbane: Queensland Council of Social Services (QCOSS).

Tang, A. (1997) 'Contracting Out in Community Services', in L. Pearson (ed.), *Administrative Law: Setting the Pace or Being Left Behind?*, Sydney: Australian Institute of Administrative Law.

Taperell, G. (1995) *National Competition Policy and its Implementation*, Sydney, Australia: Public Sector Research Centre.

Tonking, A. (1992) 'Gentleman and Players: Application of the Trade Practices Act to Government Bodies, Including those Corporatised or Privatised', *Queensland University of Technology Law Journal* 2:75.

Yeatman, A. (1991) *Educating the Clever Country*, Canberra: Australian Government Publishing Service.

12

CAUTIONARY REFLECTIONS ON THE PRIVATISATION PUSH

Charles Sampford

Introduction

We are in the midst of public sector reform. The key to that reform lies in the identification of goals for public organisations and determining the means for achieving those goals, including regulatory, institutional and management means. Regulatory means can include specific laws aimed at the relevant industry or privatised enterprise, the application of general competition law and the general promotion of ethics.[1] Privatisation and corporatisation are institutional means for addressing problems of public sector performance and as a means for achieving identified goals. However, they may also be considered management means, as the corporation, especially the corporation owned by shareholders, is seen as a different model for the management of assets and the achievement of goals from that found in traditional civil service departments and statutory corporations.

This book has been designed to examine the advantages and disadvantages of corporatisation and privatisation. In this concluding chapter, I reflect upon the earlier contributions and suggest some reasons in too readily adopting privatisation as the model means for the reform of the public sector and the achievement of its goals. These words of warning are prompted by the widespread ideological assumptions that underlie much of the debate, the multiple goals of organisations, the transaction costs of privatisation, the redistributive and public disinvestment effects, the difficulties of privatising infrastructure networks and natural monopolies and the discouraging example set by the flagship of privatisation (the United Kingdom). These warnings do not amount to a blanket rejection of privatisation. Indeed, where the vast bulk of economic activity is carried on by non-government corporations, the possibility that more might usefully be carried on that way must always be an option. But it is not necessarily obvious which option should be preferred: private or public or some combination of the two.

Avoiding ideological assumptions

In considering whether privatisation is an appropriate means for achieving the goals of current government organisations, it is common to hear two ideological responses: *always* and *never*.

Privatisation is a means for achieving the goals of organisations currently within the public sector rather than a solution that is to be pursued (or eschewed) in all cases. Nonetheless, much public debate has been affected by one of the two ideological positions noted above. Some of those who have been the most fervent advocates of privatisation tend to see fundamental differences between public and private organisations. They tend to idealise the market place and demonise or dismiss governments as being incapable of ever doing better than private organisations. Such idealisation of free markets might be understandable in countries with no recent experience of free markets (such as those in Eastern Europe) but seems very strange to anyone who has lived through the excesses and failure of financial markets in the 1980s. The difficulty lies in the common tendency to compare the idealised version of markets with the inefficient practices of some government agencies (or, for some ideologies, the excesses of Stalinist state bureaucracies). One must avoid comparing an idealised version of the system you like with real versions of the systems you dislike.[2] This is as foolish as contrasting the failings of contemporary capitalism and the communist ideal. We must look at *real* markets, *real* public companies, *real* government organisations and consider the ways in which they can be improved. There is no surer way of turning the debate into an ideological fight (and also losing the plot) than to compare the idealised version of the market place with the reality of government or vice versa.

What is privatisation? Privatisation involves taking a 'public' body and turning it into a 'public' company. The verbal confusion which shows the different conceptions of 'public'[3] and in which public companies are seen as part of the 'private' sector is only a linguistic symptom of the confusion surrounding the public/private divide about which I have written elsewhere.[4] The private sphere is sometimes characterised as personal (referring to private space and personal privacy) and as non-governmental. However, the use of the term 'public company' can also refer to the public nature and public purposes of corporations. The attempt to use the language of private individuals to cover huge organisations that straddle the life of hundreds and thousands of workers and affect millions of customers should be seen for the ideological foolishness it is.[5] As I have argued before,[6] the alleged divide between public and private can actually obscure some of the more important differences between different organisations (e.g. size, range of products and services offered and expertise required, degree of competition). We should avoid ideologically-driven distinctions between public and 'private' organisations and the accompanying assumptions about the vices of the former and the virtues of the latter.

Winnie Goh provides an excellent antidote for such sloppy ideologically-based assumptions. She notes that one of the greatest increases in productivity in Malaysia was achieved within a container terminal retained in public ownership whereas the performance of the wholly privatised postal service declined significantly.[7] The nature of corporate ownership is *not* the single key to the success or failure of companies, as will be made clear below.

The multiple goals of organisations

One of the reasons why privatisation is so strongly supported is the imagined simplicity of purpose. Public sector organisations are seen as having to pursue a range of social and economic goals (creating employment, maintaining a national presence in key industries, sustaining local businesses, developing domestic technology, providing vocational training in high-technology industries, decentralising industry). Planning for such a range of goals is complicated; some goals contradict others and it is difficult to maintain accountability when the partial achievement of one goal may be used by managers to offset significant failures to achieve others (most notably, profitability). By contrast, corporations are seen as single-minded profit maximisers, simplifying both management and accountability.

Yet public bodies are not alone in pursuing multiple goals. Indeed, the effective pursuit of multiple goals is a characteristic of all organisations for two reasons deriving from: the number of individuals involved in any organisation and the number of goals individuals may set for any organisation.

However clear any initial goals of an organisation's founders or funders, the goals of the directors and employees will not necessarily be the same and cannot be ensured to be the same. People join organisations for their own reasons, generally based on what they can achieve personally through joining. Organisations can be powerful and potentially very effective because they pool the resources of many. However, their weaknesses may be found in the fact that those resources must be exercised through the actions of many who may be pursuing either their own agenda or their own conception of the organisation's agenda. Accordingly, an organisation is 'a powerful but very blunt and unwieldy instrument. It is not always clear *whose* instrument it is and for what purpose, if any, it is wielded'.[8]

Second, few of us will suggest there exists only a single goal for any organisation, public or private. Some directors of public companies seem to genuinely believe that their sole duty is to maximise the return on shares. However, in addition to the private selfish ends they may pursue through the organisation (which may be independent or even antithetical to increasing shareholder value), most directors would suggest that they would pursue a number of other goals. These would include contributions to the nation's economic well-being: delivering higher quality and/or lower prices and making a contribution to development of the technological base of industry, the education of the workforce and gross domestic product. They would generally also mention promoting equal opportunity and respecting environmental concerns and ethical values. Most shareholders and the general public would agree that these were goals to strive for.

However, the prioritisation in delegating resources to accomplish such goals may not be a point of such easy agreement. Even so, I have not seen many mission statements emanating from corporations that state maximising the profit of shareholders by any legal means as the sole goal!

When we move beyond the question of 'What goals should this organisation pursue?' to 'Why should we have such organisations at all?', the single profit-maximising goal seems absurd. Why is it that democracies like Australia have something between three-quarters and four-fifths of their productive capacity in the hands of 'private' business and, largely, 'public' corporations? The justification does not lie in the enrichment of the shareholders of those businesses. That is an end to which the majority of a democracy are either indifferent or hostile. The justification lies in the supposed benefits that an economy largely comprised of such organisations offers to the members of the society of which they are a part (e.g. greater national wealth, social mobility and individual autonomy).

These are very 'public' goals for the 'private' sector. Indeed, they are public goals which further justify the use of the term 'public' companies. Of course, it might be argued that all these other goals will follow if organisations in fact pursue the single goal of profit maximisation. Even if such an heroic assumption were fully accepted, it still leaves the broader social goals as fundamental to the corporate enterprise, with the pursuit of profit merely becoming instrumental rather than the primary justification or goal.

Other, perhaps more realistic, people would suggest that these other goals be encouraged by one or more of the following: ethical persuasion, ethical investment, consumer pressure, industry self-regulation, government guidance or state regulation.

Whatever position is taken, the consequence is that real organisations, including 'public companies', pursue a variety of goals other than profit maximisation. Thus, the means by which this plurality of goals is addressed is an issue for all organisations.

The plurality of goals for public bodies is generally greater than for public companies including, as it does, what are called 'community service obligations'. However, this plurality is one of degree rather than kind. Privatisation does not carry with it the creation of simple organisations with simple and singular goals. Nor should it be assumed that public bodies, or their corporatised and privatised successors, should be forced into an ideological profit-maximising model that is too simplistic for existing corporations, let alone the formerly public newcomers.

Pursuing the broader goals of public enterprises

Even the most avid privatisers acknowledge the broader goals pursued by government business enterprises (GBEs).[9] However, their belief in the possibility and desirability of single-minded corporate profit maximisers means that they seek to take these broader goals from the core responsibilities of the GBE and reintroduce them through other means.

These further goals may be imposed by regulation or incentives (the government payment for community service obligations). Where the privatised body is in a monopoly or duopoly position, some form of regulation will often be necessary to ensure that a fair price is charged for these obligations. Indeed, where privatisation produces a monopoly or oligopoly, restrictions on price increases are required to protect all consumers.

Caution must be expressed about this approach to pursuing the broader goals of GBEs. First, most of the supporters of privatisation are also supporters of deregulation who, in other contexts, decry the ineffectiveness and inefficiency of government regulation, citing the problems of rent seeking, regulatory capture by those supposedly regulated and the difficulties of enforcing compliance by coercive means. If regulation is so ineffective, then we should be worried that our only protection against monopolistic gouging and the denial of community service obligations is entrusted to a mechanism over which so much doubt has been expressed, especially by the privatising governments of the UK, New Zealand and, more recently, Australia. On the other hand, if regulation is going to be effective in this case, then we are entitled to demand a re-examination of regulation in other areas.

Second, even if the doubts about regulation are unfounded (allowing us to return some sanity to other areas of government policy), caution must be expressed about the contradictory tensions introduced into privatised corporations by this kind of regime. If the GBE is turned into an ideal profit-maximising organisation, then the existence of such regulations will put many of the key personnel under conflicting pressures. This could lead either to the pursuit of the same contradictory goals that were seen to be a core problem for GBEs or the broader goals being marginalised and compliance minimised.

Under these circumstances, the traditional public service model for dealing with a plurality of goals deserves to be reconsidered. This involves identifying and articulating the various goals to be achieved, prioritising them and developing a plan for simultaneously progressing towards several of those goals with targets for each. This plan is then negotiated with a governing body and/or minister and monitored. All goals are addressed in the plan and there is an attempt to avoid the placing of contradictory obligations on individual officials and employees. Public sector organisations are used to such processes, as are large organisations in the private sector.

I have to admit that I am deeply sceptical about a privatisation process that involves disaggregating the multiple goals of public organisations and establishing separate organisations to pursue them, e.g. a privatised body seeking profits and a regulatory body to ensure that this new body pursues other goals. This may appear organisationally simple, with separate organisations determinedly pursuing different goals. Yet to me it appears to be a recipe for either collusion or conflict. At some point, the various goals have to be reconciled. The public sector model seeks to do this at the beginning rather than at an indeterminate end.

Transaction costs

Transfers of ownership are not without cost. Transaction costs include the costs of legislation, legal advice, due diligence, brokerage and underwriting fees. The fees can easily reach 2–3 per cent of the value of the enterprise and are not irrelevant to the excitement privatisation generates among the legal and stockbroking industries – and the uncritical support they offer for it.

To this must be added the tendency to underprice the asset to ensure that the privatisation is a 'success'.[10] Politicians pushing privatisation are less concerned that the price be maximised than that the sale go through. In this they will be aided and abetted by the underwriters who want to minimise their own risk.[11]

Another cost-incurring element in privatisation is that of contracting. Its substantial costs arise at both the tendering stage as well as after the contract is awarded. Indeed, if the original award is only for a 'test' period, the entire process, with its accompanying costs, must be revisited following the test period.

Finally, there are ethical dangers in the privatisation of government bodies. These are very large and very valuable enterprises. Those who buy these enterprises will seek the best deal for themselves. Governments are in a position to determine who will take them over and to influence their level of profitability, especially where they retain monopoly or near-monopoly privileges. This raises great temptations: for direct corruption, for the favouring of political supporters or for the creation of a group of businesses sufficiently beholden to government to attract an unhealthy flow of campaign donations. Ironically, those who seek to privatise government in order to reduce its supposedly corrupting influence are giving those who privatise an opportunity for corruption not seen since public monopolies were sold and peddled in the days of the charter companies.

Another ethical difficulty in privatising government bodies is that these organisations often provide very volatile and potentially problematic services, such as health care and penal services. The shift to 'private' management of such bodies can prove to be extremely dangerous, as the factor of accountability becomes increasingly intangible (even if previous accountability was only reflected in decreased votes for the government). The fiasco of privatisation of sectors of the prison service in the UK (where prisoners seemed to regularly abscond under privatised custody) demonstrates this difficulty quite clearly.

Redistributive effects

Like many of the economic changes promoted on the grounds of economic efficiency, privatisation involves redistribution of power and wealth.[12] The state power abdicated in deregulation and privatisation does not disappear; it is merely transferred to other people. Some might hope that it is distributed equally, with deregulation leading to an increase in the power of individuals and privatisation leading to a 'share-owning democracy'.

The benefits are, of course, not so randomly distributed. Privatisation does involve distinct benefits for some, certainly to the stockbroker, underwriters and lawyers. These 'beneficiaries' are certainly the most active and vocal in their advocacy of the advantages of privatisation. This in itself should send a cautionary signal. Most economic argument assumes that the behaviour of human beings can be approximated to that of those acting in pure self-interest. I am inclined to Shakespeare's retort that 'there are more things in heaven and earth . . . than are dreamed of in your philosophy'[13] and to mention some of the additions that have been suggested by philosophers, social scientists and politicians from Mill and Maslow to Macmillan. But however inadequate such an interpretation for understanding human behaviour, one cannot doubt its explanatory power for the actions of those who espouse it. To do otherwise would be to doubt their own integrity. However, to accept this philosophy is to doubt the word of those involved when they make claims beyond what is in their self-interest. For if an exaggeration of the public benefits of what was in their private interests suited their private interests, one would presume that an economic rationalist would be bound to engage in that exaggeration.[14]

Less directly, there are much greater transfers of power involved than the incidental wealth generated by the transaction costs. Deregulation leaves those who would otherwise be regulated more powerful. Privatisation reduces the area of the economy subject to state control and extends the areas of the economy subject to market power. Even though powers to control GBEs and to regulate others do not involve direct or pure democracy, they are exercised by those who are ultimately responsible to the electorate.

A common 'winner' in the redistribution of power in privatisation is often the incumbent (as is often the case in political races). It is not uncommon for what was the public body to be reinvented, lock, stock and managing barrel, as a single privatised entity, thus avoiding the potential competitive costs and delays of establishing new infrastructure, procedures, personnel, etc. Meek makes this point most effectively in his analysis of telecommunications in the UK while Goh underlines its veracity in discussing the continuity of ownership in Malaysia's process of privatisation.[15]

In areas subject to the market, those with greater bargaining power can acquire further power through its exercise. Some may see the market as 'democratic' because individuals have a direct say in market outcomes. However, the voting principles are very different in this kind of democracy. Instead of one person/one vote, the principle is one dollar/one vote. This has an obvious attraction for those who possess more than the average number of dollars.[16]

Deregulation and privatisation are part of what might be seen as privatisation of power, an abdication of power by state institutions and its assumption by individuals and large corporations.[17] Once given away, it is very difficult to take back. The power assumed will be used to resist its retaking or its limitation. Indeed, it may well be used to seek extensions of that very power. If a media baron is allowed to extend his shareholding to 25 per cent in the hope that his papers will be 'even handed', he is likely to demand more next time – as Conrad Black did with the Australian newspaper group he bought.

Externalising costs

It is generally assumed that privatised industries will be more 'efficient'. Efficiency gains can be made by producing more with the same workforce and capital stock or they can be made by producing the same output with a smaller workforce or capital stock. In the case of telecommunications, for example, there are very significant prospective increases in consumption expected. In such an environment, corporatised and privatised bodies can engage in both and there is a real chance that many employees losing jobs in the privatised entity will be employed by competitors.

However, in the case of water and power, there are strong environmental reasons against increasing output (and consumption); thus, efficiency gains can only be achieved by cutting the workforce. In a full-employment economy, it could be expected that such labour would generally be taken up by other areas of the economy. In an economy with 9–10 per cent unemployment, workers shed from one firm will largely produce increases in unemployment equal to or greater than (if 'multiplier' effects are established) workers shed. This may increase the profit of the corporation concerned but it increases the economic costs of unemployment (along with the indirect economic and other costs of unemployment, like reduced educational opportunity and increased criminal activity). When large corporations shed labour, thereby increasing their profits but externalising significant costs which are borne by the government, this constitutes a general problem for the economy of considerable complexity. Where the labour is shed from a government business enterprise, the result is potentially bizarre. The government is externalising costs onto itself! While cost shifting between departments and levels of government is as old as bureaucracy, it is considered to be an example of unrealistic bureaucratic waste rather than clever economic thinking. If GBEs are privatised as a part of this process, it does not alter the economic consequences of what is being done.

Public disinvestment

The next caution is a reminder that privatisation is a form of disinvestment. As such, it has both an economic and a symbolic effect. The economic effect lies in the billions of dollars that are spent in buying the assets in which the government has invested. This can have extremely powerful negative knock-on effects. For example, Australia is currently in desperate need of investment in the kinds of goods and services that can be marketed internationally. If investors are encouraged to spend billions of dollars investing in government assets, either less will be invested in these new productive investments or more will be invested from overseas and Australian control of both new business and former GBEs will be reduced. There is a danger that GBEs and new investment will have to compete with each other and must then seek to offer higher returns. If the new investments cannot offer the higher returns, then the privatisation of GBEs may actually hold off investment in new productive activity. They may 'crowd out' such investments in the way that government borrowing was once supposed to do. Indeed, there is a danger that mass privatisations will turn them into 'the only game in town'.

There is also an important symbolic dimension. While the government is urging others to save and invest in the nation's own productive capacity, it is in fact giving the opposite lead.

Difficulties in privatising infrastructure networks

There are particular problems in privatising infrastructure networks (water, gas, power, roads and telecommunications). The traditional approach has been to treat such networks as 'natural monopolies', in that duplication is enormously expensive and thus makes competition inherently inefficient.

Those who hail the value of private organisations and their goal of profit maximisation should recognise the simple point that profit maximisation may be achieved in three ways: increase in market share, cost minimisation and price maximisation. Of these, the one that involves the least work is price maximisation. Price rises have a disproportionate contribution to profits as all price rises flow directly into profit (e.g. if a product or service costs 80 per cent of its sale price to produce, a 10 per cent increase in cost will produce a 33 per cent increase in profits (assuming steady sales), meaning that a company could sustain a 25 per cent drop in sales and still be ahead). Sales have to drop very significantly to alter the logic of this 'calculus'. This will only occur if there is real competition.

The current preferred answer is to provide either a strong regulatory regime or competition. The United Kingdom has concentrated on the former, Australia on the latter; however, there is a tendency to move from the former to the latter. Doubts about the former have already been expressed above. Some services can be offered competitively but there are enormous difficulties in introducing real competition into networks. The idea of duplicating some of these networks seems bizarre to say the least. The fact that two companies are each spending over two billion dollars laying fibre-optic cables to the same streets in Australia, for example, does not reduce the absurdity of the exercise; it merely increases the wonder that ideology could blind anyone to it. Rather than the apotheosis of competition, it seems more like its *reductio ad absurdum*.

Other problems lie in pricing access to networks. Colin Meek emphasises the value of maintaining the integrity of the telephone network.[18] In suggesting that non-paying clients have only their outgoing calls barred, he points out the value to other members of the network of being able to call the disconnected subscriber. This reflects a very important and obvious feature of some public sector communication networks: they connect people to each other and each benefits from the connection. If only half the population were connected, the entire network would be much less valuable and the costs of communicating with those who were not on the network would be much higher.[19] Accordingly, the costs of connecting remote users should not be seen as entirely attributable to, and to be borne by, the remote user. Some of the extra costs should be borne by the remote user or by the government as part of community service obligations.[20] However, part of it should be seen as part of the costs of expanding the system for all subscribers and properly attributable to the standard costs of network access.

It may be argued that the inefficiencies of monopolies exceed the inefficiencies of duplication and quadruplication. I would suggest that this is a management problem which should not be beyond the wit of human beings to solve. If someone continues to argue that the efficiency losses of monopoly are so great as to counter the inefficiencies of duplication, one has to ask two questions. First, is this an empirical observation or an indication of ideological bias? Second, where does the argument stop? Does this mean that everything done by the government has to be duplicated?

The response to a departmental head or minister who argues thus is not to privatise the body but to accept the statement as an honest acknowledgement of the incompetence of the head/minister and appoint the person with the strongest claim to competence. In short, natural monopolies would seem to be the best candidates for the public sector model of managing multiple goals, of which efficiency and price minimisation are but two.

For whom the road tolls

New roads are generally built for two purposes: to enable the traffic to move more quickly, and to attract traffic from alternative routes. The imposition of road tolls is a means of paying for the road that seems perfectly designed to minimise the achievement of either end. By imposing a toll, a disincentive is placed on using the new road by those for whose use it was designed and leaves more traffic on the alternative routes which the road was designed to alleviate. Where the difference in time and distance saved is not great, the new road may be used very little.[21] Where the difference is significant but the alternative route is a slower but feasible alternative, there are very significant leakages to alternative routes (as in much of rural France). The existence of free alternative routes creates problems. If these are maintained and upgraded, then there is duplication and a reduction in tolls collected. There may also be a temptation to avoid making optimal decisions on other roads in order to maximise toll revenue.[22] Where the savings in fuel or time make the tollway much more economical to use, then it obviously will be used, despite the grumbles, the cost and delay that the toll imposes (e.g. bridges which face no free competition or motorways through particularly mountainous terrain).[23]

Even if the disincentive of the toll does not cost too many motorists, it will raise objections on the grounds of equity. Why charge a toll for this road, this motorway, this bridge and not for that one? The answer that the market will bear charging for one and not for another is hardly convincing. An alternative approach could be to impose a tax on petrol, which is much more evenly directed, being based upon road use (nicely weighted against heavier and speeding vehicles).[24] It is also less costly to collect an increased existing tax than to collect a toll.

Despite the simple and obvious economic arguments against tolls, whether imposed by governments or privately owned corporations, the adverse political consequences should be even more obvious. Road tolls are almost uniquely unpopular; as the New South Wales, Victorian and Queensland governments in Australia have found (with the latter losing all seats surrounding the Sunshine Coast and proposed Gold Coast tollways, and, consequently, government). I would argue that the deep and abiding dislike of tolls is not merely the aversion to paying taxes and charges. No other tax or charge of this magnitude produces such a reaction. Normally, when a new road is proposed, the negative reaction comes from the relative few who are adversely affected because of proximity. Those who use it are generally supportive as they can see themselves using it, reducing their journey times and increasing the value of their property. However, if a new road is a toll road, especially if it is privately owned, the property owners do not see themselves using the road but rejecting its use because of the toll. They are alienated from the road. They do not see it as 'their' road, a 'public' road. They see it as an intrusion and an expense. Roads are seen as quintessentially public and their removal from the public domain is not appreciated.[25]

There is, of course, a simple supposed argument in favour of tolls and privatised infrastructure: that the public cannot afford such developments of infrastructure. This view is entirely spurious. The public pay in one way or another, whether through general revenue taxes, specific taxes or tolls. The question here is: What is the most efficient means of collecting from the public? The answer is not via the means of tolls, privatised or otherwise.

The burden of proof

None of these cautions suggest 'never privatise'. That would be an ideological assumption rather than a logical conclusion. However, they do suggest that a positive burden of proof is placed upon those who wish to privatise; indeed, transaction costs alone impose that burden. It is common to ask, 'Why should the government own an airline, or a bank, or . . . ?'. These are good questions if you are proposing to purchase an airline or a bank, and they remain issues for debate. However, the central questions are: Why should we decide to sell the service? Why should we decide to change it? In a world of real transaction costs, the burden of proof must be on those who demand the transaction. This should be a burden that the privatisation proponents should be more than happy to accept. If either we or they do not believe that they can discharge that burden, one wonders why they should be listened to at all.

A rather discouraging example: theory put to practice

Most of the above discussion has dwelt on the theoretical problems that are likely to arise. These debates may continue indefinitely. However, the point of the theory is to inform practice. When we examine the practice of privatisation in the country that has led the rest of the herd (the UK), one is confronted by the greatest cautions of them all.

In evaluating privatisation, we need to consider the ultimate goals of policy. The claim made for the market economy and the privatised corporations that join it is that it maximises gross domestic product and the standard of living of the people. This is the recent history of the United Kingdom. Colin Meek provides an excellent summary of the detrimental effects of privatisation in Chapter 5. The overall performance of the economy, society and polity are even more discouraging.

Although the few who have benefited from the redistribution of wealth and power may be exceedingly pleased with the eighteen years since Mrs Thatcher came to power and look to current growth rates, the periods of economic 'success' involve recoveries from the disastrous recessions induced by government economic policy in 1979–80 and 1989–90. Given that the period coincided with the first, and best, eighteen years of North Sea oil, this is a sorry record. The first Thatcher government provides a wonderful example of ideologically-driven economic failure. She aimed to increase gross domestic products by changing the tax system and she aimed to reduce inflation by increasing interest rates. Unfortunately, inflation was more than doubled by her changes to the tax system and increasing interest rates drove the economy into a massive recession, more than trebling unemployment and cutting industrial capacity by 25 per cent. Indeed, it was 1988 before England returned to the 1979 levels of industrial production – just in time for the second Thatcher recession.[26] The last Thatcher government fell amidst the ideologically-driven shift of local council rates from charges based on property values to per capita charges. At the time of writing, her successors face decimation in the 1997 election.

The great irony is that the action that saved her first government from electoral oblivion and came to be the symbol of the Thatcher years centred on the use of the ultimate public sector organisation, the military. She pulled the country together in what seemed like, and was, a noble and common purpose. The Falklands War not only saved a small number of islanders from a particularly nasty dictatorship but also delivered the Argentinian people from that same dictatorship in circumstances which so humiliated the Argentinian military that they have a reasonable chance of a democratic future. However, this is a noble and wonderful and common purpose which benefits greatly the people of Argentina; it benefited very little the people of England. One only wishes that Mrs Thatcher could have pulled her country together to fight an economic war which was much more vital to the interests of the English.

An Australian parallel

The push to privatisation in Australia is gathering pace as part of a general adoption of market ideology in Australia. This is supported by most of the political, bureaucratic and financial elites but not by the electorate. It would seem that the current liberal government was elected on a backlash against the economic reforms introduced by the Australian Labor Party rather than an enthusiasm for their continuation. Whether the electorate will turn on the conservative government that promised a reduction in the pace of reform and delivered the opposite (as in New Zealand), only time will tell.

However, it is interesting to reflect upon the most popular and most lauded move of its first year. After the world's worst massacre by a lone gunman was committed in Port Arthur, Tasmania, in April 1996, Prime Minister Howard pushed through a plan for the toughening of gun laws, the buy-back of guns and the funding of this by a compulsory levy on all income. Despite a noisy minority, this move received strong support from the overwhelming majority in all opinion polls conducted on the issue. Yet this was an exercise in the coercive power of the state, for a stated public good, overriding the settled rights of citizens to the property that they had, paid for by the state levying a charge on all citizens.

This was quintessentially an exercise of public power for the public good. The contrast between this and the unpopularity of the abrogation of public power for private gain could not be more marked.

Conclusion

Why, then, have those who most readily adopted the market ideology in their policies performed so badly in competition with other countries? Economic theorists may believe that, by privatising, they ensure that every decision is more efficient and that hence the nation will become more efficient because every decision is being made on the most efficient grounds. However, when it comes to this kind of efficiency, the whole is very often less than the sum of the parts.

One example that easily comes to mind is overseas investment of superannuation funds. Some may say that superannuation funds should invest wherever they can maximise their returns for the individual policyholders. However, the individual policyholders are also workers and parents of current and potential workers as well. It may well be that a domestic investment which produces a slightly lesser return to the individual policyholder as policyholder may in fact produce a greater return to the policyholder as worker or parent of worker. Of course, the benefits are not confined to the workers or parents who are policyholders in that superannuation fund. Thus, it is even more possible that, where a number of superannuation funds invest in domestic job-creating industries, the net benefits to policyholders in their various roles are greater.

It is classically the role of governments to ensure that the whole is at least as great as the sum of the parts. It seems to me that those governments who have succeeded best and those economies which have succeeded best have been the very ones in which the government has attempted to ensure that the whole is greater than the sum of the parts; in short, that corporations (whether they be government owned, partly privatised, fully privatised or always in private hands) should all contribute to the well-being of the nation and ultimately to the greater well-being of themselves.

My greatest caution about privatisation is that we may in fact be following the models of those societies which have in fact introduced a feverish degree of market competition within their own countries but have failed in the international competition on which those companies and ultimately their people depend. I find it exceptionally difficult to regard the British government for the last eighteen years as a model for anything; rather it is a cautionary tale of that which should be avoided. There are indeed worse disasters to observe over that period, most notably the former Soviet Union. But the fact that some have done worse does not hide the fact that virtually all have done better than the UK. One of the greatest tragedies of the post-Cold War world is that so much of the former East thought it best to follow the model provided by the UK rather than the model provided by their far more successful Western allies in Central Europe. Whereas the greater natural advantages and generally greater common sense of many countries such as Australia mean that I do not believe they will fail as badly as any of these, I find it bizarre that we should even contemplate following them. I only wish we could look to some really successful economies for inspiration.

Notes

1 These are the subject of extensive research by the National Institute for Law, Ethics and Public Affairs, Brisbane, with the key ideas outlined in C.A.J. Coady and C.J.G. Sampford (eds) (1993) *Business, Ethics and Law*, Federation Press, Sydney. In particular, see C.J.G. Sampford and D. Wood, 'The Future of Business Ethics'.

2 Whincop and Rowland refer to this as the 'Nirvana complex' (see Chapter 3). The idea is further developed in C. Sampford, 'Law, Ethics and Institutional Reform: Finding Philosophy, Displacing Ideology' (1994) 3 *Griffith Law Review* 1.

3 Alternately, 'a part of the government' and 'managed and usually owned by non-government or "private" individuals'.

4 C. Sampford, 'Law, Institutions and the Public/Private Divide' (1992) 20 *Federal Law Review* 185.

5 Another aspect to this private/public debate is the assumption that government business enterprises may 'emulate the performance of the private sector'.

6 Sampford (1992).

7 See Goh, Chapter 8, 'Review of Various Corporatised and Privatised Entities' and 'Conclusion'.

8 C. Sampford (1989) *The Disorder of Law*, Blackwell, Oxford, Chapter 7.

9 Most of the targets established for privatisation were expected to serve goals beyond producing a return to government. Some of these involved securing access to certain kinds of service (water, power, telecommunications) for all members of the community even where they could not afford the economic costs of their provision. Others were more general, as in the contributions that telecommunications industries could make to the skilling of the workforce and the development of high-technology industries.

10 See Whincop and Rowland, Chapter 3, 'A Theoretical Analysis of Efficient Governance'.

11 There is merit in the Victorian view that sale by tender has lower transaction costs and a lower chance of producing an undervaluation.

12 One of the many ironies of those who press for market solutions on the grounds of efficiency is the frequent inability to produce results that are Pareto efficient.

13 *Hamlet* II. v. 166.

14 It is interesting to note that George Soros, long known as a proponent of *laissez-faire* economics, now recognises that common interest should take precedence over particular interests. Indeed, he warns that the present, market-driven system will collapse unless such a recognition occurs and is acted upon. See G. Soros, 'The Capitalist Threat' (1997) 279(2) *The Atlantic Monthly*, February, pp. 45–58.

15 See Meek, Chapter 5, and Goh, Chapter 8.
16 See further discussion of this factor in Sampford (1992) and C. Sampford, 'Law, Ethics and Institutional Reform: Finding Philosophy, Displacing Ideology' (1994) 3 *Griffith Law Review* 1.
17 This is not to say that the power either belongs to or is exercised by shareholders in any simple sense, any more than state power is exercised by voters.
18 See Chapter 5.
19 The costs of access to those outside the road or communications network would be very great indeed.
20 This does not apply so clearly to gas, water and electricity because the resource is a one-way flow. But where there is a two-way flow, as in road and telecommunications, this is a more appropriate cost allocation.
21 This has been the case with the Sunshine Coast Motorway in Queensland, Australia. A two-lane toll road was built parallel to the existing coastal highway. Its toll was so unpopular with voters that, over the period from 1992 to 1995, it led to a loss of all State seats through which the motorway passed.
22 In privatising the Southeastern arterial road in Melbourne, clearways are to be removed to reduce traffic flow on an alternative route.
23 Yet such cases are not necessarily clear-cut, as is demonstrated by the response in Scotland when a toll bridge was constructed between the Scottish mainland and the Isle of Skye. Commuters were so incensed at the construction (which they had not supported), the high cost of the toll (substantially higher than the long-running ferry) and the forced unemployment of the ferryman (whose family had captained the Skye ferry for generations) that they undertook a virtual 'park-in' on the bridge. After refusing to pay the toll, drivers, passengers and cars waited on the bridge for the police to come and take them away. Commuter after commuter did this, causing a traffic jam to the effect that no one, toll payer or not, could cross the bridge.
24 Of course, vehicle-recognition technology can reduce the delays of toll collection but does not reduce the disincentive to road use.
25 As the case of Skye noted above proves, even the shift from private to public is not always accepted.
26 The figures are discussed in C. Sampford, 'Dworkin's Claim to a Socialist Inheritance' (1991) *Bulletin of the Australian Society of Legal Philosophy* 16: 37.

References

Coady, C.A.J and Samford, C.J.G. (eds) (1993) *Business. Ethics and Law*, Sydney: Federation Press.

Sampford, C. (1989) *The Disorder of Law*, London: Blackwell.

—— (1991) 'Dworkin's Claim to a Socialist Inheritance', *Bulletin of the Australian Society of Legal Philosophy* 16: 37.

—— (1992) 'Law, Institutions and the Public/Private Divide', *Federal Law Review* 20: 185.

—— (1994) 'Law, Ethics and Institutional Reform: Finding Philosophy, Displacing Ideology', *Griffith Law Review* 3: 1.

Sampford, C.J.G. and Wood, D. (1993) 'The Future of Business Ethics', in C.A.J. Coady and C.J.G. Sampford (eds), *Business, Ethics and Law*, Sydney: Federation Press.

Shakespeare, W., *Hamlet* II, v. 166.

Soros, G. (1997) 'The Capitalist Threat', *The Atlantic Monthly* 279(2): 45–58.

APPENDIX

Corporatisation and privatisation: in whose interest?

A review of a conference held by Griffith University Law School and Griffith University School of International Business in conjunction with RIPAA on 18 March 1996

by Robert Troedson, Queensland Parliamentary Library

A philosophy of corporatisation and privatisation of government business enterprises (GBEs) has been strongly advocated in many OECD and Asian countries over the last fifteen years. This approach is part of a range of measures described as economic rationalism. The concept is that GBEs should operate on a commercial basis, or be subject to fair competition, or be wholly or partially sold to private interests. In Australia the most widely known examples are the corporatisation of Telstra and the partial sale of Qantas and the Commonwealth Bank. In Queensland most government business activities have been commercialised or corporatised over the last three years, for example QIDC, GoPrint and Q-Build.

In April 1995 the National Competition Policy was formally initiated. The Council of Australian Governments adopted a package of proposals based on the recommendations of the Committee of Inquiry chaired by Professor Fred Hilmer. Competition Policy encompasses more than corporatisation and privatisation, although they are part of it. Moreover, Competition Policy does not necessarily require corporatisation or privatisation of GBEs, but it does recommend such an approach when it is demonstrably in the public interest. The conference programme provided a synthesis of these related issues. Corporatisation and privatisation aspects of Australia's competition policy were considered along with reports on developments in New Zealand, the United Kingdom and Malaysia.

The conference title asked the question *In whose interest?*. Although the details varied, the international speakers gave the general impression that individual consumers had experienced relatively few benefits from corporatisation or privatisation programmes to date. In Malaysia, the emphasis of government policy has been on privatisation rather than competition. In many cases, prices charged by privatised enterprises have risen considerably and service standards have fallen. In the UK and New Zealand, policies have endeavoured to facilitate competition in markets previously dominated by a monopoly GBE. The success of these efforts has been limited by the practical difficulties of providing competitive access to existing networks such as for water and electricity reticulation, apparent resistance on the part of the traditional enterprise, and the extensive litigation that has often occurred.

In Australia, corporatisation and privatisation initiatives tend to be more recent, and apart from Telstra and Optus there is little clear evidence of the transformation from monopoly to competition. A common view expressed was that Australia was in a good position to proceed with caution and learn from the mistakes of the older overseas players. However, views diverged on the actual benefits likely to flow from privatisations currently in progress or being planned.

Economic theory has identified several potential advantages of corporatisation and privatisation. These derive from the elimination of direct political interference and reduction of the productive and allocative inefficiencies that are assumed to be inherent in non-private enterprises. However, formal analyses have questioned these assumptions and concluded that supposed advantages may not occur or may be smaller than previously thought.

By contrast, the current programme in Victoria, described as a mix of commercialisation, corporatisation and privatisation of GBEs, and introduction of competition, was stated by one of its architects to be highly successful. The programme has three primary goals: not corporatisation or privatisation *per se*, but rather increased efficiency and the effective use of resources; maximisation of customer choice; and reduction of state debt. It was predicted that the Victorian programme would become a model that other states would follow. Victoria was the only state other than Queensland to be represented on the conference programme.

The appropriate answer to the title question *In whose interest?* is presumably that the customer should ultimately receive at least some benefit. The mood of the conference seemed to be that while favourable consumer impacts are often predicted, their realisation in Australia faces several hurdles. For example, the information on which to base consumer choices or to quantify outcomes may be difficult or expensive to obtain. Unforeseen costs, such as those associated with the duplication necessary to enable competition, or benefits forgone, such as dividends to government from retaining ownership and dividends for investors and the community from alternative investments, may seriously limit the actual advantages to consumers from corporatisation and privatisation programmes.

Again, the Victorian situation was presented as a model for others to follow. The Office of the Regulator-General has, among other objectives, responsibility to prevent misuse of monopoly or market power and to ensure that users and customers benefit from competition and efficiency. A Customer Consultative Committee and an Electricity Industry Ombudsman scheme have been established as vehicles for communication of issues and dispute resolution. In view of the focus of the conference on the interests of stakeholders, it was perhaps unfortunate that the programme did not include a counterbalancing view from an Australian consumer perspective.

Overall, the conference provided an interesting insight into some overseas experiences of corporatisation, privatisation and competition, and informed discussion of some of the issues that are facing similar programmes in Australia. It lacked debate on current outcomes and immediate prospects. No doubt partly because few analyses of these issues have yet been conducted.

The seminar was presented jointly by Griffith University Law School and Griffith University School of International Business in conjunction with the Royal Institute of Public Administration Australia, Queensland Branch. It was held at Bardon Professional Centre on 18 March 1996. The conference organisers expect to publish the proceedings in book form in due course.

INDEX